D0489127

and
Rotorcraft

Bell 407 new light single in flight over Atlanta, Georgia, where it was one of 18 aircraft provided by Bell Helicopter Textron in support of the '96 Olympics.

Airlife's Helicopters and Rotorcraft

R. W. Simpson

Airlife
England

Copyright © 1998 R. W. Simpson

First published in the UK in 1998
by Airlife Publishing Ltd

British Library Cataloguing-in-Publication Data
A catalogue record for this book
is available from the British Library

ISBN 1 85310 968 1

Typeset by Phoenix Typesetting, Ilkley, West Yorkshire.
Printed in England by Biddles Ltd., Guildford and King's Lynn.

Airlife Publishing Ltd
101 Longden Road, Shrewsbury, SY3 9EB, England

CONTENTS

Other Manufacturers

INTRODUCTION

When *Airlife's General Aviation* was written in 1990, it was intended that helicopters should be included. This became impractical, both for reasons of space and because of the impossibility of excluding military helicopters from what was, essentially, a civil aircraft book. *Airlife's Helicopters and Rotorcraft* seeks to remedy this while following a similar format to the earlier volume.

Airlife's Helicopters and Rotorcraft covers the principal rotating wing aircraft built commercially since 1945. It includes a great variety of machines including true helicopters, autogyros, tilt-wing aircraft, flying platforms, strap-on personal helicopters and compound helicopters. It has not been possible to cover every prototype produced since 1945, but the principal small-production helicopters and the most popular types of kit-built amateur helicopters and autogyros are included in the section on Other Manufacturers. For reasons of space, no attempt is made to cover the myriad of one-off amateur built machines. Each major manufacturer is given a section covering the general history of the company and its products, and tables identifying the different models built and the quantities produced, together with the constructors' serial numbers (c/n) of these aircraft.

It is estimated that 27,300 civil and approximately 30,000 military helicopters are currently in operation, worldwide. Helicopters have become a part of daily life – yet there remains an attitudinal gulf between fixed wing and rotary wing flyers. On the one hand, fixed-wing flyers may declare that 'You wouldn't get me up in one of those things'. By contrast, the helicopter devotee will argue that 'normal' aircraft are limited to operating from fixed runways and this makes them vulnerable in emergencies and that the helicopter is far more flexible operationally. The truth is that both categories aim to fulfil similar objectives in complementary ways, and are the product of remarkable engineering development and the experimentation of industry pioneers.

The idea of the helicopter goes back to the Leonardo da Vinci concepts of 1493 – and perhaps farther. In the twentieth century numerous experiments with rotating wing machines were carried out during the thirty years leading up to the start of World War II. Very satisfactory autogyros produced by Cierva, Kellett and others were developed during this period. The real potential of helicopters with powered rotors (as compared with the autogyro which uses a conventional engine and propeller but replaces a fixed wing with a freely rotating rotor) was recognised during World War II, and was led by the work of the great Igor Sikorsky. Other inspiration came from the designs of Professor Focke and the British experiments of G & J Weir Ltd.

By the end of the war, Sikorsky's R-4 and R-6 were already operational. Whilst a curiosity, the helicopter's worth for crucial tasks such as air-sea rescue was being recognised. The two biggest challenges for the early engineers were ground resonance and the problem of the torque effect of the helicopter's engine interreacting with that of the rotor. Ground resonance was eventually conquered by detailed design but rotor torque found solutions which were many and various. Focke had used twin side-by-side counter-turning rotors, Piasecki fitted tandem rotors and many designers used a pair of counter-directional rotors on a common mast – although this involved complicated coaxial drive systems. Charles Kaman's unique answer was to fit two intermeshing rotors on closely set pylons. The problem could also be solved if the shaft was not driven from a central engine but the rotor blades powered independently. This led to a variety of tip-jet systems the most successful of which was probably that fitted to the Sud Djinn.

In the end, the simplest solution was to have a separate small tail rotor driven off the main engine to offset the torque. Though this had certain disadvantages, it turned out to be the most popular formula. The main problem with a tail rotor is that it is normally out of sight of the pilot and therefore vulnerable to striking other objects when the helicopter operates from confined spaces. This difficulty has been reduced in recent times by the introduction of Aérospatiale's 'Fenestron' and by the McDonnell Douglas NOTAR system of ducting air to a control nozzle at the end of the tail boom.

The 1950s were a decade of experimentation led by the American military authorities. Great enthusiasm was shown for 'personal' helicopters for military troops in the field and many manufacturers produced single-seat helicopters ranging from basic 'strap-on' machines to substantial fully-enclosed types. There was also a vogue for flying platforms with rotors beneath the pilot's feet or in ducted enclosures, fore and aft. In the end all of these failed because they were found to be too complicated to operate effectively in battle-field conditions. As the benefits offered by helicopters became evident, spurred by the wars in Korea and Vietnam, the roles and specifications became clearer. With the year 2000 approaching, the helicopter has achieved a certain maturity – but the concept has a dynamism which offers scope for increasing technological advance as future decades offer new challenges to this unique form of flight.

In writing *Airlife's Helicopters and Rotorcraft* I have been fortunate to have had the help of many experts and friends in various aviation fields. I have to give special thanks to Eric Myall of Air-Britain who has critically reviewed the manuscript and kept me on the straight and narrow, and Mike Hooks and Michael Stroud who have been more than generous with their advice and photographic assistance. I am also most thankful to the staff of Aviation Data Service in Wichita – John Zimmerman, Dave Richardson (DR) and Peter Simmonds for a mass of information on American helicopters. David H Napier of the Aerospace Industries Association kindly provided the information on American helicopter deliveries. For the patience of my wife, Valerie, I am also eternally grateful. The photographic coverage would have been much poorer without the assistance of John M Davis, who provided access to the Kansas Aviation Museum's Robert Pickett archive of unique photographs by Harold G Martin. The illustrations in *Airlife's Helicopters and Rotorcraft* are acknowledged with specific references – Harold G Martin/Kansas Aviation Museum (HGM Collection), Eric Myall (EM), Mike Hooks (MJH), Peter Keating (PRK) and Michael Stroud (MS). Other illustrations are from the author's collection and from manufacturers' archives which are individually acknowledged. This book has also drawn heavily on the knowledge of the writers and compilers of numerous reference works published in the UK and elsewhere. Their contribution to knowledge is enormous and I thank every fellow author for the jigsaw of information which I have been able to access.

R. W. Simpson, April 1998

ABBREVIATIONS.

A number of abbreviations are used in the book. Definitions or explanations of these are shown below. For convenience, the title 'Soviet Union' has been generally referred to throughout, even though this has now been broken into the separate parts of the Commonwealth of Independent States.

ALAT	=	French Army Aviation
ASW	=	Anti-Submarine Warfare
AV-MF	=	Soviet Naval Aviation
a/c	=	Aircraft
CAA	=	Civil Aviation Authority
COD	=	Carrier on Deck (Navy logistics)
Cont.	=	Teledyne Continental Motors
c/n	=	Construction Number
DGAC	=	French Civil Aviation Authority
ECM	=	Electronic Counter Measures
ESM	=	Electronic Signal Monitoring
FAA	=	Federal Aviation Administration
FF	=	First Flight date
FLIR	=	Forward Looking Infra-Red
GE	=	General Electric Aircraft Engines
GRP	=	Glass Reinforced Plastic
h.p.	=	Horsepower
IFR	=	Instrument Flight Rules
JASDF	=	Japanese Air Self Defense Force
JGSDF	=	Japanese Ground SDF
JMSDF	=	Japanese Maritime SDF
Lyc.	=	Textron Lycoming
MBB	=	Messerschmitt-Bolkow-Blohm
MDAP	=	Military Defence Aid Program

MoS	=	Ministry of Supply
NASA	=	National Aeronautics & Space Admin.
NOTAR	=	No Tail Rotor
PADC	=	Philippine Aviation Development Corp.
pax	=	Passengers
Prot.	=	Prototype
P&W	=	Pratt & Whitney
RSV	=	Italian Flight Test Establishment
SAAF	=	South African Air Force
SAR	=	Search and Rescue
shp	=	Shaft Horsepower (turbine engines)
SNCAN	=	Nord Aviation.
SNCASE	=	Sud Est
SNCASO	=	Sud Ouest
s/n	=	Serial Number (normally military)
TBO	=	Time Between Overhauls
TOGW	=	Takeoff Gross Weight
USAF	=	United States Air Force
USCG	=	United States Coast Guard
USMC	=	United States Marine Corps.
USN	=	United States Navy
u/c	=	Undercarriage
VERTREP	=	Vertical Replenishment
VTOL	=	Vertical Takeoff and Landing
V/STOL	=	Vertical or Short Takeoff and Landing

HELICOPTER DELIVERIES BY UNITED STATES MANUFACTURERS, 1977 TO 1995

Model	1995	1994	1993	1992	1991	1990	1989	1988	1987	1986	1985	1984	1983	1982	1981	1980	1979	1978	1977
Bell 205A															2				
Bell 206								13	74	67	87	94	107	193	476	550	469	322	283
Bell 212						1	3	18	11	11	8	18	6	32	49	116	86	50	47
Bell 214			2	1		1	2	11	13	15	10	13	11	12	12	7	8	16	9
Bell 222								20	12	20	22	26	17	15	21	41			
Bell 412					4	14	17	24	17	12	19	16	18	24	51				
Bell AH.1S	9	7	12			5				13	37		19	11	21	1	7		7
Bell AH.1W	24	22	7	10	22	7		8	24	13									
Bell TH.57											47	21	69	7					
Bell TH.67	55	63	0																
Bell UH-1H											15	12				70	61	27	17
Boeing 234											4		4	1	6				
Boeing CH.47	2			6	9	11		1	4	7	3	3		8	23	6	4	4	12
Brantly B2B																	2	11	1
Brantly H5T										4									
Enstrom 280				3	9	15	18	10	5	7	7	3	1	7	17	30	19	47	52
Enstrom 480	8	4	2																
Enstrom F28	3	13	8	3	8	12	6	7	7	3	11	2	8	17	29	18	27	44	44
Hiller 1100														3	1				
Hiller UH-12E	1			3	2		3	4	6	10	2		7	29	29	49	43	52	40
Kaman SH.2F		5									17	12	1						
Kaman K.1200	6																		
McDD 500	12	3	5	23	42	65	64	39	37	40	48	85	70	108	136	265	196	196	211

Model	1995	1994	1993	1992	1991	1990	1989	1988	1987	1986	1985	1984	1983	1982	1981	1980	1979	1978	1977
McDD 500MD/ME								19	11		29	24	26	14					
McDD 520N	10	9	21	17	3														
McDD 530	12	22		11	5	12	9	5	4	24	8	7							
McDD 900	12	2																	
McDD AH.64	36	26	88	61	65	96	112	118	125	117	51	16							
McDD H.300										1			67	54	50	136	110	116	125
Robinson R22	83	89	135	222	402	384	310	204	127	90	79	79	64	88	156	78			
Robinson R44	96	106	31																
Schweizer 330	4	5	5																
Schweizer 300C	22	35	40	39	78	83	69	45	43	27	32	11							
Schweizer 300CB	21																		
Sikorsky CH.53	7	4	11	8	6	14	14	10	10	7	10	18	20	24	15	2			
Sikorsky HH.60H	14	2			7	3	2												
Sikorsky MH.53		13						9		3									
Sikorsky MH.60G				15	19	22	18	16											
Sikorsky S-61																5	5		25
Sikorsky S-70	19	29	64	24	36	35	17	13	1	3	28	11							
Sikorsky S-76	14	15	9	12	18	16	17	11	13	10	19	31	36	28	50	85	36	27	
Sikorsky S-80		1		11		2	3												
Sikorsky SH-60	11	18	17	23	24	28	21	19	19	24	24	22	2						
Sikorsky UH-60	64	65	60	38	72	85	83	72	81	79	111	123	137	126	120				
Total Deliveries	**533**	**558**	**520**	**530**	**831**	**911**	**788**	**696**	**644**	**607**	**728**	**647**	**690**	**801**	**1264**	**1459**	**1073**	**912**	**873**

Notes:
1. Bell transferred production of Model 206, 212, 222 etc to Textron Canada from 1989 onwards
2. Deliveries include all civil, US Military and export aircraft

A twin-engined Aérospatiale AS.355M Ecureuil works in support of ground-based units for battlefield liaison and to provide much needed firepower.

AÉROSPATIALE FRANCE

Nationalisation of the French aviation industry in the years immediately prior to World War II had resulted in the formation of the Société Nationale de Constructions Aéronautiques Sud-Est (SNCASE) and the Société Nationale de Constructions Aéronautiques Sud-Ouest (SNCASO). During the early years of peace both companies pursued a myriad of projects including development of helicopters to meet a wide range of missions. Sud-Est made the greatest progress with rotary wing aircraft, and when the two organisations merged on 1 March 1957 to form Sud-Aviation it was the team from SNCASE which dominated the Helicopter Division. The other national company, SNCAN, also experimented with rotary wing aircraft but was not able to bring any of them to production status.

Sud-Ouest took an early initiative after the war using research carried out in Germany into helicopters with rotor-tip propulsion. The diminutive SO.1100 Ariel I was a tiny streamlined machine with a three-blade main rotor and a tail stabilising rotor inside an annular duct which was displayed at the Aviation Salon of 1946. A series of developed Ariels followed but Sud Ouest finally went into production with a much more basic machine – the Djinn – which was adopted by the French Army and subsequently found a role as a crop-sprayer. The Djinn retained the principle of rotor-tip propulsion with tip nozzles ejecting compressed air generated by a Turboméca Artouste turbine engine.

At Sud-Est the inspiration for future helicopter design also came from Germany. The company's research was initially based on the work of Professor Focke which resulted in a French version of the Focke Achgelis Fa.223 twin rotor helicopter. The struggle to make this aircraft sufficiently laterally stable soon gave way to a more straightforward solution. Professor Focke and M. Renoux had also designed a single-seat machine, the SE.3101, which had an engine mounted centrally in the fuselage driving a three-blade main rotor and twin stabilising tail rotors. This provided the basis for refinement of SNCASE's helicopter engineering and led to the three-seat prototype Alouette I which used a single tail rotor and featured a more developed tubular steel fuselage structure with clear separation between the cabin section, tailboom and engine installation.

The Sud-Est development had taken some years during which Bell and other manufacturers had been producing substantial numbers of helicopters However, the Alouette was ahead in having turbine power from the start and the definitive Alouette II, which flew at the hands of Jean Boulet in March, 1955, soon broke the world helicopter altitude record and the first production aircraft appeared early the following year. The Alouette II had, by this time, grown to five-seat capacity and featured a streamlined cabin pod although it retained the open tubular rear boom design. Sud Aviation went on to build over 1600 examples of the Alouette II and its derivatives and delivered them to military and civil

13

Aérospatiale SE.3130 Alouette II, F-ZBDB

users in approximately 50 countries. The French Army, Navy and Gendarmerie took substantial numbers and other military customers included Belgium, the United Kingdom, Germany, Lebanon, Sweden, Switzerland and Turkey. A high-altitude version, the Lama, was produced in France and in Brazil (where it was built under licence by Helibras) and in India where Hindustan produced it as the Cheetah. In the United States, an unsuccessful agreement was reached between Sud Aviation and Republic Aviation Corporation to assemble and manufacture the Alouette II as the Republic Lark.

With the Alouette II firmly established in production Sud Aviation followed on, in 1959, with a more powerful model, the Alouette III. This was, essentially, a completely new design with a wholly metal-clad fuselage and a wheeled undercarriage rather than the skid landing gear of the earlier helicopter. A number of variants of the Alouette III were produced with increasingly powerful engines and, again, the type was built under licence in Switzerland, India (as the Chetak), and Romania (as the IAR.316B). Atlas Aircraft in South Africa, which maintained a large fleet of Alouette IIIs for the SAAF, has recently experimented with a substantially modified version of the SA.316 which embodies a NOTAR anti-torque tail system somewhat similar to that of the McDonnell Douglas MD.520N.

At around the same time that the Alouette III entered development, Sud-Aviation were studying a French military requirement for a heavy transport helicopter. The result was the SE.3200 Frelon. This was designed with the entire engine module, housing three Turboméca Turmo turbines, being positioned on top of the fuselage, which resulted in a completely unobstructed cabin. Two Frelons were built and successfully tested but the military requirement had expanded in the meanwhile. So, the company followed on with the SA.321 Super Frelon which had almost twice the gross weight of the earlier proto-types. The Super Frelon featured a boat hull, a separate tail boom which allowed a rear loading ramp to be fitted and the ability to carry up to 30 troops. Most of the 104 production Super Frelons were delivered to the French military forces, with the Aéronavale receiving a number for anti-submarine warfare. Israel, Libya, Iraq and China also purchased the Super Frelon and the type was built under licence in China as the Changhe Z-8. A civil version was developed but not delivered to any commercial users.

During the early 1960s the capabilities of helicopters were becoming recognised and the Alouette offered insufficient capacity for the French Army. Sud-Aviation had manu-factured the Sikorsky S-55 helicopter under the title 'Elephant Joyeux'. This was followed

Aérospatiale SA.316B Alouette III, 9H-AAV

by a batch of 180 Sikorsky H-34s under licence for the Army and the Aéronavale (HSS-1 Seabat standard) and five SAR versions for the Belgian Air Force. However, in 1962 the French Army issued a requirement for a tactical transport helicopter which could rapidly carry up to 20 soldiers to the battlefront and perform a wide range of cargo-carrying and heavy-lift tasks. Sud-Aviation had experimented with an upgraded H-34 (No.76) fitted with a twin turbine 'Bi-Bastan' installation, but the S-58/H-34 structure offered insufficient capacity to meet the new specification and was, in any case, an outmoded design.

The result was a completely new design, the SA.330 Puma. Development commenced in 1963 with French Government funding, and the prototype flew two years later, followed by a batch of six pre production machines. Like the Frelon it had the power unit positioned on top of the fuselage. This allowed a clear internal volume designed to carry up to 18 troops plus two crew. The SA.330 had the classic layout of a main fuselage pod with tailboom and fin structure, and the twin Bastan VII turbines drove a four-blade main rotor and five-blade tail anti-torque propeller. During development the Bastans were replaced by a pair of Turboméca Turmo III turboshafts similar to those used on the Super Frelon.

Substantial orders for the Puma were received from the French Army, and the Royal Air Force also selected the Puma. In February 1967, Sud-Aviation entered into a co-production agreement with Westland Helicopters under which the SA.330, the SA.341 and the WG.13 would be produced in collaboration. This resulted in the Puma being partially manufactured in England – and the 48 British military Pumas were completely assembled by Westland at Yeovil. This arrangement continued in force until 1988.

The Puma became a popular choice for offshore oil operations with significant orders being placed by Bristow Helicopters. Military purchasers of the SA.330 included Chile, Indonesia, Morocco, South Africa and Spain. The SA.330 was manufactured under licence in Romania as the IAR-330 with approximately 90 being delivered to Romanian military and civil users and to the air forces of Ethiopia and Guinea. Atlas Aircraft in South Africa carried out a major upgrade programme on the South African Air Force Pumas. This involved installing the more powerful Makila 1A turboshafts with associated modifications to the tail unit, and extensive upgrading to offensive systems capability and developed avionics and nose-mounted radar. These were known as the Oryx in SAAF service.

HELICOPTERS AND ROTORCRAFT

The SA.330 was replaced in production in 1980 by the SA.332 Super Puma, which retained the same basic airframe but had a 30% increase in engine power and a redesigned transmission to go with it. Many other modifications were introduced including a new undercarriage, composite main and tail rotors, redesigned tail and a longer nose section. The later Super Puma Mk.2 had a stretched fuselage, and progressive improvements to the rotor head and transmission were introduced over the life of the type. Again, Bristow Helicopters acquired more than 30 aircraft which they named 'Tiger'. The military AS.332 was renamed 'Cougar' in 1990 and was delivered to more than 30 countries. IPTN in Indonesia, which had been building the SA.330 under licence, completed a batch of Super Pumas for domestic civil and military use.

On 1 January 1970, Sud-Aviation, Nord Aviation and SEREB merged to form the Société Nationale Industrielle Aérospatiale. Just prior to this date Sud-Aviation had flown a new light helicopter, the SA.340, which was intended as a replacement for the Alouette. This streamlined all-metal machine was tested initially with a conventional tail rotor but was subsequently fitted with a 'fenestron' multi-blade anti-torque device housed in a circular tail shroud within the tail fin structure. Its main rotors were designed in cooperation with Messerschmitt-Bölkow-Blohm in Germany. Four production prototypes of the definitive SA.341 Gazelle were flown and the type was incorporated into the joint production agreement with Westland so that parallel production started at Toulouse and Yeovil to meet initial orders from the French ALAT and the Royal Navy and Army Air Corps. A civil Gazelle was developed and sold in some numbers and a variety of military models were offered – some with dual controls and many with extensive externally-mounted armament. The largest Gazelle users were Egypt, which acquired almost 100 examples, and Iraq, Libya and Kuwait. In Yugoslavia the Gazelle was built under licence by Soko which completed 132 of the SA.321H 'Partizan' and a number of the SA.342L which had an improved fenestron tail rotor.

With the Puma and Gazelle in production, Aérospatiale found itself with a gap in the six to ten seat helicopter category. Design work started in 1970 on the SA.360 Dauphin which was, initially, derived from the Alouette III and used the rotor blades from that helicopter. In its early form, the SA.360 had a fixed tailwheel undercarriage, a fenestron tail similar to that of the Gazelle and a single Astazou XVI turboshaft engine. Eventually, the engine power was upgraded and Aérospatiale decided to offer both single- and twin-engined versions of the Dauphin equipped with new composite main blades.

The Dauphin turned out to be a highly efficient performer and gained several closed circuit speed records early in its career. It was the twin-engined model which received the

Sud Ouest SO.1120 Ariel 3, F-WFUY *(via MJH)*

Aérospatiale AS.565 Panther, EB 2001 *(Aérospatiale)*

bulk of orders and Aérospatiale fitted this SA.365 with their new 'Starflex' glass-fibre rotor head which used a central fibreglass 'star' and maintenance-free steel/rubber ball joints in place of the traditional root hinges. This drastically reduced the normal number of parts required for a normally very complex assembly. The SA.365C received its French DGAC type certificate in July, 1978 and deliveries, largely to civil users, commenced shortly thereafter. Many examples of the basic Dauphin were sold to police authorities but only a handful were sold for military transport.

A requirement for a U.S. Coast Guard replacement for its Sikorsky S-62 fleet led Aérospatiale to produce the modified SA.366. This was based on a developed version of the Dauphin – named SA.365N Dauphin 2 – which featured a retractable tricycle under-carriage and remodelled nose section. The U.S. Coast Guard version was tasked with short range rescue missions and had extensive equipment bays in the rear cabin and a pair of Lycoming LTS101 turboshafts which were based on the Turboméca Arriel. A total of 96 were delivered as the HH-65A Dolphin but it was not long before it was realised that the Dolphin was short on range for Coast Guard requirements and, with the LTS101, was underpowered. As a result of an unacceptably high in-flight shutdown rate and low TBO consideration was given to replacement of the engines by Allison-Garrett T800 turbines but this has not so far been pursued.

The civil SA.365N has had a smoother ride and is now well established as a corporate transport with substantial sales in North America for executive use and for healthcare emergency operations. It has led to the fully-militarised AS.565 Panther which has been sold to a number of air arms including Brazil (36), India, Ireland, Thailand and Saudi Arabia. The Panther is capable of carrying a range of externally mounted weapons including Exocet missiles but a number of aircraft have been equipped in a naval role for operation from corvettes and are fitted with harpoon landing systems for this application.

One of Aérospatiale's most successful designs is the six-seat AS.350 Ecureuil (Squirrel) which was aimed at the civil market dominated by the Bell Jet Ranger. Aérospatiale produced a simple structure for the Ecureuil with a minimal number of parts so as to achieve low production cost and good maintainability. The Starflex rotor head, comprising only 70 component parts and offering greatly reduced maintenance cost, was used and the airframe incorporated a mixture of composites and pre-formed light alloy panels. The Ecureuil made its first flight in 1974 and was certificated in France in October 1977. The AS.350 was sold in North America as the 'A-Star' with a Lycoming LTS101 engine and elsewhere with the French-built Turboméca Arriel.

Having successfully launched the AS.350, Aérospatiale added a twin-engined equivalent, the AS.355. Known as the Twin-Star in America and Twin Squirrel in Europe, the AS.355

Aérospatiale SA.361H Dauphin, F-WZAK *(Aérospatiale)*

was substantially the same as its single-engined brother but had a strengthened airframe, redesigned transmission, modified rotor blades and two Allison 250 turboshafts mounted side-by-side above and behind the cabin. Production deliveries followed shortly after type approval was received in October, 1980. The company soon followed the civil Ecureuils with a military armed version named 'Fennec' which was offered in various configurations including anti-tank and ground attack versions. Customers for the Fennec included Denmark, Ecuador and Australia – which acquired a number for naval ship-based communications.

In 1992, Aérospatiale became a part of Eurocopter. Sometimes referred to as Eurocopter-France, its current activities are described under the Eurocopter section.

Production details

A number of different serial number sequences were used over the span of Aérospatiale's development – which is understandable when the number of changes of corporate structure are considered. Details are given below. It should be noted that the 187 examples of the SA.342M HOT Gazelle for the French ALAT were given amended serial numbers with the first digits increased by 2 (i.e. changed to 3 or 4). Thus, c/n 1547 became 3547, c/n 1904 became 3904 and c/n 2231 became 4231.

Model	Prototype Serials	Main production	Number Built	Notes
SO.1221		FR-1 to FR-150	150	Also allocated military c/ns 1 to 100 or civil c/n 1001 to 1050. Military to civil conversions have c/n 1100 to 1114.
SE.313 SE.318 Lama		c/n 1001 to 2679	1679	All models included in overall serial number sequence.
SA.316 SA.319		c/n 1001 to 2392	1392	Includes c/ns allocated to Romanian prodn. Also some 5000-series c/ns.
Sikorsky S-55D		SA.1 to SA.135	135	Information unconfirmed.

Model	Prototype Serials	Main production	Number Built	Notes
Sikorsky S-58		SA1 to SA185	185	Also assembly of Sikorsky-built airframes with 'SKY' in front of the Sikorsky c/n (e.g. SKY-281).
SA.321	c/n 001 & 002 01 to 06 (pre-prod)	c/n 101 to 204	112	
SA.330	Pre-series c/n 330.01 to 330.08	c/n 1001 to 1678	686	Romanian production unknown. Includes Westland-built aircraft.
SA.332 AS.532	332.01	c/n 2001 to 2439+	440	Includes Nurtanio (Indonesian production) with dual c/ns shown below.
NAS.332		c/n NSP1 to NSP024	19	Local Indonesian c/ns. Aircraft also have Aérospatiale serial as above.
SA.341 SA.342	c/n 341.01 to 341.04	c/n 1001 to 2234	1234	See narrative note on HOT Gazelle.
AS.350 AS.550		c/n 1001 to 2932+	1932	
AS.355 AS.555	c/n 355.01 and 355.02	c/n 5001 to 5607+	609	
SA.360	c/n 360.001 & 002	c/n 1001 to 1034	36	
SA.365	c/n 366.003 & 365.004	c/n 5001 to 5079	81	
SA.365F SA.365N SA.366	c/n 5100 and some production airframes as shown in type table	c/n 6001 to 6501 up	502	

Model information

The companies which made up Aérospatiale produced a large number of models and sub-models. In the following table, the AS prefix denotes an Aérospatiale design and SA relates to Sud Aviation. The SA prefixes were replaced by AS as a result of the Aérospatiale takeover and applied to all new models introduced after 1957. There was a delay in changing the prefix for models which had already been in production in 1957 and designations for these only started to alter in 1968. The designation change was not applied retrospectively to pre-1957 production machines.

Sud Ouest SO.1221 Djinn, F-BIEV

Helibras AS.305B Esquilo, PT-HYV

HELICOPTERS AND ROTORCRAFT

Type No.	Name	Notes
SE.700		Experimental all-metal autogyro with nose-mounted 330 h.p. Bearn 6D-07 engine, stub wings with end fins and retractable tricycle u/c. FF May 1945. 2 built.
SNCAN N1700	Norelic	Single-seat experimental helicopter with shrouded tail rotor and adjustable rotor head. One Prot. FF 17 Nov. 1947.
SO.1100	Ariel 1	Two-seat helicopter with rotor-tip jet propulsors powered by compressor from a 220 h.p. Mathis G8 engine. Pod fuselage with tricycle u/c and shrouded rear prop. Later modified with tail boom. One Prot. F-WFKM FF 14 May 1947.
SO.1110	Ariel 2	Developed Ariel 1 with modified control system and Turboméca compressor. First of two Prots. F-WFRQ FF 21 May 1950.
SO.1120	Ariel 3	Three-seat all-metal helicopter with fixed tricycle u/c and one 275 shp Turboméca Artouste turbine driving rotor-tip propulsors via an air compressor. first of two Prots. F-WFUY (c/n 01) FF 18 Apl. 1951.
SO.1220	Djinn	Single-seat experimental army support helicopter with open frame structure and landing skids and powered by one 250 shp Turboméca Palouste turbine providing compressed air to rotor tips. First of two Prots. F-WCZX (c/n 01) FF 2 Jan. 1953.
SO.1221	Djinn	Production version of SO.1220 for French Army with enclosed transparent cockpit structure and enlarged tail with tailplane and end fins. Prot. F-WGVH (c/n 001) FF 14 Dec. 1953.
SO.1310	Farfadet	All-metal three-seat compound helicopter with small wings, fixed tricycle u/c and four-blade main rotor driven by a 360 shp Turboméca Arrius II turboshaft and forward propulsion from a 360 shp Turboméca Artouste II. Single Prot. F-WBGD (c/n 01). FF 8 May 1953.
N.1750	Norelfe	Three-seat Aerotecnica AC.13 all-metal streamlined pod & boom helicopter built by Nord with a 280 shp Turboméca Artouste I turbine positioned behind cabin driving three-blade main rotor and tail compressed air unit. First of two Prots. F-WGVZ (c/n 01) FF 28 Dec. 1954.
NC.2001		Experimental helicopter with two meshing rotors on separate pylons, powered by one 450 h.p. Renault 12 S00 engine. Three built. Prot. FF 28 June 1949.
SE.3000		Experimental helicopter with two rotors on outrigger pylons, powered by one 1000 h.p. BMW-323-R2 engine. Three built. Prot. F-WFDR. FF 23 Oct. 1948.
SE.3101		Experimental single seat open-frame helicopter with 100 h.p. Mathis engine driving three-blade main rotor and V-tail mounting two stabilising rotors. Single Prot. F-WFDQ (c/n 01) FF 15 June 1948.
SE.3110		Developed SE.3101 with all metal airframe and 200 h.p. Salmson engine. Single Prot. F-WFUE FF 10 June 1950.

Type No.	Name	Notes
SE.3120	Alouette I	Three-seat helicopter with enclosed cabin, open-frame rear boom, fixed tricycle u/c (later skids) and one Salmson 9NH engine positioned behind cabin driving 3-blade rotor. Two built. Prot. F-WGGD (c/n 01). FF 31 Jul. 1951.
SE.3130	Alouette II	New design incorporating components of SE.3120 with streamlined cabin pod for five seats in two rows, open frame rear fuselage, skid u/c and one 450 shp Turboméca Artouste II turboshaft. Prot F-WHHE (C/n 01) FF 12 Mar. 1955.
SE.313B	Alouette II	New designation for SE.3130 revised in 1967.
SE.3131	Gouverneur	Alouette II with fully enclosed centre and rear fuselage and deluxe cabin. Single Prot F-BIEA (c/n 01). FF 10 May 1957.
SE.3140		Experimental Alouette II with shorter main rotor blades and 400 shp Turboméca Turmo turboshaft. F-WIEB (c/n 01) FF 16 May 1957.
SE.3150	Lama	Alouette II fitted with larger main rotor, 3-blade tail rotor and 500 shp Turboméca Artouste III turboshaft. Two built. Prot. F-ZWVN (c/n 001) FF. 11 Mar. 1958. Second prot. F-ZWVM fitted with Turmo II and FF 19 May 1958
SA.315A	Lama	Production-standard SE.3150 for hot and high operations powered by one 570 shp Artouste IIIB turboshaft. Prot. F-BPXJ FF 17 Mar. 1969.
SA.315B	Lama	SA.315A with taller u/c and minor alterations
SA.315B	Cheetah	Indian built Lama by Hindustan. FF 6 Oct. 1973. Appx. 190 built.
H.315B	Gaviao	Brazilian built Lama by Helibras.
SE.3160	Alouette III	Redesigned Alouette II with all-metal monocoque fuselage, fully enclosed seven-seat cabin and fixed tricycle u/c, powered by one 870/550 shp Turboméca Artouste IIIB. Prot. F-ZWVQ (c/n 001) FF 28 Feb. 1959.
SA.316A	Alouette III	New designation for SE.3160 revised in 1968.
SA.316B	Alouette III	SA.316A with strengthened transmission and 220 lb. TOGW increase.
IAR-316B	Alouette III	SA.316B built in Romania by IAR.
SA.316C	Alouette III	SA.316B fitted with a 870/660 shp Artouste IIID turboshaft.
IAR-317	Airfox	Light attack helicopter prototype built in Romania by IAR. Based on IAR-316B with new stepped two-seat armoured cockpit and external weapons points.
SA.3164		Alouette III with stepped windshield and nose-mounted 20mm canon and external missile points. Prot FF 24 June 1964.
SA.3180	Alouette Astazou	Alouette II fitted with 450 shp Turboméca Artouste II turbine for high-altitude operation. Prot. F-WHHF FF 31 Jan. 1961.
SA.318C	Alouette Astazou	New designation for SE.3180 revised in 1967.
SA.319	Alouette III	SA.316 fitted with 600 shp Turboméca Astazou XIV turboshaft. Prot F-ZWVQ.

HELICOPTERS AND ROTORCRAFT

Type No.	Name	Notes
SA.319B	Alouette III	Production version of SA.319 for military and civil users.
HSA.316B	Chetak	SA.316B manufactured by Hindustan in India. 200 built.
IAR.316B		SA.316B manufactured by ICA-Brasov in Romania.
SA.316B	Alouette III	SA.316B manufactured by FFA in Switzerland. 60 built.
SE.3200	Frelon	Heavy transport helicopter with single four-blade main rotor powered by three 750 shp Turboméca Turmo IIIB turboshafts positioned in housing on top of fuselage. Fitted with outrigged sponsons mounting u/c. First of two Prots. F-ZWVS (c/n 001) FF 10 June 1959.
SA.320	Frelon	New designation for SE.3200.
SE.3210/ SA.321	Super Frelon	Larger development of SA.320 with boat hull and outrigger floats, rear loading doors, boom tail, six-blade main rotor driven by three 1320 shp Turboméca Turmo IIIC turboshafts. Prot. F-ZWWE FF 7 Dec. 1962.
SA.321B	Super Frelon	Standard French Air Force/Army Super Frelon.
SA.321D	Super Frelon	Standard French Navy Super Frelon.
SA.321F	Super Frelon	Civil Super Frelon with streamlined external sponsons.
SA.321G	Super Frelon	Anti-submarine Super Frelon for Aéronavale.
SA.321H	Super Frelon	Simplified military version of SA.321.
SA.321J	Super Frelon	27-passenger civil utility version of SA.321.
SA.330	Puma	Medium-lift 20-troop military helicopter with retractable tricycle u/c and four-blade main rotor driven by two 1320 shp Turboméca Turmo III.C4 turboshafts positioned in housing above main cabin. Prot. F-ZWWN (c/n 01). FF. 14 Apl. 1965. Jointly built by Aérospatiale and Westland. Originally named Alouette IV.
SA.330B	Puma	SA.330 for French ALAT.
SA.330C	Puma	Military export version of SA.330B.
SA.330E	Puma	SA.330 for RAF designated HC.1.
SA.330F	Puma	SA.330 for civil customers.
SA.330G	Puma	SA.330F for commercial customers with 1575 shp Turmo IVC turboshafts.
SA.330H	Puma	SA.330G for ALAT and overseas military customers.
SA.330J	Puma	SA.330G with composite main rotor blades and higher weights. Some assembled by IPTN in Indonesia.
SA.330L	Puma	SA.330H with composite main rotor blades and higher weights.
SA.330R	Puma	Stretched SA.330 used as development aircraft for Super Puma.
SA.330S	Puma	Portuguese SA.330C modified by OGMA with composite main rotor and two 1700 shp Turboméca Makila I turboshafts.
SA.330Z	Puma	SA.330 fitted with experimental tail fenestron. Prot F-ZWRR (C/n 05).
IAR.330L	Puma	Puma manufactured in Romania by IAR with 1588 shp Turboméca Turmo IV-CA turboshafts.

Type No.	Name	Notes
SA.331	Puma	SA.330 used as development aircraft for SA.332 Super Puma with two 1755 shp Turboméca Makila turboshafts and redesigned rotor head. Also known as SA.330R. F-ZWWO (c/n 02) FF 5 Sept. 1977.
AS.332	Super Puma	SA.330 with extended forward fuselage providing 21-troop capacity, ventral tailfin, two 1775 shp Turboméca Makila 1A turboshafts, new rotor head, faired sponsons. Prot F-WZJA (c/n 01) FF 13 Sep. 1978.
AS.332B	Super Puma	Military transport version of AS.332.
AS.332B1	Super Puma	AS.332B with 1877 shp Makila 1A1 turboshafts. Redesignated AS.532UC.
AS.332C	Super Puma	Civil version of AS.332 with 19-pax capacity.
AS.332F	Super Puma	Naval AS.332 equipped with Exocet missile system or anti-submarine search equipment.
AS.332F1	Super Puma	AS.332F with 1877 shp Makila 1A1 turboshafts. Redesignated AS.532MC.
AS.332L	Super Puma	AS.332C with lengthened forward fuselage and 22-pax cabin. Prot. F-WZJN FF 10 Oct. 1980.
AS.332L1	Super Puma	AS.332L with 1877 shp Makila 1A1 turboshafts.
AS.332L2	Super Puma Mk.2	AS.332L1 with 2109 shp Makila 1A2 turboshafts, redesigned rotor blades and spheriflex rotor head, rear fuselage stretch and optional exterior baggage pod.
AS.332M	Super Puma	AS.332B with lengthened forward fuselage, interior cabin extended to house 24 troops and fuel tankage reduced.
AS.332M1	Super Puma	AS.332M with 1877 shp Makila 1A1 turboshafts. Redesignated AS.532UL.
AS.332M2	Super Puma Mk.2	AS.332M1 with 2109 shp Makila 1A2 turboshafts, redesigned rotor blades and spheriflex rotor head, and rear fuselage stretch. Redesignated AS.532U2. Also built in Combat-SAR configuration.

Aérospatiale/Westland SA.341B Gazelle AH.1, XW843 *(Westland)*

Type No.	Name	Notes
SA.340		Light five-seat helicopter initially designated X-300 with streamlined fuselage, skid u/c, SA.316 tail rotor, three-blade main rotor driven by a Turboméca Astazou IIN2 turboshaft. Prot. F-WOFH (later F-ZWRF) c/n 001. FF 7 Apl. 1967. Later fitted with tail fin and buried 'fenestron' tail rotor. Two built.
SA.341	Gazelle	Production SA.340 with longer cabin, enlarged tail fin etc. powered by one 590 shp Astazou IIIN.
SA.341A		Designation not used.
SA.341B	Gazelle AH.1	British Army cooperation version with Astazou IIIN engine.
SA.341C	Gazelle HT.2	Royal Navy version with Astazou IIIN engine and dual controls.
SA.341D	Gazelle HT.3	Training version of AH.1 for RAF.
SA.341E	Gazelle HCC.4	RAF communication model.
SA.341F	Gazelle	Army cooperation model for ALAT with Astazou IIIC engine.
SA.341G	Gazelle	Civil model with Astazou IIIA engine.
SA.341H	Gazelle	Export military model with Astazou IIIB engine. Also built under licence by Mostar (Yugoslavia).
SA.341L1	Gazelle	SA.341F with increased gross weight and 858 shp Astazou XIVM turboshaft.
SA.342K	Gazelle	Military SA.341 powered by a 858 shp Astazou XIVH engine and fitted with improved 'fenestron' tail and increased gross weight.
SA.342L	Gazelle	SA.342K for civil customers.
SA.342M	Gazelle	ALAT Anti-tank version of SA.342K with four Aérospatiale HOT missiles, autopilot and infra-red exhaust suppressor.
SA.349		Experimental SA.341 with additional fixed wing for high-speed compound helicopter research. Prot. F-ZWRF (c/n 001).

Sud Est SE.3101 *(via MJH)*

Type No.	Name	Notes
AS.350	Ecureuil A-Star	Six seat multi-task helicopter with conventional fuselage design, tail fin and tailplane, skid u/c, three-blade main rotor with 'starflex' hub and one 592 shp Textron-Lycoming LTS.101 turboshaft. Prot. F-WVKH (c/n 001) FF. 26 June, 1974. Second prototype fitted with 641 shp Turboméca Arriel engine.
AS.350B	Ecureuil	Production civil AS.350 with one 641 shp Turboméca Arriel 1B turboshaft and 4300 lb TOGW.
AS.350BA	Ecureuil	AS.350B with AS.355 rotorhead and 4630 lb TOGW.
AS.350B1	Ecureuil	Civil AS.350B with 684 shp Arriel 1D engine and 4850 lb TOGW.
AS.350B2	Ecureuil	AS.350B1 with 732 shp Arriel 1D1 engine and 4961 lb TOGW.
AS.350B3	Ecureuil	AS.350B2 with one FADEC – electronically controlled 847 shp Arriel 2B engine. Prot. FF 4 March 1997.
AS.350C	A-Star	AS.350B for North American customers with 592 shp Textron-Lycoming LTS.101-600 engine. 4300 lb TOGW.
AS.350D	A-Star Mk.III	AS.350C with 615 shp Textron-Lycoming LTS.101-600A2 engine. 4300 lb TOGW.
AS.350D1	A-Star Mk.III	AS.350D with 4000 lb TOGW.
AS.350L	Ecureuil	Military armed version of AS.350B fitted with Hughes TOW anti-tank missiles, GIAT 20mm cannon and twin 7.62mm gun pods.
AS.350L1	Ecureuil	Military AS.350L with 684 shp Arriel 1D turboshaft.
AS.350Z	Ecureuil	AS.350B tested experimentally with scaled-down AS.365 tail fenestron and fin unit. Prot. F-WYMZ (c/n 1013).
AS.355E	Twin Star Ecureuil 2	AS.350 fitted with two 425 shp Allison 250-C20F turboshafts, modified transmission and fuel system and 4628 lb TOGW. Prot. F-WZLA (c/n 01) FF 28 Sep. 1979.
AS.355F	Twin Star Ecureuil 2	AS.355E with dual hydraulic systems, larger main rotor blades and 5071 lb TOGW.
AS.355F1	Twin Star Ecureuil 2	AS.355F with 5291 lb TOGW.
AS.355F2	Twin Star Ecureuil 2	AS.355F1 with modified yaw compensation system, higher external load weight and 5600 lb TOGW.
AS.355M	Ecureuil 2	Armed surveillance version for Armée de l'Air with HOT or TOW missiles and a 20mm GIAT M-621 cannon.
AS.355M2	Ecureuil 2	Military AS.355 powered by two Allison 250-C20F turboshafts and fitted with external 20mm cannon, machine-guns and rockets.
AS.355N	Ecureuil 2	Civil AS.355 powered by two Turboméca TM-319 turboshafts.
SA.360		11-seat helicopter with streamlined fuselage, fixed spatted tailwheel u/c, fenestron tail rotor, and single 4-blade rotor driven by one 940 shp Turbomeca Astazou XVIIIA turboshaft. Prot. F-WSQL (c/n 360-001) FF 2 June 1972.
SA.360A	Dauphin	SA.360 for Aéronavale. 1 built.
SA.360C	Dauphin	SA.360 for commercial customers. Some fitted with skids.
SA.361	Dauphin	SA.360 fitted with Astazou XX turboshaft and 'starflex' rotor head. Prot. F-BSQX/F-ZWVF FF 12 Jul. 1976. Three converted from SA.360Cs.

Type No.	Name	Notes
SA.361H/ HCL	Dauphin	Anti-tank SA.361 with nose-mounted FLIR system, eight HOT missiles. Prot. F-WZAK c/n 1012.
SA.365	Dauphin 2	SA.360 fitted with two 650 shp Turboméca Arriel 1A turboshafts Prot. F-WVKE (c/n 365.004) FF. 24 Jan. 1975. Second prot. (F-WVKD c/n 365.003) used for testing retractable u/c.
SA.365C	Dauphin 2	Civil production version of SA.365 with 7500 lb TOGW.
SA.365C1	Dauphin 2	SA.365C with 667 shp Arriel 1A1 turboshafts.
SA.365C2	Dauphin 2	SA.365C with 670 shp Arriel 1A2 turboshafts, 7715 lb TOGW and modified transmission system.
SA.365N	Dauphin 2	SA.365C with retractable tricycle u/c, lengthened cabin with max 11 pax separated from crew, pointed nose, composite rotors new air intakes and redesigned under-floor fuel tanks. 710 shp Turboméca Arriel IC turboshaft. 8818 lb TOGW. FF 31 Mar. 1979. Prot. F-WZJD (c/n 5100).
SA.365N1	Dauphin 2	SA.365 with 724 shp Arriel 1C1 turboshafts, 9038 lb TOGW and recontoured lower tail section eliminating ventral fin.
AS.365N2	Dauphin 2	SA-365N with two 763 shp Turboméca Arriel 1C2 turboshafts, new gearbox, 9371 lb TOGW.
AS.365N3	Dauphin 2	AS.365N with quiet tail rotor and two Arriel 2C turboshafts. Prot. FF Oct. 1996.
AS.365N4	Dauphin	AS.365N3 with wide 12-passenger fuselage, five-blade main rotor and improved avionics suite. Prot. FF 16 Jun. 1997. Redesignated EC-155.
SA.365F	Dauphin 2	Navalised SA.365N for Saudi Arabia etc. with pointed radar nose and either under-nose radar dish or anti-submarine missile system and 700 shp Arriel 1M turboshafts. Prot. F-WZJD (c/n 5100) FF in this form 22 Feb. 1982.

Aérospatiale SE.3210 Super Frelon, F-ZWWJ *(Aérospatiale)*

Type No.	Name	Notes
SA.365M	Dauphin 2	Army light tactical version of SA.365N1 with 12-troop capacity. Powered by two 913 shp Turboméca TM.333-1M turboshafts. 9039 lb TOGW. Prot. F-WZJV (c/n 6005) FF 29 Feb. 1984. Later named Panther.
Harbin Z.9		Chinese licence-built SA.365M.
AS.365K	Panther	SA.365M with 748 shp Arriel 1M1 turboshafts. Redesignated AS.565.
X.380	Dauphin	SA.365N with combined composite rotorhub/mast, 5-blade rotor with swept tips, and 837 shp Turboméca Arriel 1X turboshafts.
AS.366G	Dolphin HH-65A	Three-seat SA.365N for US Coast Guard short-range recovery tasks with internal stretcher fittings, rescue hoist, pop-out flotation bags etc. 8928 lb. TOGW. Powered by two 680 shp Textron-Lycoming LTS.101-750A-1 turboshafts. Prot. USCG.4101 (c/n 6002) FF 23 Jul. 1980. Four built.
AS.366G1	Dolphin	Production AS.366G with LTS.101-750B-2 turboshafts and 8950 lb TOGW. 92 built.
AS.532	Super Puma	Revised designation for AS.332 issued in 1990.
AS.532UB/ AB	Cougar	Reduced-cost AS.532 without external sponsons and with new strutted main u/c legs, modified comms equipment etc.
AS.532UC	Cougar	New designation for short fuselage unarmed AS.332B1 from 1990.
AS.532AC	Cougar	New designation for short fuselage armed AS.332B1 from 1990.
AS.532MC	Cougar	New designation for long fuselage unarmed AS.332F1 from 1990.
AS.532SC	Cougar	New designation for long fuselage armed AS.332F1 Navalised version with Exocet missiles from 1990.
AS.532UL	Cougar	Revised designation for unarmed AS.332M1 issued in 1990. Some equipped as 'Horizon' surveillance platform with under-fuselage extendable radar antenna.
AS.532AL	Cougar	Revised designation for armed AS.332M1 issued in 1990.

Aérospatiale/Westland SA.330E Puma HC.1, XW201

HELICOPTERS AND ROTORCRAFT

Type No.	Name	Notes
AS.532U2	Cougar	Revised designation for unarmed AS.332M2 issued in 1990.
AS.532A2	Cougar	Revised designation for armed AS.332M2 issued in 1990.
AS.550	Fennec	Revised designaton for AS.350L1.
AS.550A2	Fennec	Armed AS.550 with cannons and rockets.
AS.550C2	Fennec	Armed anti-tank AS.550 with ESCO Heli-TOW system.
AS.550M2	Fennec	Unarmed AS.550 for naval transport and ship support.
AS.550S2	Fennec	Armed AS.550 for Naval anti-shipping missions with torpedoes.
AS.550U2	Fennec	Unarmed AS.550 for general military transport and support.
AS.555	Fennec	AS.355 to military specification similar to that of AS.550 but with twin 456 shp Turboméca Arrius TM.319 turboshafts.
AS.555AN	Fennec	AS.555 with 20mm cannon and external rocket pods.
AS.555AR	Fennec	Naval AS.555 with cannons and rockets.
AS.555CN	Fennec	Missile armed version of AS.555.
AS.555MN	Fennec	Naval version of Fennec with 360-degree radar under nose.
AS.555MR	Fennec	Unarmed naval version of AS.555.
AS.555SN	Fennec	Naval version with torpedoes.
AS.555SR	Fennec	Naval anti-submarine version of AS.555 with search radar, dunking sonar and two underslung homing torpedoes.
AS.555UN	Fennec	AS.555 for ALAT for IFR training and general utility missions.
AS.565AA	Panther	Redesignation of SA.365K for general military transport.
AS.565CA	Panther	Redesignation of SA.365K for anti-tank operations with 8 HOT missiles. Optional 849 shp Arriel 2C turboshafts.
AS.565SA	Panther	Redesignation of SA.365F1 for Naval anti-submarine operations.
AS.565MA	Panther	Redesignation of SA.365F1 for unarmed Naval operations.
AS.565UA	Panther	Redesignation of SA.365K for military attack operations.

Aérospatiale AS.332L Super Puma, N721SW (*Aérospatiale*)

AEROTECNICA   SPAIN

The story of the Aerotecnica helicopters goes back to the original research carried out in the early 1950s by Jean Cantinieau in France. Cantinieau, an engineer with Sud Ouest (SNCASO), designed his C.100 in cooperation with M. Decroze. It was an open frame single-seat machine with a triangulated tube structure surrounding the pilot and carrying the engine and rotor installation at its apex above the pilot's head. The engine was mounted just forward of the rotorhead so as to reduce the extent of mechanical linkages and the C.100 had a three-wheel undercarriage and high-set tubular tailboom structure carrying a small tail rotor. The C.100 made its first of a total of three flights on 10 November, 1951 at St. Cyr and performed reasonably well.

Cantinieau quickly moved on to a two-seater, the MC.101, which retained the general layout of the first machine but with a much cleaned-up structure and a 105 h.p. Hirth engine. Two examples of the MC.101 were built by Matra (F-WGIX and F-WGIY, c/n 01 and 02), the first of which was flown by Gerard Henry at Buc on 11 November 1952. It was shortly after this that Cantinieau gained the interest of the Marquis del Merito, a Spanish industrialist, who had established Aerotecnica SA as an aerial photography and crop spraying business based at Cuatro Vientos near Madrid.

In 1953, Cantinieau took his designs to Spain where the C.101 became the Aerotecnica AC.11. It soon became evident that the aircraft was underpowered in Madrid's hot and high conditions and a 150 h.p. Lycoming was installed – in which form it became the Model AC.12. With Spanish Government funding, two AC.12 prototypes were built. These differed from the AC.11 in having a full all-metal monocoque fuselage with a large overhead 'spine' encompassing the boom and engine installation. The powerplant, which was upgraded to a 170 h.p. O-320-B2A, was attached in front of the three-blade rotor head and the AC.12 had a fully enclosed two-seat cabin and small skid undercarriage.

Cantinieau had also been working on another project for a three-seat turbine-powered helicopter, the designs for which he had sold to SNCAN. The layout of this machine was very close to that of the AC.12. SNCAN built two prototypes of this helicopter as the Nord N.1750 Norelfe which was a rather futuristic all-metal machine with a large bubble canopy and a Turboméca Artouste I turbine mounted above and behind the cockpit. The three-blade rotor was positioned directly over the engine and had a rotorhead enclosed in a large spherical fairing. The tail rotor was replaced by a ducted exhaust gas arrangement similar to that employed forty years later on the McDonnell Douglas NOTAR designs. This was controlled by the pilot through pedals.

The three-seat Norelfe prototype, F-WGVZ, was flown on 28 December 1954 but SNCAN was occupied with other projects and sold both the aircraft and the rights to Aerotecnica who designated them AC.13A. After further testing in Spain, Aerotecnica moved to a larger five-seat version known as the AC.14. The prototype AC.14 used part of the structure of one of the AC.13s but had a lengthened cabin section with a rear seating area and a larger 400 shp Turboméca Artouste IIB turboshaft engine.

Having funded much of the Aerotecnica helicopter project, the Spanish Government placed orders for twelve examples of the piston engined AC.12 and ten of the AC.14. These were delivered to the Spanish Air Force, with the designations EC-XZ-2 and EC-XZ-4 respectively, where they served for a relatively short period before being retired. Aerotecnica also started construction of a prototype of the much larger AC-21 which was a 12/14 passenger machine with twin Turboméca Turmo III turbines and a massive ducted-air tailboom. A turbine version of the AC.12 was planned and they also started working on the AC-15 development of the AC.14 with a 260 h.p. Lycoming O-435-V engine. Unfortunately, in 1962 the Spanish Government withdrew further financial support and Aerotecnica went into liquidation.

Following the collapse of Aerotecnica, Jean Cantinieau returned to France where he joined Matra. There, he designed and completed a single example of the 'Bamby'. This single-seat machine closely resembled the Aerotecnica machines but embodied a triangular end to the tailboom which provided a better direction and control of exhaust gas. After brief testing in 1963 the Bamby suffered a power train failure and was abandoned.

Aerotecnica AC-12 *(via MJH)*

Aerotecnica AC-14
(via MJH)

AGUSTA   ITALY

The Agusta Group has its origins in the Costruzioni Aeronautiche Giovanni Agusta which was formed by Giovanni Agusta in 1907. It built a number of small aircraft during the pre-war period in factories at Cascina Costa, Milan and Benghazi, including over 100 examples of the IMAM RO.41 military training biplane.

Following the war, the company had a long period in which it was not involved in aircraft production but became well known for producing its line of world class MV Agusta motorcycles. However, Domenico Agusta, who had taken over on his father's death in 1927, saw the rapid advance of the helicopter industry and, in 1952, he took out a licence to build and market Bell helicopters for European customers.

Since then the Grupo Agusta has expanded through acquisition to become the largest aerospace group in Italy. Today, Agusta comprises C.A.G. Agusta S.p.A., Bredanardi C.A. S.p.A., SIAI Marchetti S.p.A., Caproni Vizzola S.p.A. and Industria Aeronautica Meridionale S.p.A. together with a substantial aerospace systems division. In addition, Agusta is a 50% partner with GKN-Westland in European Helicopter Industries Ltd. which is developing the EH-101.

The first licence-built Agusta Bell 47G flew in May 1954 and over 700 of various marks of Bell 47 were completed with more than a third being delivered to the Italian Air Force, Army, Navy and Carabinieri. This production activity provided Agusta with an excellent manufacturing and skills base and led to the design of a number of new aircraft. In association with Filippo Zappata, they conceived the AZ.1 twin-engined transport aircraft and this eventually led to the four-engined AZ.8, which flew in 1958.

The AZ.8 was unsuccessful, but Zappata then designed the AZ.101 38-seat heavy transport helicopter which fell into the Sud Frelon and Sikorsky S-61 category. The sole prototype flew in 1964 as the A.101G powered by three Rolls-Royce-Bristol Gnome turboshaft engines which drove the large five-bladed single rotor. A long period of A.101G development ensued with the aircraft undergoing tests at the Reparto Sperimentale Volo (RSV) between January 1969 and mid-1971. The A.101G failed to meet requirements and the expected Italian military orders did not materialise. The prototype was eventually abandoned at Vergiate in 1980. However, by this time Agusta was entering into licence agreements with Sikorsky and Boeing-Vertol to build helicopters which would more closely meet the needs of the Aeronautica Militare Italiana.

With volume production in the 1950s concentrating on the small Bell 47 models, Agusta's attentions turned to new designs which would, at one end, offer greater passenger capacity and lifting power, and at the other would replace the existing Bell models. The first of these was a redesign of the experimental Bell 48 (YH-12B) which had first flown in 1946.

Agusta A.104, I-AGUM

Agusta obtained one of the prototype Bell 48s and married the dynamic components to a new fuselage which provided 9-seat capacity in its unusually wide cabin. It became the first helicopter to gain a type certificate in Italy and a couple of A.102s were sold to a commercial customer (Elivie). The prototypes operated with the RSV for a while, but the design was not a commercial success, largely because of the advent of turbine powerplants for helicopters.

Agusta's response was to build a new version of the Bell 47G powered by a Turboméca Astazou turboshaft engine. This hybrid model was fitted with a fully enclosed cabin section but only flew as a prototype. At the same time, the design department was pursuing a series of very light helicopters led by the Agusta A.103 which was intended for military observation, small volume crop spraying and training. This prototype was followed by a more practical two-seater, the A.104 Helicar, which was also powered by a 140 h.p. MV-Agusta piston engine, and then by the 104BT which used a light turbine engine. The final variant, which flew in 1965, was the Agusta A.105 with a more substantial airframe and a larger Turboméca – Agusta turboshaft engine. By this time Agusta recognised that the two seaters were not what the market really needed and they built a four-seat version – the A.105B. By this time however the Bell Jet Ranger had appeared on the scene and Agusta decided to extend their existing relationship with Bell by taking a production licence for the Model 206 rather than the costly option of further development of the A.104B.

The Jet Ranger proved to be a highly important programme for Agusta and eventually they built over 900 examples. At the same time, other Bell models were taken in hand and substantial numbers of the Bell 204, 205, 212 and 412 were completed both for civil and military customers and included specialised miltary variants such as the AB.212ASW search helicopter for the Italian Navy.

The opportunities for licence production also brought Agusta and Sikorsky together. In 1967, production started on an initial batch of 26 of the Sikorsky ASH-3D (AS-61A-4) for use by the Italian Navy. Agusta also built a pair of ASH-3D/TS VIP versions of the Sea King which were used for Italian governmental and Papal transport. Sales were subsequently made to Libya, Peru, Iran and Saudi Arabia with total Sea King production reaching 80 aircraft.

In addition to the Sea Kings, Agusta developed the AS-61N1 Silver, based on the Sikorsky S-61N with a shorter fuselage and greater payload. Sikorsky had closed its production line in 1980 and the Silver was announced in the following year with a view to filling this market gap, but it appeared just as the North Sea oil industry boom subsided and no commercial sales were made. The Sikorsky connection also embraced the HH-3F Pelican which was built to fulfill the AMI's role of search and rescue. Twenty examples were delivered to the 15th Stormo and positioned at bases around the Italian coast. SIAI-Marchetti was also included in the production activity for the HH-3F and the SH-3D, AB-205, AB212 and AB-412. Through its associated company, Elicotteri Meridionali SpA, Agusta has built over 160 examples of the CH-47C Chinook under licence from Boeing. All such sales have been to military customers including Italy, Egypt, Libya, Morocco, Greece and Iran.

In 1981, as a result of a complex state reorganisation of industry, BredaNardi was brought into the Agusta Group. This company had been established in February 1971 by Breda, a state-owned concern in the EFIM Group, and Nardi which had a long history of design and production of light aircraft including the FN.333 amphibian and the pre-war FN.305. BredaNardi took out licences for production of Hughes helicopters and initially produced the piston-engined Hughes 300C at its Milan plant, with the Greek Air Force being a major customer for 20 aircraft as trainers. This was followed by further agreements to build the turbine-powered 500 series. It appears that over 150 examples of the various NH.500 models were constructed and more recent deliveries included 50 NH.500Es to the Italian Air Force. The BredaNardi factory has now been renamed the Monteprandone Works of Agusta, but production has been substantially reduced.

Many years of licensed production had proved profitable for Agusta, but it had its drawbacks. The needs of the domestic Italian military system were becoming satisfied by the late-1960s and Agusta's licences restricted the market area in which they could operate. In particular, North America was not available to them under the Bell and Sikorsky agreements. Agusta therefore looked again to their own design to take them forward.

Early design work started in 1964 and the resultant A.109 emerged as a single-cabin seven-seat helicopter with a streamlined pod-and-boom layout. It was envisaged that the Turboméca Astazou 12 turboshaft would be used to power the new machine. As the design became enlarged and refined the six-passenger accommodation was separated from the two-seat flight deck and power requirements were changed to a pair of Allison 250-C14 turboshafts. Eventually the Agusta team redesigned the fuselage, making it a tapered streamlined design with the engine and rotor system positioned above the main cabin and a prominent tailfin at the end of a long integral boom. Five prototype airframes (including one for static test) were put in hand in 1970 and the prototype flew in the following summer. The A.109 received its type certificate in mid-1975 and went into production at Cascina Costa.

The A.109 was targeted at civil executive operators and at military users. Agusta established an American marketing arm in Philadelphia and has been successful in selling the A.109 to corporate users and in the growing hospital support and police sectors. Out of the 430 examples completed by mid-1996 over 80 have been delivered to the Italian Army, Guardia di Finanza and Carabinieri. Agusta has been imaginative in creating customised variants for special requirements and in its latest form, the A.109 Koala has reverted to the original single-engined concept.

By the early 1980s, Agusta was suffering from the financial strains of a declining military market and the startup costs of the A.109, together with its dependence on American components paid for at detrimental exchange rates. 1992 found Agusta in the ownership of the Italian state holding company EFIM, but with the liquidation of EFIM Agusta was transferred to the temporary ownership of IRI-Finmeccanica and a period of financial and organisational uncertainty ensued, despite the governmental decision to wipe out the company's long-term debt. The financial restructuring was essential as attention moved to development of the A.129 Mangusta attack helicopter.

HELICOPTERS AND ROTORCRAFT

The Mangusta, which is currently in production to meet an Italian Army requirement for up to 66 aircraft, is a tandem seat all-weather anti-tank helicopter powered by a pair of Rolls-Royce Gem turboshafts. It has the ability to fire its externally mounted TOW missiles at night by means of a pilot helmet display, and other equipment includes infrared suppressors on its twin exhausts, and a laser jammer and laser warning display. A scout version of the A.129 is planned to provide battlefield support to the attack models of the Mangusta and it is to be expected that there will be considerable development in weapons fit as the aircraft matures.

Production details

Agusta issues serial numbers in separate blocks to each basic aircraft type. In certain cases, prototypes have had unique individual numbers but generally they are allocated the initial numbers in the relevant block. Meridionali use a system of unique serial blocks for each customer with a letter prefix. A simple numbering system was used by Nardi for the NH.269 but their allocations for the NH.500 helicopters is unknown and is believed to be based on the Hughes/McDonnell Douglas system used for the American-built equivalents. Production details up to mid-1996 are:

Model	Serial Batch	Number Built	Notes
Agusta-Bell 47G and 47G-2	001 to 304	304	
Agusta A.102	001 to 005	5	
Agusta-Bell 47J	1001 to 1152	152	
Agusta-Bell 47G3B-1	1501 to 1643	143	

Agusta A-106 *(Agusta)*

Model	Serial Batch	Number Built	Notes
Agusta-Bell 47J2 and 47J3	2001 to 2123	123	
Agusta-Bell 47G-4A	2501 to 2562	62	
Agusta-Bell 204B	3000 to 3238	238	
Agusta A.104	4001 to 4002	2	
Agusta-Bell 205A	4001 to4485	485	
Agusta-Bell 205A-1	4501 to 4517	17	
Agusta-Bell 212	5501 to 5724	224	
Agusta-Bell 212ASW	001 to 040	40	
Agusta-Sikorsky HH-3F	6201 to 6220	20	
Agusta-Sikorsky AS-61 A-4	Unknown	70	
Agusta AS-61N1 Silver	6401 up	2	
Agusta A.109A	7101 to 7252	152	
Agusta A.109 Mk.II	7253 to 7436	184	
Agusta A.109C and A.109K	7601 to 7679	79	
Agusta-Bell 206A/B Jet Ranger 2	8001 to 8556	556	
Agusta-Bell 206B Jet Ranger 3	8557 to 8740	184	
Agusta-Bell 206A-1 Jet Ranger	9001 to 9170	170	Military deliveries.
Agusta A.109K2	10001 to 10031	31	
Agusta A.119 Koala	10001 to 10002	2	
Agusta A.109P Power	11001 to 11002	2	
Agusta-Bell 412	25501 to 25677	177	
Meridionali CH-47C	M.001 to M.026, P.001 to P.079, R.001 to R.020, S.001 to S.009, B734 to B744	76	Individual serial batches for separate customers: M=Italy, P=Iran, R=Libya, S=Morocco, B=US Army.
BredaNardi NH.300C	001 to 025	25	
BredaNardi NH.500 series	Unknown	170	Poss. Hughes/McD-D system.
EH.101	50001 to 50006	6	Also EH prototype numbers.

Model List

Details of the models designed or built by Agusta are as follows:

Type No.	Name	Notes
A.101D		Proposed medium single rotor helicopter of classic fuselage and boom configuration with 27-pax capacity and powered by three 750 shp. Turboméca Turmo III turboshafts.

Type No.	Name	Notes
A.101G		Developed A.101D with three 1400 shp. R-R-Bristol Gnome 1400 turboshafts driving 5-blade main rotor, tricycle u/c. 35-pax capacity. One Prot. MM80358 FF 19 Oct. 1964 .
AB102		Medium single-rotor helicopter based on Bell 48 with streamlined all-metal fuselage, 8/10-seat capacity, Bell rotor sytem and one 600 h.p. P&W R-1340 piston engine driving a single main rotor. Prot. I-AGUT (c/n 001) FF 3 Feb. 1959.
A.103		Light single-seat single rotor 'pod & boom' helicopter powered by one 85 h.p. Agusta MV-GA70 piston engine. One Prot. FF Oct. 1959.
A.104	Helicar	Light 2-seat all-metal helicopter developed from A.103 with single stabilised rotor, skid u/c and powered by one 120 h.p. Agusta MV-A120 piston engine. First of two Prots. I-AGUM FF Dec. 1960.
A.104BT		A.104 with 270 shp Agusta A.270 turboshaft engine. One built.
A.105A		Two-seat utility helicopter derived from A.104 powered by one 275 shp Turboméca-Agusta TAA.230 turboshaft engine. One Prot. MM80415 FF 1 Nov. 1964.
A.105B		A.105 with lengthened rear cabin and four seats and 7 imp. Gal fuel increase. One Prot. MM80416 FF 1965.
A.106		Single-seat ASW helicopter for frigate deck operations with tail skid u/c allowing two torpedoes to be underslung; powered by one 320 shp Turboméca-Agusta TAA.230 turboshaft. First of two Prots. MM5001N. FF Nov. 1965.
A.109	Hirundo	Eight-seat executive helicopter with streamlined fuselage incorporating vertical fin and tailplane, 4-blade main rotor, retractable tricycle u/c, 5200 lb TOGW and powered by two 420 shp Allison 250-C20B turboshafts. Prot. 'NC7101' FF 4 Aug. 1971.
A.109A		A.109 with additional ventral fin, structural strengthening and 5730 lb. TOGW.
A.109A Mk.II		Single-pilot IFR certificated version of A.109A with two 450 shp Allison 250 C20R/1 engines.
A.109 EOA		Military A.109A for Italian Army with sliding doors, fixed u/c, external ordnance points and two 450 shp Allison 250 C20R/1 turboshafts.
A.109BA		Anti-tank version for Belgian Army.
A.109C		A.109A with improved transmission system, composite main rotor, stronger u/c, 5996 lb TOGW and 'wide body' cabin. Military version A.109CM.
A.109 MAX		Medevac version with transverse stretcher stowage and bulged side door transparencies.
A.109A TOW		Military A.109A with externally mounted Hughes TOW missile tubes and nose-mounted ranging module.

Type No.	Name	Notes
A.109K		Military version of A.109A with revised nose profile, redesigned engine compartment and uprated transmission, external stores hardpoints, optional fixed u/c and 722 shp Turboméca Arriel 1K turboshafts for enhanced hot & high operations. Also known as A.109KM and A.109KN (Naval version).
A.109K2		Civil hot and high rescue version with special avionics, fixed u/c, new fuel tanks, Tail skid replacing ventral fin, 771 shp Arriel 1K1 engines, rescue hoist etc. Prot. HB-XWA (c/n 10001).
A.109KM		Military version of A.109K2 with external braced hardpoints.
A.109D		Experimental A.109K2 with retractable u/c, new rotor head with titanium hub and Allison 250-C22 turboshaft.
A.109E	Power	A.109D with fixed u/c, wider cabin, redesigned instrument panel and controls, modified tailfin and two 732 shp Pratt & Whitney PW206C turboshafts. Prot. I-EPWR (c/n 11001).
A.115		Developed version of the Bell 47J-3 with open rear fuselage structure and powered by a 480 shp Turboméca Astazou II turboshaft. One prot. I-AGUC.
A.119	Koala	A.109 with one Pratt & Whitney PT6B-37/1 turboshaft engine, fixed skid u/c . Prot. I-KOAL (c/n 10001) FF Feb. 1995.
EMA.124		Light three-seat helicopter derived from Bell 47 with open frame rear fuselage, skid u/c and one 305 hp Lyc. VO-540-B1B3 piston engine. Intended for production by Elicotteri Meridionali SpA. One Prot. I-EMAF (c/n 7501) FF 28 May 1970.

Agusta A.109A, 3A-MOR

Agusta A.129 Mangusta, MM593 *(Agusta)*

Type No.	Name	Notes
A.129	Mangusta	Advanced tandem-two-seat combat helicopter with fixed tailwheel u/c and stub wings mounting anti-tank missiles or guns and rockets. Powered by two Rolls-Royce Gem II-1004 or Allison-Garrett LHTEC-T800 turboshafts. Prot. MM590 FF 11 Sep. 1983.
A.129U		Proposed utility tactical transport version of A.129 with enlarged fuselage. Not built.
NH.300C		Hughes 269 built under licence by BredaNardi.
NH.500C		Hughes 500C built under licence by BredaNardi.
NH.500M		Hughes 500M built under licence by BredaNardi.
NH.500MC		Hughes 500M upgraded and built under licence by Breda-Nardi.
AB.47G		Agusta-built Bell 47G light helicopter. Prot. I-SIAP (c/n 001) FF 22 May 1954.
AB.47G2		Agusta-built Bell 47G 2.
AB.47G2A		Agusta-built Bell 47G 2A.
AB.47G3	Super Alpino	Agusta-built Bell 47G 3.
AB.47G3B		Agusta-built Bell 47G 3B.
AB.47G3B1		Agusta-built Bell 47G 3B1 Prot. MM573.
AB.47G-4A		Agusta-built Bell 47G -4A Prot. I-FLAM (c/n 2501).
AB.47J		Agusta-built Bell 47J Prot. MM574/ I-AGIZ.
AB.47J-2		Agusta-built Bell 47J-2.
AB.47J-3		Agusta-built Bell 47J-3.
AB.47J3B		Agusta-built Bell 47J3B.
AB.47J3B-1		High altitude version of 47J-3 with supercharged Lyc. 270 hp. TVO-435-B1 engine.
AB.204B		Agusta-built Bell 204 re-engined with a 1050 shp Bristol-Siddeley Gnome H.1000 turboshaft engine. Prot. I-AGUG FF 10 May 1961.

Type No.	Name	Notes
AB.204AS		Anti-submarine version of AB.204B.
AB.205		Agusta-built Bell 205 14-seat helicopter powered by one Bristol-Siddeley Gnome H.1200 turboshaft. Prot. I-AGUH (c/n 4001).
AB.205A-1		Agusta-built Bell 205A-1 Prot. I-ACUO (c/n 4501).
AB.205TA		Twin engined version of AB.205 with two Turboméca Astazou XII turboshafts.
AB.205BG		Twin engined version of AB.205 with two Bristol-Siddeley Gnome H.1200 turboshafts.
AB.206A	Jet Ranger	Agusta-built Bell 206A.
AB.206B	Jet Ranger	Agusta-built Bell 206B Jet Ranger 2 and Jet Ranger 3.
AB.206L1	Long Ranger	Agusta-built Bell 206L.1.
AB.212		Agusta-built Bell 212. Prot. I-AGUR (c/n 5501).
AB.212ASW		Agusta-built Bell 212 for anti-submarine warfare with 1875 shp Twinpac PT6T-6 turboshaft, Bendix ASW avionics, dipping sonar and strengthened corrosion proofed structure.
AB.412	Griffon	Agusta-built Bell 412. Griffon is military version.
AS-61A	ASH-3D	Agusta-built Sikorsky SH-3D for Italian Navy with AN/APN-195 radar in nose radome and under-fuselage APQ-706 Marte missile guidance radar.
AS-61N-1	Silver	Sikorsky S-61N with a 50-inch shorter forward fuselage, increased fuel capacity and capacity for 24 pax plus 3 crew. Prot. I-RAIE/I-AGSI (c/n 6401) FF 25 June 1984.
AS-61 VIP		One VIP model delivered to Libya.
AS-61R	HH-3F Pelican	Agusta-built Sikorsky HH-3F for Italian Air Force search & rescue operations.
EMB-CH47C	Chinook	Boeing CH-47C Chinook built by Meridionali.
EH-101		See European Helicopter Industry chapter.

BELL HELICOPTER TEXTRON

USA

With a public image forged from 'MASH', 'The Whirlybirds' and the extraction of the last evacuees from Saigon, Bell must be the best known of the world's helicopter manufacturers. Founded by Larry Bell in July 1935, the Bell Aircraft Corporation made its name during World War II as the producer of the P-39 Airacobra and as a major subcontractor to the other aircraft companies in the American war effort. Bell also took a major part in the development of high speed flight with its creation of the P-59 Airacomet and the X-1 and X-2 supersonic rocket planes.

Bell's helicopter business originated with Larry Bell's interest in the helicopter models which were the basis of experiments by Arthur M. Young. Young, who was actually a mathematics graduate rather than an engineer became fascinated by the possibilities of helicopters during the 1930s. The key to Young's helicopter models was his rotor system which embodied a mass-balanced stabilising bar set at right-angles to the main rotor which, combined with a teetering hinge mechanism, achieved a satisfactory level of stability for his helicopter models. Young joined Bell following demonstrations of his techniques in 1941 and based himself at Gardenville, New York near to Bell's main Buffalo plant where he used his research to create the Model 30. This had a metal fuselage with an open cockpit at the front and followed the now-familiar classic helicopter layout with a main two-blade rotor driven by a Franklin engine buried behind the cockpit and an anti-torque propeller/rotor at the tail. The second prototype was further refined with an enclosed cabin and a fuselage which foreshadowed future helicopter design by having a separate cabin pod and tail boom structure.

Three model 30 prototypes were tested and refined to the point that Bell was able to produce the prototype Model 47 which flew in December, 1945 and was to become the most famous of the company's products. A side-by-side two seater, the Bell 47 had a simple structure built around the cockpit shell with an open tubular tailboom to carry the tail rotor, the Franklin engine positioned behind the cockpit rear bulkhead driving the main rotor (duly fitted with its stabilising bar) and a simple four-wheeled undercarriage. The cockpit had a large windshield which could be fitted with an upper section to provide a completely enclosed cabin. Early in the development of the Bell 47 this was changed to the well-known bubble canopy.

On 8 May 1946, the Bell 47 became the world's first commercially certificated helicopter. It was immediately evaluated by the U.S. Navy (as the HTL) and the U.S. Air Force (YR-13) which led to a 1948 order for 65 H-13Bs for the U.S. Army where it acquired the name 'Sioux'. The success of the H-13 in Korea is legendary and a range of civil and military Bell 47s followed with various power units and configurations. The 1,000th Bell 47 was completed in April 1953. With the Bell 47B, the company introduced a fully enclosed cabin and fabric-covered rear fuselage – which proved to be very sensitive to side wind effects. Several further versions with enclosed all-metal monocoque fuselages were developed including the Model 47H and 47J. The design formed the basis for several variants produced by other manufacturers including the Kawasaki KH-1 and dedicated crop spraying variants such as the Continental Copters El Tomcat. The Bell 47 was constructed under licence by Westland, Kawasaki and Agusta, and by the end of 1973 when production ceased, over 6,300 examples of the Bell 47 had been completed.

With the Model 47 in production, Bell concluded that there was a market for a larger helicopter with seating for five or six people. This resulted in them building the Model 42 which was a very streamlined all-metal helicopter with a completely enclosed fuselage pod and boom and a fixed tricycle undercarriage. Like the Model 47, it had a stabilising bar on the main rotor. Three prototypes were buiilt and though Bell could not find much enthusiasm from the civil market, the Model 42 led to the Model 48 for the U.S. Air Force. As the XR-12, this performed well with a more powerful engine than the Model 42 and further led to the Model 48 (YH-12B) which had a four-leg undercarriage and reshaped cabin section. Because of difficulties in resolving various stability and rotor control problems Bell only built a small batch of ten aircraft.

In 1950, in response to a U.S. Navy requirement, Bell was successful in gaining the contract for a new anti-submarine helicopter. The HSL-1 was radically different from any Bell design which had gone before (or which has appeared since). It used two rotors mounted at the extreme front and rear of the box-section fuselage, driven by a massive 2,400 h.p. Pratt & Whitney R.2800 engine positioned behind the main cabin section. A useful feature was the autopilot which allowed the HSL-1 to hover for extended periods on station while using its 'dunking sonar' gear. It was because of the size of the HSL-1 production effort that Bell decided to move its manufacturing plant from Buffalo, New York to its present base at Fort Worth, Texas. In fact, the HSL-1 was a disappointment with development being protracted due to vibration problems. The result was that only 50 examples were built and these were employed on testing towed minesweeping systems for much of their service career.

Bell's next design, the Model 204, was possibly its most successful insofar as it formed the basis for a family of helicopters which have survived in production for 40 years. Again, it was spurred by a U.S. Army specification for a general utility helicopter capable of casualty evacuation. Bell's design was its first to use a turbine engine and it had large doors on both sides of the main cabin which resulted in a large square space facilitating rapid

Bell 206 Jet Ranger III *(Bell)*

loading and unloading of troops and equipment. The XH-40 prototype flew in October, 1956 (on the same day that Larry Bell died). The U.S. Army designated the production version HU-1 – from which came the unofficial name 'Huey'. The HU-1 was officially known as the Iroquois and later became the UH-1 in the 1962 tri-service consolidation exercise.

In 1960, Bell Aerospace Corporation was acquired by Textron Inc. and in 1976 its helicopter design and manufacturing division was renamed Bell Helicopter Textron. Production of the enlarging range of helicopters expanded and the advent of the Vietnam War brought fame and fortune for the Huey. The UH-1 assumed many unplanned roles and, in particular, sprouted external weapons points to carry rocket launching pods, SS-11 wire-guided missiles and various combinations of machine-guns, 20-mm cannon and other weapons. Bell delivered UH-1s to numerous foreign air arms including the Australian Air Force and Navy, Colombia, Norway, Spain, Thailand and Turkey. The AB.204B was built by Agusta with over 100 examples being delivered to the Italian armed services. Bell 204s were also sold to many civil operators and a production licence was granted to Fuji in Japan.

From the Model 204, Bell moved on to the stretched Model 205. This had increased power and was delivered in large numbers to the United States Army and a range of overseas military users. It provided an ideal platform for upgrading to the twin-engined Model 212, which was fitted with a pair of Continental T72 turboshafts mounted side-by-side driving the classic Huey two-blade rotor through a mixer gearbox. The Model 212 (initially Model 208) proved particularly valuable to the offshore oil industry. Bristow Helicopters used a considerable number for shuttling between North Sea oil platforms on short sectors where it was important to have the confidence given by twin engines. The Bell 212 was also sold to the Canadian Armed Forces who bought 50 CH-135s, and to the Greek Navy for ASW duties and to the Peruvian Navy for on-board service for frigates.

Bell experimented extensively with the Model 204 and other aircraft to achieve increasingly high speed performance. In 1965 they flew the YUH-1B compound helicopter based on a Model 204 with fixed wings and externally mounted turbines at a speed of 250 mph. In 1968, a further development machine reached 316 mph. However, the Model 204 design was heading in a different direction. In 1962, Bell mated the dynamic components of the Huey to a new streamlined two-seat fuselage to create the D-255 Iroquois Warrior. This aircraft with its tandem two-seat cockpit was conceived as a dedicated high speed helicopter gunship with a very narrow head-on profile and provision for a wide range of externally-mounted weapons. It sparked off the Army AAFSS design competition which Bell failed to win, but Bell then decided to build a simpler and smaller aircraft. They built the experimental Model 207 Sioux Scout and this formed the basis for the Model 209 which first flew in September 1965.

The Model 209 was evaluated by the Army and ordered into production as an interim machine to meet the urgent needs in Vietnam. The initial AH-1G Cobra led to a series of 'Hueycobra' variants, not only for the Army but also for use by the U.S. Marines and the Navy. Cobras were sold to many foreign air arms including Iran, Pakistan, South Korea, Israel, Spain, Thailand and Turkey. Inevitably, the users of Cobras found reasons for needing to upgrade them and obtain improved performance and this led firstly to the AH-1J which traded the single Lycoming T53 turboshaft for a Pratt & Whitney PT6T-3 TwinPac engine. In turn, this was upgraded to a more powerful variant in the AH-1T – and eventually the AH-1W was substantially redesigned to take a pair of 3250 shp General Electric T700 engines in which guise it was named 'SuperCobra'.

Bell's Model 212 had become a versatile workhorse for the oil and construction industries and in 1970 a project was put in place to stretch the airframe to provide higher load capacity. The Model 214 Huey-Plus, which flew in October of that year, had a higher-powered Lycoming T53 engine and a larger two-blade rotor. This variant was ordered for Iran in large numbers and it was contemplated that a factory would be established in Tehran to manufacture further helicopters to meet the needs of the Imperial Iranian Army Aviation. However, the Islamic revolution in December 1978 put an end to this plan. It was during this period of relationship with Iran that the Model 214ST (Super Transport) was developed as a joint production project. This was a stretched version of the Model 214 with a 14-passenger cabin and a pair of 2250 shp T700 engines. When the Iranian production plan collapsed, Bell continued with the 214ST and marketed it as a new model fitted either with skids or with a tricycle undercarrriage.

The 1960 U.S. Army competition for a light observation helicopter resulted in Bell submitting their YHO-4 design but, as it turned out, the contract was awarded to Hughes and Bell took the opportunity of looking at a commercial application for the design. This actually meant an almost complete redesign and the resultant Model 206 was a very attractive four/five-seat machine with a classic fuselage-pod and boom layout and an Allison 250 turboshaft mounted above the cabin. The prototype flew in December 1965, and deliveries under the name Jet Ranger commenced a year later. The Jet Ranger was highly successful and the second round of Army helicopter re-equipment led to Bell receiving a large order for the OH-58 Kiowa variant of the Jet Ranger. Successive variants of the Jet Ranger were sold worldwide and licence production was carried out in Italy by Agusta. Military orders came from over 30 countries including a large batch for the Canadian Armed Forces. Bell has also developed the Model 406CS Combat Scout, which is an advanced military derivative of the Kiowa fitted with external armament and a rotor-mast mounted sighting system in a ball housing.

Eventually, in 1986, Bell transferred all production of the Jet Ranger to the new Textron Canada factory at Montreal-Mirabel. This factory has also built the Model 206L Long Ranger which has a lengthened fuselage to provide club seating and capacity for another three passengers. The Model 206L has now been developed into the Model 407 with a four-blade main rotor and improved systems. They also experimented with a twin-engined version – the Model 400 – which used a pair of Allison 250 engines and had a ring-shroud to protect the tail rotor. This project was eventually cancelled in 1989 due to uncertainty about the future market but Jet Rangers are being converted to twin-engined 'Gemini ST' configuration by Tridair using a Soloy Dual Pac engine installation. An equivalent twin engined conversion, the Model 206LT, is also marketed by Bell. The company is now working on the new Model 427 which is a larger derivative of the Long Ranger with a new simplified transmission system, a Pratt & Whitney PW.206D twin turbine engine and an enlarged cabin with a central bulkhead between the fore cabin and the after cabin that contains the fuel tank.

Bell's other commercial helicopter is the Model 222, which was a completely new executive helicopter designed in the mid-1970s. Like the Long Ranger, this has a separate cockpit and main cabin area but features a retractable tricycle undercarriage with the main

Bell 209 AH-1W Cobra Plus *(Bell)*

43

units retracting into fuselage sponsons. Whilst it was aimed at business operators, the Bell 222 has been widely used for civil medical work and for municipal departments. Many police forces adopted the Model 222 including the Metropolitan Police for operations in the greater London area. Bell has subsequently upgraded the Model 222 to the Model 230. This was followed by the higher powered Model 430 which used the 400-series model designation to indicate the redesigned four-blade rotor. It is also offered with a skid under-carriage for utility applications. The Model 430 is manufactured at Mirabel alongside the Jet Ranger variants.

Over the years, Bell has explored many experimental helicopter developments including a variety of tilt-rotor concepts such as the XV-3, the X-22 and the XV-15. These experiments eventually led to the joint project between Bell and Boeing which became the V-22 Osprey and which first flew in March, 1989. Details of the Osprey programme are described in the chapter on Boeing-Vertol. The two companies also cooperated in design of a commercial 6/9 passenger tilt-rotor aircraft designated Bell-Boeing 609. Using Osprey technology, the Model 609 will have a conventional aircraft fuselage with four rows of seat pairs in the main cabin and swivelling wingtip rotor pods mounting Pratt & Whitney PT6C-67A turboshafts driving three-blade prop-rotors. Bell took 100% control of this programme in early 1998.

Bell has consistently pursued opportunities to maintain its overseas markets and has been highly successful in supplying many overseas military and civil customers. In a recent

Bell 214 ST Super Transport, N3186W *(Bell)*

Bell 222, LN-OSB *(Bell)*

move and with the objective of widening its international capability, Bell agreed in May 1997 to acquire a 70% majority stake in the Romanian company IAR which has traditionally manufactured helicopters from the Aérospatiale range. IAR is currently developing the 'AH-1RO Dracula' gunship which is based on the AH-1W SuperCobra powered by General Electric T700 turboshafts and will build 96 examples to a Romanian military order, subject to financing for the programme being arranged..

In 1997, Bell Helicopter Textron is selling a basic range of ten commercial helicopters including the Model 206B3, 206L4, 206LT, 407, 230, 430, 212, 412, AH-1W and the OH-58D.

Production details

Detailed information on serial numbers and the number of aircraft built by Bell are as follows:

Model	Serial Batch	Number Built	Notes
42	c/n 1 to 3	3	
47	c/n 1 to 11	11	
47A	c/n 1 to 28	28	inc. 18 YR-13 & 10 HTL-1.
47B, 47B3	c/n 1 to 78 (excl. c/n 46)	77	Civil deliveries.
47D, 47D-1	c/n 1 to 665	665	Civil deliveries plus HTL-2, HTL-4, HTL-5, H-13B, H-13D, H-13E.
47G, 47G-2, 47G-2A, 47G-3B, 47G-4, 47H, 47J 47J-2,	c/n 666 to 3851 (Not built: c/n 1582 to 1591, c/n 1616, c/n 2571 to 2585)	3160	Civil deliveries plus H-13E, H-13G, H-13H, TH-13T, H-13S, HTL-6.
47G-3B-1	c/n 3901 to 4013	113	Civil deliveries plus OH-13S.
47G-3B-1, -2, -2A	c/n 6501 to 6871	371	Civil deliveries.
47G-3B-1	c/n 7401 to 7418	18	Australian military.
47G-4A	c/n 7501 to 7769	269	Civil deliveries.
47G-5	c/n 7800 to 7976	176	Civil deliveries.
47G-5 and -5A	c/n 25001 to 25160	160	Civil deliveries.
61	c/n 1 to 53	53	HSL-1.
204	c/n 1 to 19	19	XH-40 and YH-40 (XHU-1 and YUH-1B).
204	c/n 10 to 3117	3107	HU-1A, UH-1A, UH-1B, UH-1C .
204	c/n 3202 to 3207	6	SH-1D for Brazil.
204	c/n 4001 to 6000	2000	UH-1D.
204	c/n 6001 to 6192	192	UH-1E.
204	c/n 2001 to 2199	199	Civil deliveries.
204	c/n 6301 to 6327	27	HH-1K.
204	c/n 6401 to 6490	90	TH-1L.
204	c/n 7001 to 7120 c/n 7301 to 7326	146	UH-1F, TH-1F.

Model	Serial Batch	Number Built	Notes
204	c/n 8051 to 8066 c/n 8101 to 8240 c/n 8301 to 8504	360	Dornier-built UH-1D for German Government.
204	c/n 8501 to 13934 c/n 13997 to 14003 c/n 16001 to 16054 c/n 17001 to 17025 c/n 17101 to 17130	5550	UH-1H.
204	c/n 31001 to 31079 c/n 31401 to 31456 c/n 31501 to 31759	394	UH-1N, VH-1N.
205	c/n 30001 to 30332	332	
206A	c/n 1 to 660 (excl. 252, 253) c/n 672 to 715	702	Fort Worth built civil Jet Ranger.
206B	c/n 661 to 671 c/n 716 to 3958, c/n 4048 (excl, c/n 2520, 2529, 2536, 2538, 2542, 2581, 2585, 2589, 2601, 2605)	3245	Fort Worth built civil Jet Ranger.
206B	c/n 3959 to 4421 (excl. c/n 4048)	462	Mirabel built civil Jet Ranger.
206	c/n 5001 to 5040	40	TH-57.
TH206	c/n 5101 to 5257	157	TH-67.
206	c/n 39998 to 42250 c/n 44001 to 44074 c/n 44501 to 44506	2332	OH-58A.

Bell Model 30, NX41867 *(Bell)*

Model	Serial Batch	Number Built	Notes
206L	c/n 45001 to 45790	790	
206L-2	c/n 46601 to 46617	17	
206L-3	c/n 51001 to 51214	214	Fort Worth built Long Ranger III.
206L-3	c/n 51215 to 51612	398	Mirabel built Long Ranger III.
206L-4	c/n 52001 to 52182	182	Mirabel built Long Ranger IV.
407	c/n 52901 to 52902 c/n 53001 to 53214	78	Mirabel built Model 407.
209	c/n 19291 to 19296 c/n 20001 to 21127	1133	AH-1G.
209	c/n 21501 to 21508 c/n 21701 to 21730 c/n 22101 to 22347 c/n 22501 to 22520 c/n 22601 to 22624	329	AH-1F, AH-1E.
209	c/n 24001 to 24100	100	AH-1P.
209	c/n 26001 to 26124	124	AH-1J, AH-1T for USN.
209	c/n 26201 to 26245 c/n 26501 to 26640 c/n 29001 to 29070	255	Export deliveries, AH-1J, AH-1T.
209	c/n 73401 to 73424	24	Fuji built AH-1F.
212	c/n 30501 to 30999 (excl. 30604 to 30610) c/n 31101 to 31399 c/n 32101 to 32199 c/n 32201 to 32262	952	
212	c/n 35001 to 35100	100	Mirabel built Model 212.
214A	c/n 27004 to 27295	290	Mostly for Iran.
214B	c/n 28001 to 28070, c/n 27001 to 27003	73	
214C	c/n 17201 to 17239	39	Iran.
214ST	c/n 18401 to 18403 c/n 28101 to 28200	103	
412	c/n 33001 to 33213 (excl. 30604 to 30610)	206	
412	c/n 34001 to 34025	25	Indonesian production by Nurtanio.
412	c/n 36001 to 36140	140	Mirabel built Model 412.
412CF	c/n 46401 to 46411	11	Model 412 for Canadian Armed Forces.
222	c/n 47001 to 47130	130	
222B	c/n 47131 to 47156	26	
222UT	c/n 47501 to 47574	74	
230	c/n 23001 to 23038	38	
400	c/n 48001 to 48004	4	
430	c/n 49001 to 49013	13	

HELICOPTERS AND ROTORCRAFT

Model Information

Bell's first helicopter, the Model 30, was given its designation within a simple model sequence which started at the Model 3 and 4 (which became the Model 12 or YP-39) and continued through the Model 5 Airabonita and the production Airacobras which became the Model 13, Model 15 and Model 26. The Model 33 and 41 were Kingcobra variants and the Model 27 was the Airacomet jet fighter. The Bell helicopters are detailed in the following table and the type numbers follow an approximate sequence of their design although in later years the designations were more randomly allocated for marketing rather than engineering purposes.

Type No.	Name or designation	Notes
30		Experimental single- seat helicopter with open frame fuselage structure (later enclosed), pilot seat in nose, three-leg tailwheel u/c and 160 h.p. Franklin engine mounted in centre section driving tail rotor and 2-blade wooden main rotor with transverse stabilising bar. Prot. NX41867 (c/n 1) FF 29 Dec. 1942 subsequently rebuilt with monocoque fuselage. Second prot. NX41868 with two seats and enclosed cabin. Third prot. NX41860 with open cockpit and revised tailboom structure.
42		Streamlined five-seat helicopter with all-metal fuselage and boom, tricycle u/c. Powered by one 450 h.p. Pratt & Whitney R-985 piston engine mounted behind cabin driving two-blade wooden rotor with stabilising bar. First of three Prots. NX33540 (c/n 1) FF 1946.
47		Developed version of Model 30 (third prototype configuration) with two side-by-side seats, open cockpit (but later removable transparent bubble), four-leg wheel u/c, open frame rear fuselage with tail skid (later tubular tail rotor protector), ventral fin and one 175 h.p. Franklin engine driving two-blade wooden main rotor. Prot. NC41962/NC1H (c/n 1). FF 8 Dec. 1945.
47A	YR-13 YH-13 HTL-1	USAF version of Model 47 as YR-13 with enclosed rear fuselage and tail boom, powered by one 175 h.p. Franklin O-35-1 engine. 28 built.
47A	YH-13A	Three YH-13 modified for cold weather operations.
47B		Two-seat commercial Model 47 with enclosed tailboom, fully enclosed fuselage with stepped windshield, under-nose transparencies and two car-type doors, four-leg u/c. Powered by one 178 h.p. Franklin 6V4-178-B3 piston engine. 2200 lb TOGW. Prot NX41967 (c/n 2).
47B-3		Model 47 for crop dusting with modified open cockpit, engine compartment fairing, and externally mounted dusting hoppers. One 178 h.p. Franklin 6V4-178-B32 piston engine.
47D		Model 47B-3 with improved plexiglass canopy, new wheel installation with brakes, 24 volt electrical system, modified fuel system, optional float u/c (47D-S) and 178 h.p. Franklin 6V4-178-B32 engine.
47D	H-13B Sioux HTL-2	Military model similar to civil 47D with 200 h.p. Franklin O-335-3 and four-leg u/c, bubble canopy with removable top, covered rear fuselage and dual controls. 61 built.
47D	H-13C Sioux	H-13B with uncovered rear fuselage and skid u/c with external medevac litter fittings. 16 built.

Type No.	Name or designation	Notes
47D-1	H-13D Sioux	H-13C with single pilot controls and 200 h.p. Franklin O-335-5. 88 built.
47D-1	H-13E Sioux	H-13D with dual controls, three seats, modified main and tail gearboxes and main transmission. Powered by a Franklin O-335-5B. 49 built.
47D-1		Three-seat Model 47D with open frame fuselage, new canopy, gravity-feed fuel system, ventral fin, roller-bearing transmission, 29-USG fuel capacity, reduced equipment and increased useful load. 2078 lb. TOGW.
47D-1	HTL-4	US Navy version of Model 47D-1. Later TH-13L. 46 built.
47D-1	HTL-5	HTL-4 with 200 h.p. Franklin O-335-5 engine.
47E	HTL-3	Two-seat Model 47D with 200 h.p. Franklin 6V4-200-C32 engine, 2350 lb. TOGW, 33-USG fuel capacity, optional open cockpit.
47G		Three-seat Model 47D with 200 h.p. Franklin 6V4-200-C32AB engine, skid u/c, small tailplane with endplates, relocated battery, revised tail rotor gearbox, synchronised elevator and relocated 43-USG 'saddle' fuel tanks. 2350 lb TOGW.
47G-2		Model 47G with 200 h.p. Lycoming VO435-A1A engine, relocated cyclic hydraulic boost controls, bonded metal rotor blades and 2450 lb. TOGW. Also built by Kawasaki.
47	H-13G Sioux	Military model similar to 47G-2 with increased fuel and external stretcher fittings. 265 built.
47	HTL-6	US Navy dual control training version of H-13G. Later TH-13M.

Bell 407, C-GFDS *(Bell)*

Type No.	Name or designation	Notes
47	H-13H Sioux	H-13G with 250 h.p. Lycoming VO-435-23 engine, improved skid u/c and all-metal bonded rotor blades. 468 built.
47G-2	El Tomcat	Agricultural conversion by Continental Copters with single seat cockpit and two large external hoppers plus underslung spray bars.
47G-2A		Three-seat Model 47G with 240 h.p. Lycoming VO-435-A1E engine, 2850 lb TOGW. Also Kawasaki model.
47G-2A-1		47G-2A with fuel capacity inc. from 43-USG to 61.6-USG.
47G-3	H-13K Sioux	Civil and military model 47G with 225 h.p. Franklin 6VS-335-A engine, longer rotor blades and 14-inch longer tailboom. 2650 lb TOGW.
47G-3B	OH-13S Sioux	Civil and military Model 47G-3 with turbocharged 260 h.p. Lyc. TVO-435-A1A and 2850 lb. TOGW. 576 built.
47G-3B1		Model 47G-3B with 270 h.p. turbocharged Lyc. TVO-435-B1A engine, 8-inch wider 3-seat cabin, 61.6-USG fuel capacity. 2950 lb TOGW. Built also by Westland and Agusta.
47G-3B2		Model 47G-3B1 with turbocharged 280 h.p. Lyc. TVO-435-G1A. 2950 lb TOGW.
47G-3B2	TH-13T	Two/three seat military instrument trainer with extra IFR equipment. 417 built.
47G-3B2A		Model 47G-3B2 with TVO-435-F1A engine and 11-inch wider cabin
47G-4		Model 47G with 260 h.p. Lyc. VO-540-B1B3 engine, 61.6-USG fuel, hydraulically assisted controls and 2950 lb TOGW.
47G-4A		Model 47G-4 with engine uprated to 280 h.p.
47G-5		Economy 2-seat version of 47G-4 with 12 volt electrical system. 2850 lb TOGW, 28-USG fuel capacity. Can be upgraded to 3-seat configuration with synchronised elevator mod.

Bell 412SP, N412S *(Bell)*

Type No.	Name or designation	Notes
47G-5A		3-seat Model 47G-5 with 61.6-USG fuel tanks and 11-inch wider cabin.
47H-1		Model 47G with fully clad fuselage, wider three-seat deluxe cabin and rear baggage stowage locker, contoured 35-USG fuel tanks, modified skid u/c. 2350 lb TOGW.
47J		Four-seat development of Model 47H with single pilot seat and rear 3-place passenger seat. Powered by one 220 h.p. Lyc. VO-435-A1B, 2565 lb TOGW and 35-USG fuel capacity.
47J	H-13J	Model 47J for USAF with 240 h.p. Lyc. VO-435-21.
47J	HUL-1	Model 47J for US Navy with 260 h.p. Lyc VO-435-B1B. Later UH-13P. Also HUL-1G (HH-13Q) for USCG. 25 built.
47J-1		Model 47J with VO-435A engine.
47J-2	Ranger	Model 47J with 240 h.p. VO-540-B1B engine, metal rotor blades, fixed stabiliser, hydraulic controls, blue tinted bubble and windows, 48-USG fuel capacity and 2850 lb TOGW.
47J-2A		Model 47J-2 with 260 h.p. Lyc. VO-540-B1B3 engine, collective boost system and 2950 lb. TOGW. Built by Agusta.
47J-3		Naval Model 47J-2A with strengthened transmission, improved rotor brake and underslung torpedo. Agusta built.
47J-3B1		Model 47J with turbocharged Lyc. TVO-435-B1A engine for high altitude operation and modified servo control system. 2950 lb TOGW.
47K	HTL-7	US Navy 2-seat trainer based on HUL-1 with modified cockpit and IFR instrumentation. 240 h.p. Lyc. O-435-6 engine. 2565 lb TOGW, 35-USG fuel capacity. Later TH-13N. 18 built.
47L	HUL-1M	Experimental Model 47J with 250 shp Allison YT-63-A-3 turboshaft and 2850 lb TOGW. First a/c Bu.149838 FF 6 Jan, 1961. Later UH-13R. 2 built.
47	KH-4	See Kawasaki.

Bell 47D, G-ARIA

Type No.	Name or designation	Notes
48	XR-12 XH-12 H-12	Military helicopter for USAF based on Model 42 with all-metal monocoque fuselage, fixed tricycle u/c, 5-seat cabin with stepped windshield and one 540 h.p. Pratt & Whitney R-1340-AN1 engine driving 2-blade rotor with stabilising bar. Prot. s/n 46-214. FF 1947. 2 built.
48A	YR-12B XH-12B YH-12B	Model 48 with reshaped lower fuselage, wider cabin with four doors rounded nose and square side windows, four-leg u/c and 600 h.p. R-1340-55 engine. Prot. s/n 46-216. 11 built.
54	XH-15	Two-seat helicopter for USAF similar to 47B with fixed tricycle u/c (later skids), all metal fuselage and boom, powered by one 275 h.p. Continental O-470-5 engine. Prot. s/n 46-530. 3 built.
61	HSL-1	Tandem-rotor 4-crew anti-submarine helicopter for US Navy with two-blade foldable rotors on extreme front and rear, fixed four-leg u/c with twin rear wheels, outrigged rear fins and one 2400 h.p. Pratt & Whitney R-2800-50 engine buried in rear fuselage. Equipped with dipping-sonar and air-surface missiles. Prot. Bu.129133 FF 4 Mar. 1953.
65		Single-seat experimental VTOL machine with Schweizer glider fuselage and Cessna wing, skid u/c and two vertically thrusting Fairchild J44 turbojets mounted beneath the wings. Prot. N1105V (c/n 2).
68	X-14	Experimental ducted jet VTOL aircraft with Beech 35 and 45 wings, tail and other components, fixed tricycle u/c and two 1560 lb.s.t. Bristol-Siddeley Viper turbojets fitted in nose with swivelling thrust nozzles. Prot. N234NA (s/n 56 4022). First hovering flight 17 Feb. 1957.
200	XV-3	Experimental tilt-rotor machine with metal monocoque fuselage, tail fin and tailplane, skid u/c, fixed wing with two wingtip pods housing swiveling 3-blade rotor units. Powered by one 450 h.p. P&W R-985-AN-3 buried in centre fuselage. Prot. s/n 54-147 FF 23 Aug. 1955. 2 built.
201	XH-13F	Experimental H-13D fitted with one 280 shp Turboméca Artouste XT51-T-3 turboshaft. FF 1955.
204	XH-40	Utility 10-seat helicopter for US Army with all-metal monocoque fuselage, skid u/c and fin mounted 2-blade tail rotor. Powered by one 700 shp. Lyc. XT53-L-1 turboshaft mounted above and behind cabin driving two-blade metal rotor with stabiliser bar. Prot. s/n 55-4459 FF 22 Oct. 1956. 3 built.
204	YH-40	XH-40 with longer fuselage, higher skids, larger tailplane and 770 shp T53 turboshaft engine. 6 built.
204	HU-1 UH-1	Pre-production YH-40 (redesignated) with 860 shp Lyc. T53-L-1A turboshaft.
204	HU-1A UH-1A Iroquois	Production 'Huey' for U.S. Army with modified rotor mast and other detail changes.
204	TH-1A	UH-1A with dual controls and IFR equipment.
204	UH-1B Iroquois	UH-1A with 960 shp Lyc. T53-L-5 turboshaft and taller rotor mast, enlarged cabin, wider rotor blades, external armament points and 8500 lb TOGW.

Type No.	Name or designation	Notes
204	UH-1C Iroquois	UH-1B with improved rotor, enlarged fin and increased fuel.
204	UH-1M	UH-1C refitted with 1400 shp Lyc. T53-L-13 turboshaft and armed with Nord AS-11 wire-guided missiles.
204	UH-1E TH-1E	UH-1C for US Marine Corps with revised avionics, external hoist, rotor brake and various alternative external weapons fits. Dual control TH-1E. Prot. FF Feb. 1963.
204	HH-1K TH-1L UH-1L	US Navy air-sea rescue version of UH-1E with 1400 shp Lyc. T53-L-13 turboshaft. rescue hoist etc. Also training version TH-1L and utility model, UH-1L.
204	XH48A UH-1F TH-1F	USAF model for missile site support duties with 1272 shp General Electric T58-GE-3 turboshaft and redesigned transmission. Prot. s/n 63-13141 (c/n 7001) FF 20 Feb. 1964. Also TH-1F instrument trainer.
204	UH-1P	UH-1F for psycho-warfare with loudspeakers etc.
204B		Eleven-seat civil version of UH-1B with 1100 shp Lyc. T5309A turboshaft, 8500 lb TOGW and 242-USG fuel capacity. Also built by Agusta and Fuji.
204B-2		Fuji-built version of Model 205.
AB204B		Agusta-built version of 204B.
AB204AS		Agusta-built anti-submarine model.
205	YUH-1D UH-1D HH-1D Iroquois	Model 204 with 41-inch fuselage stretch with 12-troop cabin and longer tailboom, longer main rotor blades, increased fuel, double cabin windows, enlarged cabin entry door and 1100 shp Lyc.T53-L-11 turboshaft. Prot. s/n 60-6028 (c/n 701) FF 16 Aug. 1961. Also HH-1D rescue version with external hoist etc. 9500 lb TOGW.

Bell 48 YH-12B, 46-217 *(HGM Collection)*

Type No.	Name or designation	Notes
205	UH-1H Iroquois	UH-1D with 1400 shp Lyc. T53-L-13 turboshaft. Also built by Agusta, AIDC and Fuji. Canadian model CUH-1H (CH-118). Also HH-1H rescue version with external hoist etc. and JUH-1H conversions for special test purposes.
205	EH-1H EH-1X Iroquois	UH-1H converted for electronic countermeasures with AN/ALQ-144 infrared jammer, radar warning receiver etc. Also EH-1X 3-seat countermeasures version.
205	UH-1V Iroquois	UH-1H for medical evecuation with external hoist, and special instrumentation inc. DME and radar altimeter.
205A		Civil model 205 with 15 seats and extra cabin windows, 1100 shp. Lyc. T5311A turboshaft, 8500 lb TOGW and 220-USG fuel capacity.
205A-1		Civil utility Model 205 with 1250 shp Lyc. T5313A turboshaft. 9500 lb TOGW.
AB205		Model 205A-1 built by Agusta.
205B		Model 205A-1 with 1290 shp Lyc. T5317A turboshaft and 10500 lb TOGW.
206	YHO-4 OH-4A	Military four-seat light observation helicopter with all-metal monocoque fuselage and boom, tail fin and tailplane, four cabin doors, skid u/c and one Allison 250-C10 (T63-A5) turboshaft engine. 2500 lb TOGW, 76-USG fuel capacity. Prot. N73999 (c/n 1) FF 8 Dec. 1962.
206A	Jet Ranger	Development of Model 206 for civil customers with redesigned, deeper 5-seat fuselage, pointed nose with deep stepped windshield, streamlined skid u/c. Powered by one 317 shp Allison 250-C18A turboshaft positioned above cabin driving metal 2-blade rotor without stabiliser bar. 3000 lb TOGW. Some converted to 206B. Prot. N8560F (c/n 1) FF 10 Jan. 1966 Also built by Agusta.
206A-1	OH-58A OH-58B Kiowa	Four-seat Military 206A with longer rotor blades, reshaped rear windows, utility interior and military avionics. 3000 lb TOGW. 71.5-USG fuel capacity. OH-58B is variant for Austrian AF.
206A-1	OH-58C Kiowa	OH-58A upgraded with 317 shp Allison T63-A-700 with infrared suppressors, rear transmission fairing and flat-surface windshield and external minigun installation.
206A-1	TH-57A SeaRanger	Dual control Model 206A for US Navy training with revised avionics.
206B	Jet Ranger II	Model 206A with 317 shp Allison 250-C20 turboshaft and 3200 lb TOGW. Also built by Agusta.
206B3	Jet Ranger III TH-57B	Model 206B with 420 shp Allison 250-C20J turboshaft and greater diameter tail rotor. 3200 lb TOGW. Also built by Agusta.
206L	Long Ranger	Model 206 with lengthened cabin giving capacity for 1 crew and 7 pax in club seating, longer skids, enlarged tailplane with endplate fins, increased fuel and 420 shp Allison 250-C20B turboshaft driving lengthened main rotor. 4000 lb TOGW. 98-USG fuel capacity. Prot. N206L (c/n 45001) FF 11 Sept. 1974.

Type No.	Name or designation	Notes
206L-1	Long Ranger II	206L with 435 shp Allison 250-C28B engine, redesigned cabin and new engine mountings. 4050 lb TOGW.
206L3	Long Ranger III	206L-1 with 650 shp Allison 250-C30P turboshaft, port-side double doors and 'Noda-matic' rotor head system, 4150 lb TOGW and 110.7-USG fuel capacity. First a/c N1083G (c/n 51001).
206L4	Long Ranger IV	206L-3 with 4550 lb TOGW, strengthened airframe and u/c, improved tail rotor drive and strengthened transmission to handle higher max. torque. First a/c N49MA (c/n 52001).
TH206	TH-67 Creek	Military training helicopter for U.S. Army based on Jet Ranger III with two front crew seats and rear student observer position. First a/c N6220Q (c/n 5101).
206LT	Twin Ranger	Model 206L-4 with two 490 shp Allison 250-C20R turboshafts, 4550 lb TOGW.
206ST-L1 206ST-L3 206ST-L4	Gemini ST	Conversions of Bell 206L1, L3 and L4 by Tridair Helicopters Inc. with two Allison 250-C20R turboshafts married to a Soloy combining gearbox. Lower-spec Gemini BT is fitted with two Allison 250-C20B engines.
207	Sioux Scout	Experimental tandem two-seat attack helicopter with Model 47J tail section, half-glazed forward fuselage, small shoulder-mounted wings, skid u/c, chin-mounted twin machine-gun turret and one 260 h.p. Lyc. TVO-435-A1A piston engine driving two-blade rotor. Prot. N73927 FF 27 Jun. 1963.

Bell-Boeing V-22A Osprey, 163913 *(Bell)*

Type No.	Name or designation	Notes
208	Twin Delta	Model 205 fitted with two 1240 shp Cont. T72-T-2 turboshafts mounted in enlarged housing. Prot. s/n 06030 FF 29 Apl. 1965.
209	Cobra	Tandem 2-seat attack helicopter with stepped cockpit seating, slim all-metal fuselage with low-set boom and tail fin, retractable skid u/c, external armament stub wings and 1100 shp Lyc. T53-L-11 turboshaft driving UH-1 two-blade main rotor. Prot. N209J. FF 7 Sep. 1965.
209	AH-1G HueyCobra	Production Model 209 for US Army and USMC with chin-mounted turret housing 6-barrel minigun, fixed skid u/c, larger stub wings and 1400 shp Lyc. T53-L-13 turboshaft driving broad-chord rotor. First a/c s/n 66-15246 FF 15 Oct. 1966.
209	TH-1G HueyCobra	Trainer version of AH-1G with dual controls and instruments.
209	AH-1Q HueyCobra	AH-1G converted with Hughes TOW missile system and associated fire control system.
209	AH-1R HueyCobra	Development aircraft for AH-1S.
209	AH-1S TH-1S HueyCobra	AH-1Q with new glass fibre main rotor, Model 212 tail rotor and 1800 shp. Lyc. T53-L-703 turboshaft. TH-1S version for ANG with project Night Stalker system and TOW missiles.
209	AH-1E HueyCobra	AH-1S with improved broad-sweep nose turret housing M-197 Vulcan three-barrel cannon.
209	AH-1F TAH-1F HueyCobra	AH-1S with improved fire control system with HUD, laser ranging, C-NITE targeting system, IR jammers and improved avionics and IFF xpdr. Also TAH-1F dual control trainer.
209	AH-1P HueyCobra	AH-1S with modified gearboxes and transmission, flat plate windshield and other transparencies and new low-level flight control/nav system.

Bell HSL-1, 129853 *(HGM Collection)*

Type No.	Name or designation	Notes
209	AH-1J SeaCobra	AH-1G for USMC with 20mm gun in redesigned electric turret, rotor brake and 1800 shp Pratt & Whitney PT6T-3 Twin Pac twin turboshaft.
209	AH-1T SeaCobra	AH-1J with 12-inch fuselage stretch, 1970 shp P&W Twin Pac T400-WV-402 twin turboshaft, Model 214 tail rotor, small ventral fin, modified transmission and TOW missiles.
209	AH-1W Super Cobra AH-1 (4B)W Viper	AH-1T for USMC with new rotor head, two 3250 shp GE T700-GE-401 turboshafts, new gearboxes, M-197 three-barrel 20-mm cannon, AIM-9L Sidewinder, Hellfire or eight TOW-II missiles and new radar warning system and AN/ALQ-144 infrared jammer. Some AH-1T upgraded to AH-1W. Also Viper experimental version with Model 680 bearingless rotor. Prot. AH-1W s/n 161022 FF 16 Nov. 1983.
211	HueyTug	Flying crane version of UH-1C with new transmission, longer main rotor, larger tailboom, strengthened fuselage, stability augmentation system and 2650 shp Lyc. T55-L-7 turboshaft. Prot. N6256N.
212		Model 208 16-passenger helicopter with a 'Twin Pac' 1290 shp Pratt & Whitney PT6T-3 turboshaft and new semi-rigid rotor. 1200 lb TOGW and 219.6-USG fuel capacity.
212	UH-1N HH-1N VH-1N	Military Model 212 for USAF, USN and USMC with provision for externally mounted machine-guns, rockets etc. Also HH-1N SAR version and VH-1N staff transport. Canadian AF model CH-135.
AB-212		Model 212 built by Agusta.

Bell 47A, HTL-1 *(HGM Collection)*

Type No.	Name or designation	Notes
AB-212AS		Anti-submarine warfare version of 212 built by Agusta.
249		AH-1G (s/n 70-16019) converted as development aircraft for Model 412 four-blade rotor.
214	HueyPlus	Model 205 with longer nose, streamlined skids, 1900 Lyc. T53-L-702 turboshaft and Model 309 main rotor and transmission.
214A		Production Model 214 for civil and overseas military users with 2930 shp Lyc. LTC4B-8D turboshaft. First a/c N214HJ (c/n 27001).
214B	Big Lifter	Civil Model 214 with 2930 shp Lyc. T5508D turboshaft, 16 seats and extra cabin window. 13800 lb TOGW and 204-USG fuel capacity. First a/c N49631 (c/n 28001).
214B-1	Big Lifter	Model 214B with lower 12500 lb TOGW.
214C		Search & Rescue version of 214A.
214ST	Super Transport	Model 214 with 96-inch fuselage stretch and 20-seat capacity powered by two 2350 shp General Electric CT7-2A turboshafts driving two-blade main rotor. Some fitted with 5-blade rotor and some fitted with tricycle u/c. 440-USG fuel capacity. 17500 lb TOGW. First a/c N214BH (c/n 18401) Prot N224XX.
222 222A		Ten (normally eight) seat executive helicopter with streamlined fuselage and slim tailboom with dorsal/ventral fin and mid-boom mounted tailplane with endplates. Retractable tricycle u/c with main units retracting into stub wings on lower fuselage. Powered by two 592 shp Lyc. LTS101-650C-3 turboshafts driving two-blade main rotor. 7850 lb TOGW. 187.5-USG fuel capacity. Prot. N9988K (c/n 47001) FF 13 Aug. 1976. N222FV fitted with experimental fenestron tail rotor.
222B		Model 222 with 8250 lb TOGW, longer rotor blades, taller rotor mast, longer tail boom and two 685 shp Lyc. LTS101-750C-1 engines.
222UT		Utility version of 222B with 247-USG fuel capacity and skid u/c
230		Model 222 with two 700 shp Allison 250-C30G2 turboshafts and either retractable tricycle u/c or skids. Prot. C-GEXP. FF 12 Aug. 1991.
249		AH-1S fitted with shortened version of four-blade main rotor from Model 412.
D292		Advanced experimental military helicopter for US Army with two seats, reverse tricycle u/c, all-composite airframe, large mid-boom mounted tailplane, Model 222 transmission and rotor. Powered by two 685 shp Lyc. LTS101-750C turboshafts. One Prot. s/n 85-24371 FF 30 Aug. 1985.
301	XV-15	Experimental two-seat tilt-rotor aircraft with all-metal fuselage with twin fin tail unit, retractable tricycle u/c, fixed wings with swivelling Lyc. LTC1K-4K turboprops driving three-blade prop/rotors. Prot. N702NA (c/n 00001) FF 3 May, 1977. 2 built.

Type No.	Name or designation	Notes
309	King Cobra	Enlarged AH-1G with re-stressed fuselage, new tail unit with ventral fin, modified nose with turret for GE M-197 rotary cannon, transmission and rotor from Model 211 and one 2850 shp Lyc. T55-L-7C turboshaft. Second prototype (N309J c/n 2503) fitted with P&W Twin Pac T400-CP-400 twin turboshaft.
400	Twin Ranger	Bell 206L fitted with four-blade main rotor, ring shroud around tail rotor and enlarged fin, modified tailplane and end fins, Model 406 transmission and rotor head and powered by two PW209T turboshafts. First of four a/c N3185K (c/n 48001) FF 30 Jun. 1984. Twin Ranger production not implemented and supplanted by Model 206LT.
400A	Twin Ranger	Model 400 with two 937 shp PW209T turboshafts.
406	OH-58D Kiowa Warrior	Two-seat attack helicopter based on Model 206 airframe with four-blade main rotor, mast-mounted sight, external weapons mountings, advanced electronics including video downlink, IR jammers and offensive ranging. Powered by one 650 shp Allison 250-C30R turboshaft housed in enlarged engine fairing. 5500 lb TOGW. Prot. s/n 85-24716.
406CS	Combat Scout	Model 406 stripped down to 5000 lb TOGW with Allison 250-C30U engine for export customers.
407		Long Ranger with composite 4-blade main rotor, bulged cabin transparencies and FADEC fuel control system. Gemini HP is conversion by Tridair with Gemini systems. First a/c C-GFOS (c/n 52901).
409	YAH-63	Two-seat advanced attack helicopter (AAH) with tandem armoured cockpit with flat transparencies, fixed tricycle u/c, tail fin with upper and lower tailplanes, two 1500 shp GE YT700-GE-700 turboshafts mounted behind cabin driving wide chord 2-blade main rotor, nose turret for 30-mm rotary cannon and stub wings with four Hellfire missile strongpoints. Prot. s/n 73-22246 FF 1 Oct. 1975. 2 built.

Bell UH-1, 20048 *(Bell)*

Type No.	Name or designation	Notes
412		Model 212 with four-blade rotor and modified rotor head, PT6T-3B Twin Pac turboshaft and 214.2-USG fuel capacity. Also built by IPTN and Agusta. First a/c N2148K (c/n 36001).
412EP		Model 412 with 1800 shp PT6T-3D Twin Pac turboshaft, 11900 lb TOGW and improved interior seating.
412HP		Model 412 with 1800 shp PT6T-3BE Twin Pac turboshaft.
412SP		Model 412 with increased fuel and 11900 lb TOGW.
412AH		Military variant of Model 412 with machine gun turret under nose and external rocket pack mountings on fuselage sides.
427		Enlarged and lengthened version of Model 407 with wider cabin, centre-section fuel tank, OH-58D composite four-blade main rotor, 6000 lb TOGW. Powered by two 600 shp Pratt & Whitney PW206D turboshafts. To be built by Samsung, Bell and Bell Canada. Prot. C-GBLL FF 15 Dec. 1997.
430		Model 230 with four-blade '680' bearingless main rotor, 18-inch longer cabin, redesigned glass cockpit. Powered by two 808 shp Allison 250-C40 turboshafts. Prot. C-GBLL FF 25 Oct. 1994.
533		Model 204 with experimental drag reduction mods including raised rotor mast fairings and flush air intakes, streamlined skids, recontoured fin with starboard side tailplane, twin externally mounted 1700 lbs.t. Cont. J69-T9 turbojets and fixed wings for compound high speed flight tests. Prot. s/n 56-6723. FF 10 Aug. 1962.
	V-22 Osprey	Bell-Boeing advanced tilt-rotor military transport capable of carrying 24 troops with fixed forward-swept-wing mounted wingtip pods for two 6150 shp Allison T406-AD-400 turbines driving three-blade composite prop-rotors, retractable tricycle u/c, twin-fin tail unit and rear loading ramp. Prot. XV-22A s/n 163911 FF 19 Mar. 1989.

Bell 200 XV-3, 54-148 (Bell)

Type No.	Name or designation	Notes
609		Bell-Boeing developed tilt-rotor aircraft with eleven seats, conventional fuselage and T-tail and two tilt-rotor modules at wingtips.
D-2127	X-22A	Experimental two-seat VTOL aircraft with conventional all-metal fuselage and fin and forward and rear flying surfaces. Fitted with four tilting ducted rotor units on ends of wings, powered by four 1250 shp General Electric T58-GE-8B turboshafts mounted externally on rear fuselage. One Prot s/n 151520 FF 17 Mar. 1966.

U.S. Military Designations

Many of the Bell models were procured by several American military services and received appropriate designations. This principally applied to the following:

Bell Model	Name	USAF	US Army	US Navy	USMC	USCG	Total Delivered
47A		YR-13 YR-13A YH-13A		HTL-1			28
47D			H-13B	HTL-2			77
47D	Sioux		H-13C				(15)
47D	Sioux		H-13D				87
47D	Sioux		H-13E				490
47D-1				HTL-4 HTL-5 TH-13L			82
47E				HTL-3			12
47G	Sioux		H-13G	HTL-6 TH-13M			313
47G-2		UH-13H	H-13H OH-13H				470
47G-3	Sioux		H-13K				(2)
47G-3B	Sioux		OH-13S				265
47G-3B1	Sioux		TH-13T				411
47J		H-13J		HUL-1 UH-13P		HUL-1G HH-13Q	32
47K				HTL-7			18
47L				HUL-1M UH-13R			
48		XR-12 R-12A XH-12 XR-12B YH-12B					13
54		XH-15					3

Bell Model	Name	USAF	US Army	US Navy	USMC	USCG	Total Delivered
61				HSL-1			53
204	Iroquois	TH-1F UH-1F	UH-1A TH-1A UH-1B				1347
204			UH-1C UH-1M				767
204B	Seawolf			UH-1L TH-1L HH-1K	UH-1E TH-1E		337
205			UH-1D HH-1D				2008
205		HH-1H	UH-1H EH-1H				5465
206A	Kiowa		OH-58A OH-4A				2208
206A	Sea Ranger			TH-57A TH-57B TH-57C			180
209	Cobra		AH-1G AH-1P AH-1Q AH-1R AH-1S				1223
209	Cobra				AH-1T		65
209	Sea Cobra			AH-1J			69
212	Twin Huey	UH-1N	UH-1N		VH-1N		289

Continental Copters E1 Tomcat, N9092T

BOEING-VERTOL   USA

The tandem rotor Boeing Chinook is a well-known and well respected member of the helicopter world. But the credit for the series of designs leading up to the Chinook goes to Frank Piasecki. Piasecki worked for the Kellett Autogyro Company and for Platt-Lepage Aircraft and Budd Aircraft. Like many other aviation pioneers, he was a man with considerably more enthusiasm than finance. However, he formed the PV Engineering forum as an association of young engineers and this group embarked on helicopter design. The PV.1 was a remarkably advanced design for its day with a tube and fabric fuselage and a tail-mounted anti-torque system involving an enclosed fan in the rear fuselage. This design did not fly but the single-seat PV.2 which took to the air in April 1943 was very similar – but with a conventional tail-mounted anti torque propeller. It was probably the first truly rigid rotor helicopter ever to fly.

With considerable experience gained from the PV.2, Frank Piasecki managed to persuade the U.S. Navy to invest in the development of a passenger-carrying helicopter. The problem of countering the torque of the main rotor was a never-ending source of debate for helicopter engineers and Piasecki decided on a radical change from the PV.2 when he laid out the PV.3 for the Navy. Instead of the tail 'propeller' he designed the new XHRP-X with a continuous fuselage which mounted two main rotor pylon points at the front and rear. By having counter-rotating rotors the torque problem was overcome. The tandem rotor design also had the great virtue that passengers and cargo could be loaded with relatively little thought of being out of centre of gravity range.

The XHRP-X 'Dog Ship' prototype led to the more refined XHRP-1 and to the definitive production HRP-1. The new Piasecki Helicopter Corporation had been established in 1946 with a plant at Morton, Pennsylvania, and by the end of 1948, 20 examples of the HRP-1 had been delivered. These were known affectionately as 'Flying Bananas' and they served as search and rescue helicopters for the U.S. Navy and with the U.S. Coast Guard at Elizabeth City, North Carolina.

The HRP-1 still had a tube and fabric fuselage but the next development was the all-metal HRP-2 which brought a number of important improvements to the design. This was followed in 1953 by the CH-21 which had twice the power of the HRP series and was ordered by the U.S. Air Force as a long-range rescue helicopter. It was capable of operating in extreme conditions and was used in Alaska and Greenland in support of the DEW-line radar bases. For this role, the H-21 Work Horse could be fitted with inflatable pontoons on the three undercarriage legs to allow it to land on snow or marshy land. The U.S. Army also received H-21s which it named the Shawnee (in line with the policy of giving Indian tribal names to Army aircraft) and the Canadian Air Force also acquired six H-21s for rescue duties.

HELICOPTERS AND ROTORCRAFT

A total of 108 H-21s were transferred from U.S. military orders to the French Army for transporting combat troops in the war zones of Algeria and Vietnam, and 26 examples of the H-21 were built under licence for the West German Army by Weser Flugzeugbau. The civil version of the H-21, the Vertol 44, was built in small numbers to meet the needs of the developing city centre helicopter shuttles. In its airline configuration, the Vertol 44 had more cabin windows than the H-21. New York Airways used a fleet of '44s equipped with large inflatable flotation bags under the nose and rear fuselage on a route linking La Guardia, Idlewild (later John F. Kennedy) and Newark and subsequently flew them from the newly-opened Mid-Manhattan Heliport. In Belgium, Sabena operated a pair of Vertols from the Brussels heliport beside their Sikorsky S-58s. Rick Helicopters in Canada had a fleet of ten for logging and general utility work and Piasecki even delivered one Model 44 (N74056) to Russia.

In August, 1945 the Navy Bureau of Aeronautics issued a specification for a compact utility helicopter for fleet operational use. Piasecki proposed an all-metal three-seat design, the PV-11, which was to use the rotor system designed on the PV.2 with overlapping tandem rotors. The Navy requirement evolved into a larger design for which Piasecki proposed the PV-14 and its larger brother, the PV-12. As it turned out, the PV-14 was awarded an experimental development contract for three prototypes and the first of these XHJP-1s was flown in March 1948.

The XHJP-1 had the overlapping rotor arcs devised for the PV-11, and an oval-section fuselage with a prominent rear pylon section which housed the Continental R-975 piston engine. Following Navy testing at Patuxent River and operational trials on carriers and a cruiser, an initial order for 32 HUP-1 Retrievers (Piasecki designation PV-18) was placed and the first of these entered service with Squadron HU-2 at Lakehurst, New Jersey in January 1951. The later HUP-2 model was similar to the initial variant except for the deletion of the rear fins and tailplane. Piasecki started to deliver this model in the first quarter of 1952. Subsequently, the HUP-2S was selected as an anti-submarine warfare helicopter with dipping-sonar equipment and a Sperry autopilot. The U.S. Marine Corps also received a number of yellow-painted HUP-2s for air-sea rescue.

The U.S. Navy had been the main customer for Piasecki in the early days, but, in April, 1951 the U.S. Army ordered 70 H-25A Army Mules. These were similar to the HUP-1 and were engaged on medical evacuation and general transport operations. HUP-1s went to the French Navy, which used them in Indo China in 1954/55, and to the Royal

Piasecki PV-3 XHRP-1 Bu. 37968 *(HGM Collection)*

Canadian Navy which based them at HMCS Shearwater in Nova Scotia for service on its icebreaking fleet. The 339th and last HUP was handed over to the U.S. Navy on 30th June 1954 and by that time the PV-18 fleet in U.S. military service had exceeded 70,000 flight hours.

In 1948, while the HUP programme was getting under way, Piasecki commenced the ambitious YH-16 programme. The U.S. Air Force issued a specification for a very large transport helicopter which could carry forty troops. The huge YH-16, powered by two Pratt & Whitney R.1280 piston engines, flew in the early afternoon of 23rd October 1953, from Philadelphia International Airport at the hands of Harold Peterson and Phillip Camerano, and was the world's largest helicopter at that time. It would have been highly successful except that it was grossly underpowered. The second aircraft, the YH-16A Turbo Transporter, which flew in July 1955, was fitted with Allison YT.38 turbines but it broke up in the air during testing early in January 1956. The two test pilots were killed and the H-16 programme was then abandoned. Piasecki also spent considerable time in researching battlefield support vehicles for the U.S. Army and they devised the VZ-8 Airgeep. This remarkable machine was built around two ducted rotors built into the front and rear of the vehicle which gave it lift and allowed it to hover-fly at up to 70 miles per hour. The project was eventually abandoned as being too complex and offering insufficient flexibility for Army operations.

In May 1955, Frank Piasecki left the company following a management disagreement and in the following March the company was renamed Vertol Aircraft Corporation. This coincided with a new requirement being raised by the U.S. Army for a medium-lift helicopter to replace the fleet of H-37 Mojaves. The replacement needed to be large enough to cope with a wide variety of cargoes and troop loads and to have a large rear ramp to permit very rapid loading and unloading. Vertol's response was to offer the new Model 107. They had already experimented with turbine power for their helicopters with the Model 105 development of the H-21 but the Model 107 was to be the first production turbine powered

Piasecki-Vertol H-21A Work Horse, 51-15250 *(Boeing)*

design – still following the established tandem rotor configuration. It was also unusual in having a sealed fuselage allowing it to float on water

Vertol built a prototype of the Model 107 which first flew in April 1958. It introduced new low-vibration steel-sparred rotor blades and a simplified flight control system with differential collective pitch and no longitudinal cyclic pitch. The main purpose of the V.107 prototype was to provide the basis for the definitive U.S. Army submission (the YHC-1A) but the V.107 design did become a production model in its own right. The company continued its separate development and delivered civil V.107-IIs with larger airline windows for airline shuttle applications. The first customer was New York Airways which, in 1962, replaced the ageing Vertol 44s with the new helicopter and became the world's first helicopter airline with turbine equipment.

The military CH-46 assault transport variant of the V.107-II was delivered in significant numbers to the Army and to the Navy and Marine Corps where it was named 'Sea Knight'. The last CH-46 delivery was made in 1971. The Navy employed the UH-46D on 'VERTREP' on-board supply operations for the seaborne fleet and for SAR missions, medevac and general transport work. The V.107 was also delivered to the Canadian Armed Forces as the 'Labrador' and 'Voyageur' and to Sweden for use by both the Navy and Air Force. In Japan, Kawasaki took on a licence for the V.107 and built a final total of 160 aircraft including 60 for the Japanese Ground Self Defense Force, nine to the Japanese Navy and others to civil operators including Tokyo Air Lines.

March 1960 saw Vertol being acquired by the Seattle-based Boeing Aircraft Company. The U.S. Army CH-37 replacement requirement defined a helicopter which was larger than the standard Model 107. Having proved the capability of the V.107 Boeing-Vertol received a contract to build three modified YHC-1B helicopter prototypes. The resultant aircraft was virtually a redesign of the V.107 with a fuselage of squarer section, full-length external fairings containing fuel and equipment, a fixed four-leg undercarriage, a completely redesigned dynamic system, twin T55 turboshaft engines mounted on the outside of the tail pylon and an autopilot/autostabilisation system to reduce crew workload. The YHC-1A prototype flew in August 1959.

Flight testing led to the definitive YHC-1B, which was given the revised Boeing Vertol designation BV.114. Eventually, in July 1962, DoD instituted a wide-ranging redesignation of U.S. military aircraft and the HC-1B became the CH-47A Chinook. By this time, substantial production contracts were in place and the first CH-47A for the U.S. Army was handed over at Fort Rucker in August, 1962. The CH-47 was progressively improved as the CH-47B and CH-47C with higher-power turbines and modifications to the rotor system and dynamic components. The Chinook was pressed into service in Vietnam where

Vertol V.107-II-9 Voyageur *(Boeing)*

they became the 'flying trucks' of the U.S. Army, moving every type of cargo and most types of ordnance and transport equipment in the Army inventory. Roles included medical evacuation, fire fighting, parachute drops, search and rescue, transport of under-slung fuel cells and heavy construction. Over 160 Chinooks were deployed to the Persian Gulf for Operation Desert Shield and logged in excess of 16,000 hours of mission time during that conflict.

In April 1985, Boeing Vertol was contracted to upgrade existing 'A', 'B' and 'C' model Chinooks to CH-47D standard. This involved a complete strip-down of the aircraft at the Ridley, Pennsylvania plant, installation of new Avco-Lycoming T55-L-712 turbines together with redesigned composite rotor blades, new rotor transmissions, triple cargo hooks, an improved APU and single-point refuelling. The CH-47D also has a dual electrical system, advanced flight controls and a completely redesigned instrumentation and avionics suite. Boeing Vertol modified an existing CH-47A as the prototype which flew in May 1979 and the first fully converted CH-47D was delivered to the Army's 101st Airborne Division at Fort Campbell, Kentucky in February, 1983. Since then, almost all surviving CH-47 airframes have been brought up either to CH-47D or MH-47E standard and some new aircraft have also been manufactured, particularly for Australia and Singapore.

Many overseas air arms have acquired the Chinook and some U.S. Army aircraft have been transferred to other users – notably the Vietnam Air Force. The initial overseas deliveries to Spain and Australia were CH-47C standard aircraft, but Boeing Vertol introduced the Model 414 International Chinook and this was quickly upgraded to CH-47D specification (the Model 414-100). The largest user of Chinooks outside the United States is the Royal Air Force which ordered 33 aircraft in 1978 to replace the obsolete Bristol Belvederes. These were pressed into service in 1982 for the Falklands War where they performed miracles in the heat of battle. The RAF subsequently ordered another eight Chinooks which included three replacements for aircraft lost in the sinking of the Atlantic Conveyor support vessel. The RAF Chinooks were subsequently upgraded to full CH-47D standard at the Boeing factory and a further 17 new-build aircraft were also ordered.

Other purchasers of the BV.414 have included the armed forces of Canada, Italy, South Korea and Thailand. Many of the earlier export models have received factory upgrading. These include the Spanish Army fleet of 18 CH-47Cs which was rebuilt to CH-47D standard between September 1991 and April 1993. Seven of the Canadian CH-47C fleet were subsequently sold to the Netherlands and upgraded to CH-47D standard.

Boeing Vertol granted a licence for manufacture of the Chinook to the Italian associate company of Agusta, Elicotteri Meridionali SpA, and this resulted in production of 34 aircraft for the Italian Army and further sales of the Chinook to Egypt, Greece, Iran, Libya and Morocco. Meridionali also built a small batch of 11 CH-47s for the United States Air National Guard. In Japan, Kawasaki was granted a licence to build the CH-47J (which is a CH-47D standard Chinook). Following delivery of three pattern aircraft from Boeing, they commenced deliveries to the JASDF and JGSDF in 1986 based on major components and assemblies produced both at Gifu and at the parent Boeing Vertol plant.

Boeing Vertol announced the Model 234 civil variant of the Chinook in November, 1978 and flew the first aircraft in August, 1980. Four different models were offered – the 234LR (Long Range), 234ER (extended range), 234UT (Utility) and 234 Combi. Internal accommodation varies between the models depending on the extent of supplementary internal fuel tankage, but the standard 234LR can carry 44 passengers and initial deliveries were made to British Airways Helicopters for North Sea oil support and carried over 80,000 passengers in their first year of operation. BV.234s were fitted with airline-type windows and enlarged external fairings containing the fuel tanks and baggage space. They were also sold to Columbia Helicopters, ERA Helicopters and the Norwegian operator, Helikopter Service A.S. The BV.234 had a relatively short life in the North Sea and was not entirely popular with passengers who preferred the smaller Puma and the Sikorsky S-61N.

HELICOPTERS AND ROTORCRAFT

At the time of the Vietnam war, Boeing Vertol had developed the ACH-47A Armed Chinook. This armed attack variant did not get beyond the experimental stage, but the concept of using the CH-47 for Special Operations led to the design of the MH-47E for long-range all-weather intruder missions. The first MH-47E flew in May 1990 and Boeing Vertol subsequently converted a substantial number of CH-47Ds to this configuration with more powerful engines, a refuelling boom, rotor brake, rescue hoist, twin GECAL 0.50in Gatling guns, increased tankage (involving the forward undercarriage being re-positioned) and a suite of advanced avionics which are compatible with the systems fitted to the MH-60K Black Hawk. Many of the systems were flight tested in the Boeing 360 Advanced Technology demonstrator helicopter.

Boeing has also taken part in several other military development programmes. In 1972 the U.S. Army UTTAS competition was launched and Boeing-Vertol submitted its YUH-61A to compete against the Sikorsky YUH-60. This was a major departure in design philosophy for the company. The YUH-61A was a conventional medium lift helicopter with external dimensions similar to the Bell UH-1 but offering twice the cabin space of the Huey and more than three times the payload capability. It used two externally mounted General Electric T700 turboshafts to drive a single four-blade main rotor. The company also proposed a civil variant, the Model 179, which could carry up to 25 passengers in high-density operations. In the end, the Sikorsky design won the competition and Boeing decided that the civil variant was not viable in the absence of the supporting military order. With the 1997 acquisition of McDonnell Douglas, all current McDonnell Douglas helicopters are now marketed under the Boeing name.

The most recent new programmes at Boeing are both cooperative projects with competitors. The most controversial is the Bell-Boeing V-22 Osprey tiltrotor transport which has required all the engineering talent of both companies. Bell and Boeing formed a joint venture in 1982 to participate in the Joint Services Advanced Vertical Lift Aircraft Program ('JVX') competition. At the time of conception, the Osprey offered a unique combination of lifting capacity, vertical flight and high-speed performance equal to conventional turboprop tactical transport aircraft and the ability to perform different roles for each of the four American military services. Over fifty different missions were identified in the Operational Requirement.

The original need was for a total of 913 Ospreys – 552 MV-22As for the U.S. Marine

Boeing BV.414, MH-47E *(Boeing)*

68

Corps, 50 HV-22As for the U.S. Navy as combat SAR and special warfare aircraft, 80 CV-22As for the U.S. Air Force for long-range special operations and 231 MV-22As for the Army for medevac, special operations and combat support. The U.S. Navy initiated the programme with a development contract in May 1986 followed by a further $550-million engineering and manufacturing development contract in October 1992.

The first Osprey prototype flew in March 1989, followed by a further three development aircraft at approximately six-monthly intervals. Production of the aircraft was spread over a number of contractors including Grumman Aerospace, Lockheed-Georgia and General Electric. For the U.S. military forces it offered a flexible replacement for the existing fleets of CH-46, HH-53 and CH-47 helicopters. However, such a multi-capable machine brought many engineering problems, particularly in regard to vibration, and two Ospreys were destroyed during initial testing. Eventually, the U.S. Army abandoned its procurement and the USAF reduced its target number. U.S. Defense Secretary, Dick Cheney attempted to cancel the whole Osprey programme in 1990 as being too expensive. This was reversed by Congress in 1992 following a proposal by the manufacturers for a lower cost aircraft which would meet the Medium Lift reqiuirement issued by the U.S. Marine Corps. Bell-Boeing were contracted to build a further four Ospreys so that a comparison evaluation could be carried out against other helicopter options and this process is intended to be completed in 1998.

Boeing's other major cooperative project is the RAH-66 Comanche in which it is teamed with Sikorsky to develop a two-seat armed reconnaissance helicopter to replace the OH-58, AH-1 and OH-6. The Comanche proposal was submitted in late-1990 with the consortium targeted to build six prototypes of the RAH-66. Boeing has responsibility for all missions electronics integration,the rotor blades and the aft fuselage. Sikorsky handles the drive system, weapons integration and forward fuselage.The prototype Comanche made its first flight from the Sikorsky test centre at West Palm Beach in January 1996, and continues in development with a target development completion date of September 1998, and a production decision to be taken in 2003.

Production details

Model	Serial Batch	Number Built	Notes
HRP-1	c/n 1 up	23	
HRP-2	c/n 1 to 5	5	
HUP-1	c/n 1 to 32	32	
HUP-2/ H-25A	c/n 33 up	409	
H-21A, H-21B, H-21C	Not confirmed. Believed to be in range c/n 1 to approx. c/n 590	445	Some c/ns prefixed with sub-type letter (e.g. B-120, C-149).
H-21B	c/n FR-1 to FR-108	108	French Army. Additional c/ns given to aircraft with USAF serial numbers.
Model 44	c/ns within H-21 batch between c/n 417 and 538	37	
H-21C	c/n WG.1 to WG.32	32	Built by Weser-Flug.
CH-46A	c/n 2001 to 2175	175	USMC and USN deliveries.
CH-46D/ UH-46D	c/n 2176 to 2451	276	
CH-46F	c/n 2452 to 2637	186	

HELICOPTERS AND ROTORCRAFT

Model	Serial Batch	Number Built	Notes
V.107-II	c/n 1 to 11, c/n 101 to 108, c/n 301 to 304, c/n 401 to 410, c/n 501 to 503, c/n 2002 to 2003, c/n4008 to 4010	41	Information incomplete. C/n batches allocated to individual customers.
BV.114A (CH-47A)	c/n B-001 to B-005, B-007 to B-355	354	US Army. Note: B-004 Static Test.
CH-47B	c/n B-356 to B-463	108	US Army.
CH-47C, BV.234	c/n B-464 to B-736, B-747 to B-930	457	US Army and overseas customers.
CH-47C	c/n D-001 to D-045	45	Meridionali production. Allocated separate c/ns with M, P, R and S prefixes.
CH-47D	c/n M.3001 to M.3464		New c/ns for US Army CH-47A, CH-47B and CH-47C remanufactured to CH-47D standard.
MH-47E	c/n M.3701 to M.3720		New c/ns for US Army CH-47A, CH-47B and CH-47C remanufactured to MH-47E standard.
BV.308 (CH-47C)	c/n CG-071 to CG-073	3	Argentine AF.
BV.309 (CH-47C)	c/n CG-101 to CG-102	2	Argentine Army.
CH-47C	c/n E-001 to E-012	12	Australian AF.
BV.234 (CH-47C)	c/n GN-001 to GN-009	9	Canadian AF (later R.Neth.AF).
CH-47C	c/n F-001 to F-010	10	Spanish Army.

Piasecki-Vertol PV-18 HUP-1 Bu. 124588 *Boeing)*

Model	Serial Batch	Number Built	Notes
BV.414 (CH-47C)	c/n F-010 to F-015	6	Spanish Army.
BV.234	c/n M4451 to M4453, M4511 to M4516	9	Customer unknown.
BV.352	c/n M/A.001 to M/A.041	41	Chinook HC.1 for RAF.
BV.414 (CH-47D)	c/n M4009 to M4031	23	South Korea.
BV.414	c/n MA.901 to MA.904	4	Spanish Army.
BV.414	c/n MF.004 to MF.005	2	Customer unknown.
BV.414	c/n MM.819 to MM.820	2	Customer unknown.
BV.414	c/n MP.001	1	Customer unknown.
BV.234	c/n MJ.001 to MJ.023	23	Civil Model 234LR.

Model Information

Type No.	Name	Notes
PV.2		Experimental single-seat helicopter with tube and fabric fuselage, tailwheel u/c, conventional 3-blade main rotor and tail anti-torque rotor, powered by one 90 h.p. Franklin. One Prot. NX37061 FF 11 Apl. 1943.
PV.3	XHRP-X	Large tandem-rotor helicopter of 'flying banana' configuration with tube and fabric fuselage accommodating 2 crew in nose compartment and 8 pax in cabin, fitted with tricycle u/c, two counter-rotating three-blade rotors and one 600 h.p. Pratt & Whitney Wasp R-1340. One Prot. Bu.37968 FF. Mar. 1945.
PV-3	XHRP-1	XHRP-X with modified rounded nose glazing, tailplane and fins, recontoured rear fuselage. 2 built.
PV-3	HRP-1	Production version of XHRP-1 fitted with strengthened u/c, modified rotor drive system and recontoured nose. Powered by one Pratt & Whitney R-1840-AN1 piston engine.
PV-14	XHJP-1	All-metal monocoque tandem rotor helicopter with oval-section fuselage to accommodate 2 crew and 5 pax and rear pylon structure carrying rear rotor assembly, tailplane with large fins, tailwheel u/c. Powered by one 525 h.p. Continental R-975-34 piston engine. First of three Prots. Bu.37976 FF Oct. 1948.
PV-15	YH-16 Transporter YH-16A Turbo Transporter	Large tandem rotor transport helicopter of all-metal construction with 43-troop capacity, fixed tailwheel u/c, large rear pylon containing two 1650 h.p. Pratt & Whitney R-2180-11 piston engines. Prot. s/n 50-1269 later re-engined with two 3750 shp T56A turboshafts. Second prot. YH-16A (s/n 50-1270) powered by two 2925 shp T38A-6 turboshafts.
PV-16H		Experimental 2-seat helicopter with all-metal monocoque fuselage incorporating folding fixed wings and vertically set tail fan with annular ring duct, retractable tailwheel u/c, powered by one Pratt & Whitney PT6B-2 turboshaft driving foldable three-blade main rotor. One Prot. N616H (c/n 1) FF 21 Feb. 1962.

HELICOPTERS AND ROTORCRAFT

Type No.	Name	Notes
PV-17	HRP-2	Improved metal-clad version of HRP-1 with forward-angled transparent nose, longer track u/c, high-set tailplane and no tailfins, oval porthole cabin widows.
PV-18	HUP-1 Retriever	Production version of XHJP-1 for USN shipboard support with detail changes including winch etc.
PV-18	HUP-2 Retriever	HUP-1 without tailfins, fitted with autopilot and 525 h.p. R-975-42 piston engine. HUP-2S fitted with ASW search radar. Redesignated UH-25B.
PV.18	H-25A Army Mule	U.S. Army version of HUP-2 with one 575 h.p. R-975-42 engine, hydraulically boosted controls, strengthened cabin floor and internal equipment changes.
PV.18	HUP-3 Retriever	Ex-Army H-25A with hydraulically boosted controls and 550 h.p. R-975-46A engine. For Royal Canadian Navy. Redesignated UH-25C.
PD.22	YH-21 Work Horse	HRP-2 developed for USAF use with 1150 h.p. Wright R-1820 engine, increased gross weight. Prot. s/n 50-1231 FF 11 Apl. 1952.
Model 42	H-21A Work Horse	Production YH-21 with 1150 h.p. Wright R-1820-103 engine. 14-troop seats or 12-stretchers for casevac. Fitted with hoist and rescue equipment for Arctic SAR role. Some used by RCAF. Redesignated CH-21A.
Model 42	H-21B SH-21B Work Horse	H-21A fitted with autopilot, optional external fuel tankage, 1425 h.p. R-1820-103 engine and 20-troop seating, two extra windows and larger rear door. Also SH-21B SAR version. 13 transferred to French Army. Later redesignated CH-21B.
Model 42A		Ten H-21A modified by Vertol Canada for commercial use with 1425 h.p. R-1820-103 engine.
Model 42B		Civil version of Model 42.
Model 43	H-21C Shawnee	Version of H-21B with modified external winch system etc. for US Army, France & Germany. 32 built by Weser Flug in Germany.
Model 44		Civil version of H-21C with 1425 h.p. Wright R-1820-103 engine, all-metal rotor blades and roll stability system.
Model 44A		Utility transport model with 19 pax seats and provision for external cargo hoist.
Model 44B		Civil airline version with 15 seats, full soundproofing, baggage compartment and provision for external inflatable floats. Prot. N3913A (c/n B-120).
Model 44C		Executive transport version of Model 44 with custom interior. One (N74056) delivered to Russia, Oct. 1960.
Model 59	Seageep	VTOL open-frame 'flying saucer' vehicle for US Navy with pilot on centrally-placed seat, pontoon landing gear and two Turboméca Artouste IIC turbines driving fore and aft vertical lift fans. One built.
Model 59K	VZ-8P Airgeep II	US Army VTOL vehicle similar to Seageep with fixed tricycle u/c. First of two Prots. s/n 58-5510. FF 1963.
Model 63	HUP-4	Two HUP-2 fitted with an 800 h.p. R-1820 engine.

Type No.	Name	Notes
Model 71	H-21D	Two H-21C re-engined for U.S. Army tests with two G.E. T58 turboshafts. Prot. s/n 55-4203.
Model 76	VZ-2	Experimental US Army tilt-wing aircraft with open tube fuselage, Bell 47 bubble cockpit, constant chord wing pivoted around mainspar, T-tail , fixed tricycle u/c and powered by one Lycoming T53 turbine engine mounted above mid-fuselage driving two rotor-propellers mounted on wings. Prot. s/n 56-6943 FF 1958.
Model 105		Model 44 fitted with two 825 shp Lycoming T53 turboshafts. Prot. N3914A (c/n B-147) FF 20 Nov. 1957.
Model 107		All-metal tandem rotor 23-pax. commercial medium transport helicopter with sealed fuselage for water flotation, rear fuselage sponsons, fixed tricycle u/c powered by two 850 shp Lycoming T53 turboshafts. Prot. N74060 (c/n 69-1X) FF 22 Apl. 1958.
V.107-II		Enlarged 25-pax production Model 107 powered by two 1050 shp GE CT58 turboshafts. Prot. FF 25 Oct. 1960.
V.107-II-2		Five Vertol 107 for Pan American and NYA with square cabin windows, rear fuselage baggage pod and 19000 lb TOGW.
V.107-II-15		14 Vertol 107 for Swedish Air Force as Hkp.4A with large external long-range tanks on sponsons and SAR equipment and for Swedish Navy as Hkp.4B. Powered by two Bristol-Siddeley Gnome H1200 turboshafts as Hkp.4B.
V.107-II-9	CH-113 Labrador CH-113A Voyageur	18 Vertol 107 for RCAF search & rescue as CH-113 with enlarged sponsons containing long range tanks, 21400 lb TOGW. CH-113A Canadian Army tactical transport without long-range tanks. First a/c N10112/ RCAF 10403 (c/n 303).
V.107	YHC-1A YCH-46C CH-46C	Model 107 evaluated by US Army as 22-troop tactical transport with rear loading ramp, larger sponsons, strengthened u/c with twin nosewheels, revised nose transparencies, powered by two 1025 shp. GE T58 turboshafts. Prot. s/n 58-5514 FF 27 Aug. 1959.

Piasecki PV-15 YH-16A, 50-1270 (HGM Collection)

Type No.	Name	Notes
V.107M	HRB-1 CH-46A HH-46A RH-46A Sea Knight	Model 107-II assault transport for USMC with 25-troop capacity, powered main rotor folding, rear cargo loading system, powered by two 1250 shp GE T58-GE-8B turboshafts. Some converted to HH-46A base rescue model and RH-46A minesweepers for US Navy.
V.107M	CH-46D	CH-46A with redesigned main rotor blades and two 1400 shp GE T58-GE-10 turboshafts.
V.107M	CH-46E	300 CH-46A and CH-46D re-engined for US Marines under CILOP contract with two 1870 shp GE T58-GE-16 turboshafts, new protective crew seats, self-sealing fuel tanks and improved avionics.
V.107M	CH-46F	Upgraded version of CH-46D with improved avionics and equipment for USN.
V.114	YHC-1B YCH-47A Chinook	Medium lift troop transport helicopter based on Model 107 with lengthened fuselage, external lower fuselage fairings containing fuel tanks, fixed four-leg u/c with twin wheel units, tail cargo ramp and two 2200 shp Lycoming T55-L-5 turboshafts in external pods on tail driving two three-bladed rotors. 33000 lb TOGW. Prot. s/n 59-4982 (c/n B.1) FF 21 Sept. 1961.
BV.114	CH-47A HC-1B Chinook	Production Chinook for US Army. Some delivered with 2650 shp Lycoming T55-L-7 turboshafts.
BV.143	ACH-47A	Armed enemy suppression Chinook with externally-mounted 20-mm cannon, nose turret with grenade launcher, miniguns, rocket launchers etc. Prot. s/n 64-13145.
BV.114	CH-47B Chinook	CH-47A fitted with new cambered rotor blades, recontoured rear rotor pylon, rear fuselage strakes and 2850 shp T55-L-7C turboshaft engines.

Boeing BV.179 YUH-61A, 73-21658 (Boeing)

Type No.	Name	Notes
BV.234	CH-47C Chinook	CH-47B with increased fuel capacity, strengthened rotor transmission and two 3750 shp T55-L-11C turboshafts. 44800 lb TOGW. FF 14 Oct. 1967. Includes deliveries to Nigeria, Morocco, Japan etc.
BV.145	CH-47D	472 remanufactured CH-47A, CH-47B and CH-47C with T55-L-712 engines, composite blades, improved transmission, APU, redesigned cockpit with advanced flight control system etc. Prot. YCH-47D s/n 76-8008 (c/n M.3001).
BV.414-165	International Chinook	12 Chinooks for Royal Australian Air Force.
BV.414-173	CH-147	9 Chinooks for Canadian Armed Forces.
BV.414-176	Chinook	4 Chinooks for Spanish Army with T55-L-712 engines.
BV.414-308	Chinook	5 Chinooks for Argentine Air Force and Army (Model 309).
BV.414	MH-47E	Special forces clandestine operations version of CH-47D with increased fuel, terrain-following radar in Model 234 nose, extensive integrated avionics system and jammers, four-screen EFIS, window-mounted machine guns, external Stinger hardpoints and refuelling boom. First a/c s/n 90-0414 (c/n M.3701/B-595). FF 1 June, 1990.
BV.414	CH-47F	Proposed advanced Chinook rework programme with upgraded engines, extended range, new four-blade rotor system with non-lubricated rotor hub and advanced cockpit. Not ordered to date.
BV.234	CH-47J	CH-47D manufactured by Kawasaki.
BV.414-352	Chinook HC.Mk.1 HC.Mk.1B HC.Mk.2	41 CH-47C for Royal Air Force with T55-L-11E engine, rotor brake, three cargo hooks, pressure fuelling, provision for internal ferry tanks and upgraded avionics. HC.1B has composite rotor blades. HC.2 is designation for RAF fleet reworked to CH-47D standard.
BV.234LR	Commercial Chinook	CH-47C for commercial 44-passenger and freight operations with wide-chord composite rotor blades, enlarged flank fairings (for long-range tanks), pointed nose, forward positioning of front u/c legs, galley and lavatory, rear baggage compartment. Prot. FF 19 Aug. 1980.
BV.234ER	Commercial Chinook	Model 234LR with additional internal fuel tanks and reduced pax seating.
BV.234UT	Commercial Chinook	Model 234 with central tank section removed from flank fairings and fuel tanks positioned in cabin for reduced empty weight and improved lift capability.
BV.179	YUH-61A	Tactical helicopter to meet US Army UTTAS competition with 14-seat fuselage, conventional single four-blade main rotor and tail torque rotor, full tailplane, retractable tricycle u/c and powered by two 1500 shp GE T700-GE-700 turboshafts mounted externally. First of three Prots. s/n 73-21656. FF 29 Nov. 1974.

Type No.	Name	Notes
BV.179		Civil version of YUH-61A. Not proceeded with following failure of UH-61A in UTTAS competition. Prot. N179BV (c/n 101) FF 5 Aug. 1975.
BV.347		Experimental advanced-technology helicopter with stretched CH-47A fuselage, four-blade rotors, taller aft pylon, retractable u/c and lift wing mounted above centre fuselage. Prot. FF 27 May 1970.
BV.360		Advanced twin-rotor transport helicopter externally similar to Model 107 of partial-composite construction with tricycle u/c and powered by two 4200 shp Lycoming AL5512 turboshafts. Prot. N360BV (c/n 001) FF 10 June 1987.
	V-22A Osprey	Bell-Boeing advanced tilt-rotor military transport capable of carrying 24 troops with fixed forward-swept-wing mounting wingtip pods for two 6150 shp Allison T406-AD-400 turbines driving three-blade composite prop-rotors, retractable tricycle u/c, twin-fin tail unit and rear loading ramp. Prot. XV-22A s/n 163911 FF 19 Mar. 1989. Nine flown to date.
	RAH-66 Comanche	Light attack and reconnaissance helicopter developed by Boeing and Sikorsky with tandem two-seat stepped cockpit, retractable tailwheel u/c, chin-mounted 20-mm Gatling gun, shrouded 8-blade tail fan and two LHTEC T800 turboshafts driving an advanced five-blade bearingless composite main rotor. Prot. FF 4 Jan. 1996.

Boeing BV.360, N360BV (*Boeing*)

BRANTLY   USA

N.O. Brantly was one of a number of engineers experimenting with helicopters in the immediate post-war period. In 1946, he started flight testing his Brantly B.1 helicopter which had been constructed by his employer, the Pennsylvania Elastic Company. In common with other designers, he decided on a counter-rotating co-axial twin rotor layout and the B.1 prototype (NX69125) was powered by a 150 h.p. Franklin engine buried in the tube and fabric fuselage of the craft. The B.1 had a fixed tailwheel undercarriage and directional control was achieved through a small rudder on the sternpost – because the twin main rotors were expected to neutralise the normal torque effect. Brantly also designed the three-blade rotors with a fixed pitch central 'star' and articulated outer blades which would resolve the aerodynamic problems of asymmetrical forces on the advancing and retreating blades.

Following testing, the B.1 was abandoned and Brantly moved to a more conventional arrangement of a single main rotor and small stabilising tail rotor for his B-2 model. The B-2 was designed to accommodate two people in the smallest practical fuselage. It was all-metal and best described as 'tadpole' shaped with a large transparent nose containing the cockpit and individual perspex bubbles to give headroom for the two occupants. The undercarriage was initially intended to have main wheels on forward legs and a large tail skid but this was changed to a more conventional skid undercarriage attached to the fuselage by a triangulation of struts. The B-2's single 180 h.p. Lycoming VO-360-A1A engine was buried behind the cabin to drive a three-blade rotor which embodied the lead-lag hinges for the outer blades developed on the earlier prototype.

Brantly flew the first of three prototype B-2s (N9069H c/n 1) on 21 February 1953, and embarked on certification testing which was completed and the type certificate issued on 27 April 1959. By this time he had left Pennsylvnia Elastic and set up the Brantly Helicopter Corporation with a factory at Norman, Oklahoma. The B-2 went into production in 1961 and was sold widely in the United States and abroad at the fairly affordable price of $19,950. Five examples of the B-2 were evaluated by the U.S. Army in 1960 as the YHO-3BR but no further procurement was made. Several variants of the VO-360 engine (A1A, A1B, B1A) were fitted as the production process progressed and eventually Brantly built 194 examples of the initial model (c/n 4 to 197).

Accommodation in the B-2 was fairly tight and this was improved in the B-2A by fitting a new upper canopy section with greater width and height. The seats were redesigned, the soundproofing improved and the instrument console enlarged to allow for additional instrumentation. Existing B-2s could be upgraded to B-2A standard with factory kits. Only 18 B-2As were built (c/n 301 to 318) before Brantly flew a further enhanced prototype, the B-2B (N2199U c/n 319). This introduced a 180 h.p. fuel-injected IVO-360-A1A engine and an increase in gross weight from 1600 lb to 1670 lb. Once again, these changes were available for retrospective modification on older models. It was also possible to equip these aircraft with a pontoon float undercarriage and this option was seen on many B-2s. Eventually, Brantly completed 165 examples of the B-2B (c/n 319 to 483).

The B-2 was a successful programme for Brantly but there was no denying that the aircraft was small and there was an opportunity for a larger version of the design. Brantly produced an enlarged B-2, named the Brantly 305 which had a longer forward fuselage providing a rear 3-passenger bench seat. The new five seater (N2200U c/n 1000) made its first flight in January 1964, powered by a 305 h.p. Lycoming IVO-540-A1A engine and received its type certificate on 29 July 1965. Brantly immediately commenced production but the Model 305 suffered from persistent ground resonance problems and they only built 45 examples (c/n 1001 to 1045).

In 1966 Brantly was acquired by Learjet Industries Inc. which wanted to expand its product line and saw helicopters as a natural development for its business jet line. They also designed the Gates Twinjet Helicopter which was announced in 1969 – but the strategy was doomed to failure. The Brantly production line was soon closed and a buyer sought by Gates Learjet. The Brantly type certificates and tooling were sold successively to The Aeronautical R&D Corporation of Cambridge, Mass., Brantly Operators Inc. and, in January 1975, to Michael Hynes who established a new company – Brantly-Hynes Helicopter Co. This was renamed Hynes Aviation Industries in 1984. Under the Hynes banner the B-2B became the Hynes H-2 and the Model 305 became the Hynes H-5.

Hynes produced just one H-2 (N 501BH c/n 501) but also built spares for existing Brantly owners and engineered a crop-spraying modification for the B-2 incorporating a large saddle tank around the centre fuselage. In addition, they constructed a batch of drone helicopters for the U.S. Army based on the Brantly 305 airframe. In 1986, Hynes also granted a production licence to Naras Aviation of Madras, India. However, in October, 1988 Hynes was adjudged bankrupt and Naras negotiated to acquire the business.

In the event the Naras sale did not materialise and Brantly was sold to James T. Kimura who established Brantly Helicopter Industries USA Co. Ltd. at Vernon, Texas. Kimura, unfortunately, died in October 1989, but BHI moved ahead with backing from the Chinese company Foreign Enterprise Service Corp. The first new BHI B-2 (N25411 c/n 2001) was completed and flew on 12 April 1991, and production units are now trickling out of the BHI factory for non-U.S. customers (a restriction imposed because of product liability considerations).

Below: Brantly B-2B, G-ATFH

Above: Brantly 305, G-ATSJ

BRISTOL AIRCRAFT UNITED KINGDOM

In 1944, the Bristol Aeroplane Company recruited Raoul Hafner to set up its Helicopter Division. Hafner had pioneered early prewar helicopter research with his A.R.III machine which embodied a three-legged 'spider' system to control the tilting of the rotor disc through a suspended cyclic control column. Hafner was also responsible for the early wartime Rotachute and Rotabuggy military experiments.

Hafner's team designed a five-seat all-metal helicopter which followed a similar general layout to that used by Sikorsky on the R-5 and R-6. However, it was a more streamlined and sophisticated aircraft than the Sikorsky types. The Type 171 had a fully enclosed cabin in the nose with a central compartment behind which housed the 450 h.p. Pratt & Whitney R-985 Wasp Junior engine, and a slim all-metal monocoque tail boom with a three blade anti-torque rotor. The wooden main rotor followed the earlier designs established by Hafner with three elegantly curved blades attached to the hub by semi-flexible tie-bars. The first Type 171 Sycamore prototype was flown at Filton in July 1947, followed seven months later by the second example. They had been ordered by the Ministry of Supply and went straight into Service tests in the course of which it was decided to fit the British Alvis Leonides engine.

Bristol then built 15 Sycamores for evaluation by the British military forces and by British European Airways who saw a range of commercial uses for helicopters. The Sycamore was subsequently built in quantity for the RAF as the HR. Mk.14, entering service in April 1953. It was mainly employed on search and rescue and medical evacuation tasks. The Royal Australian Navy also received 13 Sycamores for carrier plane-guard operations and three were sold to Belgium for land-based SAR duties. The largest operator other than the British forces were the German Air Force and Navy who together acquired 50 Sycamores during 1957 to 1959. The Air Force machines were used for general communications and for crash rescue while the 12 used by the Navy were SAR-equipped. The German Sycamores were finally withdrawn from service in 1973 and several were sold to civil users. Production of the Sycamore was completed in 1959 with a final total of 178 aircraft having been built (including the prototypes).

While the Sycamore was in its early development stages, Bristol also responded to another Ministry of Supply specification for a 10-seat helicopter. The tandem-rotor design which emerged was an all-metal machine with a constant-section central cabin section with five large windows each side, a two-crew nose compartment similar in design to that of the Sycamore and a large tail pylon. The Type 173 had a fixed four-leg undercarriage and a sharply dihedralled tailplane at the back. Power was provided by an Alvis Leonides engine at each end of the fuselage with inter-connnected gearboxes to ensure that either engine would provide power in the event of a single engine failure. The engines each drove a three-blade rotor but these were changed to four-blade units subsequently. The Model 173 in its initial configuration proved to be underpowered and the 520 h.p. engines were replaced by 850 h.p. Leonides in the Mark 3 version. Many different tailplane configurations were tested and the Mark 2 prototype was fitted with large stub wings fore and aft to try to improve the cruising speed of the aircraft.

The five experimental Type 173s were extensively tested by the Royal Navy and also by British European Airways, but an expected order for the naval variant failed to materialise. The Type 173 design eventually gave way to a trio of new tandem rotor helicopters to meet revised military specifications. These were the Type 191 for the Royal Navy, the Type 192 for the RAF and Type 193 for the Royal Canadian Navy. In the event, Bristol Helicopters (as it had become in 1956) only proceeded with the Type 192 and this had the distinction of becoming the first British turbine-powered helicopter, equipped with two Napier Gazelle turboshafts. In layout, the Type 192 followed the Type 173 design but it was a substantially heavier machine with an under-fuselage winch for carrying slung loads and a utility main cabin with only two windows and a large upward-opening cargo hatch. The tail unit which had caused considerable problems on the previous design started out with end-plate fins but became a heavily anhedralled tailplane on the production model.

On 23 March 1960, Bristol Helicopters Ltd was taken over by Westland, but the Type 192 contract continued with an order being placed for 25 examples for the RAF designated Belvedere HC.1. The first production delivery was made in August 1961, with Belvederes being sent to various areas of unrest in the Middle and Far East. Its service life was relatively short due to continual problems with engine reliability in the difficult overseas conditions of dust and heat. Its tall tricycle undercarriage also caused difficulties in loading the aircraft. It was eventually withdrawn from service in early 1969 to be replaced by the Westland Wessex and subsequently the Sea King. Bristol did have plans for a civil Type 192C with a deeper fuselage and large cabin windows and the substantially bigger Type 194 with a rear-mounted wing, but Westland had other developments in hand and these designs were shelved. The company also investigated an enlarged slab-sided helicopter based on the Sycamore (the Model 203) and the medium-lift Model 214 but neither project progressed under the new management.

Production Details

Bristol Aircraft used a single series of construction numbers which had reached around c/n 12800 by 1947. The Bristol helicopters received serials in the range c/n 12835 to c/n 13503 but they were intermingled with Bristol's other main production models, the Type 170 Freighter and the Type 175 Britannia. Details of numbers of each model which were built are contained in the Model Information.

Bristol 173 Mk.2, G-AMJI

Model Informaton

Details of the different type numbers allocated by Bristol to the company's helicopters are as follows.

Type No.	Name	Number Built	Notes
171 Mk.1	Sycamore	2	4-seat helicopter with single 3-blade rotor, fixed tricycle u/c and streamlined all-metal monocoque fuselage incorporating an integral tail boom with angled end section. 4850 lb TOGW. Powered by one 450 h.p. P&W Wasp Junior. Prot. VL963 (c/n 12836) FF 27 Jul. 1947.
171 Mk.2	Sycamore	1	Mk.1 fitted with a 550 h.p. Alvis Leonides engine, longer rotor blades, 5200 lb TOGW.
171 Mk.3	Sycamore	7	Mk.2 with wider cabin and 5 seats, reshaped nose section and transmission modifications. 5600 lb TOGW.
171 Mk.3	Sycamore HC.10	1	Ambulance evacuation version with two extra doors incorporating external side fairings to accommodate stretchers.
171 Mk.3	Sycamore HC.11	4	Communications model for British Army liaison.
171 Mk.3	Sycamore HR.12	4	Search & rescue model for RAF Coastal Command with starboard winch and large access door.
171 Mk.3	Sycamore HR.13	2	Improved HR.12 for RAF Fighter Command.
171 Mk.3	Sycamore HR.14	85	Definitive RAF Search & Rescue version of HC.10 with pilot's seat on right side.
171 Mk.3	Sycamore HR.50	3	Mk.3 with longer u/c for Royal Australian Navy.
171 Mk.3	Sycamore HC.51	7	Mk.3 for Royal Australian Navy.

Bristol 192 Belvedere HC.1, XG459

HELICOPTERS AND ROTORCRAFT

Type No.	Name	Number Built	Notes
171 Mk.3	Sycamore Mk.52	50	Sycamore for German Air Force/Navy.
171 Mk. 3A	Sycamore	2	Mk.3 with larger baggage bay in lower rear fuselage.
171 Mk.4	Sycamore	12	Civil Mk 3A with tall u/c.
173		1	Ten-passenger tandem rotor transport helicopter with oval-section straight fuselage with tail pylon and Type 171 nose and cockpit section. Fitted with fixed four-leg u/c and large V-tailplane. Powered by two 550 h.p. Alvis Leonides – one at each end of fuselage driving three-blade rotors. Prot. G-ALBN (c/n 12871). FF 3 Jan. 1952.
173 Mk.2		1	Developed Type 173 with modified u/c, front and rear stub wings with large endplate fins on rear. Prot. G-AMJI (c/n 12872).
173 Mk.3		3	Type 173 with 850 h.p. Alvis Leonides Major engines and four-blade rotors. Prot. XE286 (c/n 13204).
191		3	Ship-based development of Type 173 with modified fuselage, u/c etc. Three built but only used for static test.
192	Belvedere	26	Production version of Model 191 for RAF use with two cabin windows only, starboard cargo hatch, cargo hoist beneath fuselage, large anhedralled tailplane and powered by two 1465 shp Napier Gazelle turboshafts. Prot. XG447 (c/n 13342). FF 5 Jul. 1958.

Bristol 171 Sycamore Mk.3, G-ALSR *(Bristol)*

CESSNA AIRCRAFT   USA

In 1952, Cessna Aircraft Company saw an opening in the personal helicopter market which it believed would be a logical addition to the company's existing large range of light fixed wing aircraft. They also saw that the market for fixed wing military aircraft was giving way to helicopters and that their strong position in providing L-19 Bird Dogs to the US Army could be overtaken by a transition to rotary-wing aircraft. As a consequence, on 1st March 1952, they acquired the Seibel Helicopter Company which had been set up in Wichita, Kansas by Charles M. Seibel.

Seibel was an experienced helicopter engineer who had started his career with Bell in Fort Worth, Texas. In 1946 he left Bell and developed several experimental helicopters starting with the S.3 (N735B c/n 1). This open-frame prototype first flew on 4 September 1947, powered by a 65 h.p. Franklin engine and was unusual in having a control system based on altering the centre of gravity by using the control stick to adjust the forward fuselage relative to the power section. The subsequent S.4 SkyHawk (N5152 c/n 1) was a two-seat development of the S.3 with a more conventional control system and a 108 h.p. Lycoming O-235-C1 engine. Two were delivered to the U.S. Army for evaluation as the YH-24 but as it turned out, the Army found them unsuitable for their light helicopter requirement. Seibel built an S.4A three-seater (N5153 c/n 2) and the two-seat S.4B (N5154 c/n 4) with a 165 h.p. engine, but did not reach the point of commercial production.

Cessna was suitably impressed with Seibel's technological achievement to set him on course to design a high-performance two-seat personal helicopter. With the S.3 as a basis, Charles Seibel created the CH-1. The aim was to carry the design of Cessna's single-engined aircraft into the appearance of the helicopter, so the CH-1 had an all-metal monocoque fuselage with a fin and tailplane and a streamlined cabin section with 360-degree vision transparencies. The supercharged 260 h.p. Continental engine was positioned in the nose with a flexible drive leading to the main rotor shaft which ran through a central pillar in the cabin.

Seibel started with an experimental test vehicle to develop the transmission and control systems and then went on to fly the CH-1 prototype (N5155). The CH-1 received its type certificate in June 1955 and later that year it achieved fame by landing on the top of the 14,000 ft Pike's Peak in Colorado. Cessna soon decided that it could be commercially successful only if it were upgraded to four seats, and they were able to achieve this within the existing CH-1 airframe. Clearly, a prime target for sales of the CH-1 was the US military forces and an evaluation order for ten YH-41 Senecas was obtained, with the first aircraft being delivered in December 1957. The YH-41s were fitted with a new Continental engine because of the unreliability of the original Continental FSO-470. Under evaluation, the YH-41s were found to have unsatisfactory stability characteristics and poor behaviour in autorotation so no production orders were forthcoming. In fact, Cessna bought back six aircraft and converted them to civilian CH-1C standard.

The CH-1C Skyhook was introduced in 1960 and it had a further increase in power and a modified control system to resolve the handling problems of the YH-41. It is believed that 45 examples were built, and exports of civil-standard CH-1Cs were made to Argentina and Canada. In addition, five were sold under the Military Assistance Program to Iran, and six to Ecuador for military use. The history of the CH-1 is somewhat obscure, but the type did suffer an unfortunate series of engine and transmission related failures.

Consequently, in 1963, Cessna decided to abandon the programme due to failure to achieve the expected military orders and citing an uncertain commercial market and product liability concerns. They bought back and destroyed most of the remaining CH-1s and the only complete example still known to exist is a YH-41 preserved at the US Army Museum, Fort Rucker.

Cessna CH-1C Skyhook, N5746 *(Cessna)*

Cessna serial numbers for the CH-1 started at c/n 45001 for the first aircraft, which was rebuilt to CH-1A standard as c/n 45002, c/n 45003 was a CH-1A for boundary layer research and c/n 45004 was the static test example. C/n 45005 to 45014 were allocated to the military YH-41s. The commercial CH-1Cs commenced at c/n 45501 and are believed to have ended at c/n 45545.

The different CH-1 models built by Cessna were as follows:

Seibel S-4, N5154 *(Cessna/Pickett/KAM)*

Type No.	Name	No. Built	Notes
CH-1		1	Two-seat light helicopter with all-metal monocoque fuselage, conventional tail fin and anti-torque rotor, fixed skid u/c, and a nose-mounted supercharged 260 h.p. Continental FSO-470-A piston engine driving two-blade steel main rotor fitted with flexible sheet-metal hinges. Prot. N5155 (c/n 45001) FF July 1954.
CH-1A		2	Four-seat development of CH-1. First aircraft (N5156 c/n 45002) converted from c/n 45001.
CH-1B	YH-41 NH-41A Seneca	10	Military CH-1A with provision for two stretchers and fitted with 270 h.p. Continental FSO-526A engine. First aircraft s/n 56-4236 (c/n 45005).
CH-1C	UH-41A Skyhook	45	Commercial CH-1 based on CH-1B with revised systems and structure. MAP deliveries as UH-41A.Some YH-41A converted to civil configuration.
CH-1D			CH-1C with improved engine installation and transmission and 100-lb increase in gross weight.

DENEL   SOUTH AFRICA

Atlas Aircraft Corporation of South Africa Pty. Ltd. was originally established in 1963 and became the sole source for aircraft manufacturing and maintenance support for the South African Air Force during the years of the United Nations sanctions. Its main manufacturing programmes were the Impala – the SAAF trainer and ground attack aircraft based on the Aermacchi MB.326 – the Cheetah development of the Mirage III and the Kudu utility aircraft derived from the Aermacchi AL-60. Atlas was incorporated into the Armscor Group in 1969, and in 1992 there was a further rationalisation which resulted in the creation of Denel Aerospace Group with Atlas Aircraft as its manufacturing division.

Atlas Aircraft has supported the maintenance and development of the SAAF's Aérospatiale helicopters over many years and has not only modified Alouette IIIs to SAAF combat requirements but manufactured major components for the Puma and Super Frelon. Atlas carried out an upgrade programme for the Puma, developed on the experimental XTP-1 Beta development aircraft, which provided the SA.330 fleet with many of the new features of the Super Puma including an enlarged tail and Makila power-plants. In this form the modified Pumas are known as the Oryx (originally Gemsbok). The

Denel Rooivalk, ZU-AHC

85

subsequent ZTP-1 Puma is a further development which is fitted with external stub wings equipped with four weapon stations and with an under-fuselage 20mm TC-20 cannon.

The main objective of Atlas was to provide the SAAF with a gunship version of the Puma, but it became clear that a smaller and more agile platform was required. Many of the systems for this proposed aircraft were developed using a concept helicopter, the XH-1 Alpha, which was based on components drawn from the Alouette III. The XH-1 had a stepped two-seat cockpit to accommodate the pilot and gunner, and a fixed tailwheel undercarriage. Powered by a 570 shp Turboméca Artouste IIIB turbine, the Alpha was fitted with a chin-turret containing a 20mm cannon which could be aimed via the gunner's helmet-mounted sight. The Alpha flew on 27 February 1986, and was eventually retired to the SAAF Museum in Pretoria.

The XH-1 led Atlas to the XH-2 Rooivalk, which was first flown on 11th February 1990. It was later redesignated CSH-2. The Rooivalk is a tandem two seater gunship and anti-tank helicopter which is flown from the rear seat and it has a tailwheel undercarriage and conventional five-blade tail rotor. It is powered by a Denel-built version of the Turboméca Makila 1A1, known as the Topaz, rated at 2000 shp, and a variety of infra-red suppression shrouds have been tested on the prototype Rooivalks. This engine drives a four-blade main rotor and has Eurocopter-supplied dynamic systems as used on the Puma. The Rooivalk is equipped with an advanced cockpit with two multi-function display screens and a navigation display and has provision for a helmet-mounted night vision system. It has stub wings each with two hardpoints, and the standard offensive weapon will be the Matra-BAe. Mistral infra-red guided missile. At the front, the Rooivalk has a chin-mounted gun together with infra-red sensor pods. Denel flew the first of two prototypes on 11 February 1990 and a pre-production aircraft in early 1997. The first of 12 production machines for the SAAF will be delivered in late-1998.

Denel Alpha XH-1

DOMAN   USA

In 1945, Glidden S. Doman formed Doman Helicopters Inc. in order to develop various helicopter engineering concepts. These included a new hub system which was essentially similar to the mechanism used on a variable pitch propeller. The rotor system also incorporated a gimbal mounting to provide the necessary tilting of the rotor disc. Doman's theories were tested initially by installing an experimental system on a USAF Sikorsky R-6. This helicopter was known as the Doman LZ-1A and it started flight tests in early 1950 with remarkably good results. It was followed by the larger LZ-2A Pelican.

Doman's system was then designed into a larger helicopter that was seen as a viable commercial production machine. The LZ-4A had a capacious fuselage with three rows of double seats in the main cabin and a two-crew flight deck in front. Large folding doors provided access for loading bulky cargo into the main compartment. The tail boom was conventional with a cranked-up rear section mounting a tail rotor, and the LZ-4A sat on a four-leg undercarriage with trailing link dampers. A 400 h.p. Lycoming SO-590-B engine was positioned in the lower nose, driving the four-blade rotor via a flexible transmission. Following its first flight in November 1950, and subsequent testing, Doman moved on to the improved LZ-5 and transferred the LZ-4A (N74147 c/n LZ4-1) to Curtiss Wright as a test vehicle.

The LZ-5 was similar to the LZ-4 but used a 400 h.p. supercharged Lycoming 580-D engine, and had numerous detail changes. The first example was N13458 (c/n 1) which flew on 27 April 1953. Doman gained a contract from the U.S. Army to supply two aircraft designated YH-31. These were evaluated following delivery in late 1953 but it was felt that the possible maintenance problems of the complex rotor system would cause problems with field maintenance. Consequently, the two aircraft were retired in 1958 following a period of use as executive transports. Doman also designed a small two-seat helicopter, the D-10, to an Army requirement. This would have been powered by an Allison 250 turbine but was not built.

Doman actually completed two more development machines in addition to the pair of YH-31s (N94561 c/n 002 and N812 c/n 003). The third aircraft was modified into a new variant – the D-10B – which had a turbocharged Lycoming HIO-720-A1A engine and minor changes and was the subject of a co-production agreement with Fleet in Canada. N812 became CF-IBG-X (c/n DF-3). A number of deals and production relationships were subsequently established by Doman in an effort to get the LZ.5 into production. Hiller were licenced to build the military version. Doman also entered into an arrangement with Ambrosini in Italy for them to market the D-10B and for production of 20 airframes to be carried out by Aeronautica Sicula at Palermo in Sicily with final assembly at Doman's factory in Danbury, Connecticut. A plan was also devised for Aeronautica

Sicula to fit a D-10B with a Turboméca Astazou turbine. The agreement with the Italians collapsed and a new company was subsequently established as Caribe Doman in Puerto Rico during 1966. Unfortunately, the LZ-5 was obsolete by this time as more modern turbine-powered helicopters flooded onto the market. A further company, Berlin-Doman was formed and a new project launched as the BD-19 but this was also stillborn and the Doman helicopters finally vanished into obscurity.

Doman-Fleet D-10B, CF-IBG-X *(HGM Collection)*

Doman YH-31, 525779 *(via MS)*

ENSTROM

USA

The R.J. Enstrom Corporation was established in 1959 at Menominee County Airport, Michigan to develop a light three-seat civil helicopter (believed to have been designated F-27) designed by Rudolph J. Enstrom. The prototype of the definitive F-28 flew in the following year and performed well enough for the company to press forward with certification. The production F-28 was generally similar to the prototype but had a fully-clad rear fuselage and engine compartment, a three-blade main rotor and many minor refinements. The main cabin structure was enclosed in an attractive fibreglass shell, and the F-28 offered substantially better performance and a higher gross weight than the competing Bell 47G. This was despite the use of a 180 horsepower engine compared with the 240 h.p. unit in the Bell.

The F-28 programme met a setback with the loss of the production prototype in November 1962, but the helicopter eventually received its type certificate on 15 April 1965. Production got under way at Menominee immediately thereafter with first deliveries being made in January 1966. The F-28 was fairly quickly modified to F-28A configuration with a changed drive ratio which resulted in higher power output from the HIO-360

Enstrom 280FX, H-181 (Enstrom)

engine, and a slightly higher gross weight. Significant numbers were exported – particularly to Brazil and the Philippines. Enstrom also experimented with a turbine-powered version of the F-28 but this was discontinued because of the potentially heavy development cost.

In 1968, financial pressures forced a partial sale of a 94.6% interest in Enstrom to the Purex Corporation, by which time approximately 60 units had been completed. Under Purex production trickled to a standstill and two years elapsed before the company was bought by F. Lee Bailey who injected new capital and reopened the factory. With new F-28As moving down the line the company built the prototype of the Model 280 Shark which introduced a more streamlined cabin section and a new tailfin and other improvements. This, in turn, led to both the Shark and the standard F-28 being fitted with a supplementary Rajay turbocharger, which allowed an increase in gross weight and substantially better hot and high performance. These two 'C' models replaced the F-28A and Model 280 in 1978.

The Shark offered an ideal platform for a larger four-seat helicopter and in January 1978 Enstrom started work on the Model 280L Hawk. This used a stretched version of the Shark fuselage to provide a rear two-passenger bench seat and two front seats for the pilot and another passenger. The first of two Hawks was flown in late 1978.

After ten years of building up Enstrom, F. Lee Bailey sold the company to Bravo Investments B.V. of the Netherlands in January 1980. It was decided at this time not to continue with development of the Hawk but production of the F-28C and 280C continued. The ownership once again changed in September 1984 to an American investor group (headed by Dean Kamen and Robert Tuttle). Production was then concentrated on the F-28F utility model which included a dedicated police operations version, and the Model 280FX which was the latest version of the Shark with improved performance and comfort modifications. The company also embarked on a number of progressive engineering improvements to the whole product line including a redesigned and stronger main-rotor-gearbox and an improved engine soundproofing system.

In 1989 the United States Army announced its SCAT (Single Contractor Aviation Training) programme, and Enstrom joined with Link Flight Simulation to compete in tendering for the fleet of new turbine trainers called for by the requirement. Initially, Enstrom tested their proposed Allison 250 turboshaft installation in a 280FX airframe that first flew in December 1988. The definitive aircraft, based on the Model 280FX, was designated Model 480 and embodied a reshaped and wider forward fuselage together with

Enstrom F-28C, G-BURI

greater headroom and four seats, in two rows as the TH-28 it was to be configured as an Army trainer with two forward seats for instructor and pupil, and an observer pupil on the rear seat.

In the event, the SCAT tender was awarded to Bell and the TH-28 has not yet found a major military purchaser. The commercial Model 480 was, however, put into production at Menominee and gained a steady flow of orders. The 480 is offered with a variety of seating layouts for up to five occupants, and uses an unusual staggered seat arrangement to provide maximum legroom.

In the most recent ownership change, Kamen and Tuttle sold their shares in Enstrom to two Los Angeles business investors. Enstrom continues to build and sell the F-28F, 280FX and the Model 480.

Production Details

Enstrom has followed a fairly simple numerical system with separate batches for major models. Details of the serial numbers allocated are as follows:

Type No.	Serial Batch	Number Built	Notes
F-28	c/n 1	1	Prototype.
F-28	c/n 2 – 14	13	
F28A	c/n 15 to 330	316	Excluding c/n 304.
F28C	c/n 331 to 450 plus c/n 304	121	
F28C-2	c/n 451-2 to 505-2 and c/n 508-2	56	
F28F Falcon	c/n 506-2 to 527-2 and c/n 700 to 809	132	
280	c/n 1001 to 1019 and c/n 1021, 1022	21	
280C	c/n 1020 and c/n 1023 to 1227	6	
280F	c/n 1500 to 1519	20	
280FX	c/n 2001 to 2080	80	
280L	c/n 2001 and 2002	2	
TH.28	c/n 3001 to 3006+	6	
480	c/n 5001 to 5105+	105	

Model Information

Full details of all the models built by Enstrom during its 38-year history are as follows:

Type No.	Name	Notes
F-28 Prototype		Side-by-side two-seat helicopter with glass-fibre cabin enclosure, open doors and open tubular frame tailboom, skid u/c and one 180 h.p. Lycoming O-360-A1A piston engine driving two-blade main rotor. 1850 lb TOGW. Prot. N915D (c/n 1) FF 12 Nov. 1960.
F-28		Three-seat production F.28 with glass fibre and aluminium fuselage cladding, transparent doors, fully-articulated three-blade main rotor and 1950 lb TOGW. Powered by one 195 h.p. Lyc. HIO-360-C1A piston engine. Prodn. Prot. N40042 (c/n 2) FF 26 May 1962.
F-28A		F-28 with modified gearing to reduce rotor rpm and increase effective power output to 205 h.p. Ceiling windows in cabin. Increased gross weight 2150 lb.
F-28B		Experimental F-28 with turbocharged engine.

HELICOPTERS AND ROTORCRAFT

T-28		Experimental F-28 with one 220 shp Garrett AiResearch TSE-36-1 turboshaft engine. Prot. FF May 1968.
F-28C	Turbo	F-28A with Rajay 301 turbocharger and 2200 lb TOGW. Tail rotor moved from starboard to port side. Optional higher 2600 lb TOGW for agricultural ops.
F-28C-1		F-28C with new single-piece bubble windshield and redesigned instrument console.
F28F	Falcon	Utility version of F-28A with single-piece windshield, improved maintenance accessibility, improved turbocharger, new throttle correlator and 225 h.p. Lyc. HIO-360-F1AD engine.
F28F-P	Sentinel	Specially configured F-28F for police operations.
280	Shark	F-28 with revised streamlined fuselage shape, tail fins (later altered to single ventral fin and tailskid) and fuel injected HIO-360-C1B engine. Prot. modified from F-28 N40043 (c/n 3).
280C	Turbo Shark	Model 280 with Rajay 301 turbocharger and 2200 lb TOGW. Tail rotor moved from starboard to port side.
280F		280 with 225 h.p. Lyc. HIO-360-F1AD engine and other detail improvements similar to F-28F.
280FX	Shark	Improved version of 280F with redesigned u/c fairings, new inlet airscoop, tail rotor driveshaft fairing, new tailplane with endplates, cockpit annunciator panel and graphic engine monitor.
280FXT		Experimental 280FX fitted with Allison 250-C20W turboshaft to test installation for Model 480. Prot. N280FX (c/n 2001). FF Dec. 1988.
280L	Turbo Hawk	Four-seat development of 280C with larger rotor blades, 36-inch fuselage stretch to accommodate second seat row, strengthened u/c, new tailplane with endplate fins and 225 h.p. turbocharged Lyc. HIO-360-F1AD engine. Prot. N696E (c/n 2001) FF 27 Dec. 1978.
TH-28		Model 280FX with wider reshaped cabin section and rear seat area proposed as three-seat TH-28 trainer for SCATS competition. Modified tail rotor. Crash-safe fuel cells. Powered by one 420 shp Allison 250-C20W turboshaft. Prot. N8631E (c/n 3003) FF 7 Oct. 1989.
480	Turbine	Commercial 4/5 seat version of TH-28 with upgraded interior etc., single instrument console.
480	Eagle	Proposed version of Model 280L with Allison 250-C20B turboshaft. Not built.

Enstrom TH-28, N8631E *(Enstrom)*

EUROCOPTER   FRANCE/GERMANY

On 1 January 1992, Aérospatiale joined with MBB to create Eurocopter Holdings. The complex structure of the new group included a 40% shareholding by Daimler-Benz Aerospace and a 60% shareholding by Aérospatiale. The management company, Eurocopter SA, is owned jointly by Eurocopter Holdings (75%) and Aérospatiale (25%). In turn it owns the renamed operating companies, Eurocopter France and Eurocopter Deutschland . The new organisation found itself with a large range of existing production helicopters and several development projects including the NH.90, Tiger, EC-120 and EC-135.

The joining of the two helicopter manufacturers already had a common thread in the four-nation cooperative NH.90 project. This was set up under governmental agreement by Aérospatiale, MBB, Agusta and Fokker – with Aérospatiale having the largest share (42.4%) in the new joint venture company, NH Industries. The feasibility development contract was awarded in September 1992 and the NH.90 was intended as a medium-lift transport helicopter with capacity for 20 troops, and flexibility to fulfil a wide variety of roles including tactical support and attack, and naval ASW and SAR roles. A total requirement was originally seen for 182 naval variants and 544 attack models although the totals have moved down to 647 actual orders during the life of the project. Eurocopter France completed the first of five flying prototype NH.90s in the summer of 1995 and the aircraft made its first flight on 18 December of that year. First deliveries of the NH.90 are expected in 2003.

The second jointly-developed military helicopter is the Tiger, which has been under development by Aérospatiale and MBB since 1988. Eurocopter France and Eurocopter Deutschland each own 50% of Eurocopter Tiger GmbH which is the prime contractor for this programme. The Tiger, originally designated PAH-2, is a tandem two-seat combat helicopter which will be produced in anti-tank and 'Gerfaut' escort/support versions. It is an all-weather aircraft with advanced avionics and weapons systems and stealth characteristics. It is designed to be able to fire both the Euromissile HOT and TRIGAT anti-tank missiles. The first Tiger was built at Ottobrunn but flown at Marignane in April 1991. The second machine, in Gerfaut configuration, flew on 22 April 1993, and three further prototypes are to be used for the test programme. The first of 427 Tigers on order for the French ALAT and German Army will be delivered in 2001.

The merger of MBB and Aérospatiale focused the new organisation on joint development and manufacture which, initially, meant some examples of the AS.350 being built at the Eurocopter Deutschland Donauworth factory. MBB (now Daimler-Benz Aerospace) had already moved forward during the mid-1980s to generate a successor to the Bö.105, and flew the prototype Bö.108 in the autumn of 1988. After the amalgamation the Bö. 108

became the basis for a new helicopter, the EC-135, which combined the best of technology from both partners. To an outward glance, the new EC-135, which flew at Ottobrun in early 1994, was made up of the front fuselage of the Bö.108 married to a classic ten-blade 'fenestron' tail from Aérospatiale. This change did, indeed, greatly reduce the noise profile

Eurocopter EC-120, F-WWPD

Eurocopter EC-135, F-GMTF *(Eurocopter)*

Eurocopter Gerfaut, F-ZWWY *(Eurocopter)*

NHI NH-90, F-ZWTI *(Eurocopter)*

of the Bö.108 and brought the EC-135 into a similar noise category to the piston-powered Robinson R-44 and Schweizer 201C which are 50% lighter. The EC-135 was certificated in Germany in July 1996, with first deliveries being made in the following month.

The smaller partner of the EC-135, the EC-120, started as Aérospatiale's P.120L project, which was launched in January 1990. As the complementary light business helicopter in the Eurocopter lineup, the EC-120 has moved forward fairly rapidly from project go-ahead in October 1992, to flight testing of two prototypes by January 1997. The EC-120 is being developed by a consortium of the Marignane (French) division of Eurocopter (61%), the Chinese organisation CATIC/HAMC (24%) and Singapore Technologies Aerospace (15%) and incorporates the latest helicopter engineering including extensive use of composite components, a lubrication-free 'Spheriflex' rotor head and the tail fenestron which has been refined by Aérospatiale over many years.

Production Details

Model	Serial Batch	Number Built	Notes
Bo. 108	c/n VT-001 and VT-002	2	Prototypes.
EC.135	c/n 0001 to 0020	22	Also prototypes S-01 to S-03.

Model Information

Details of models introduced after the merger of MBB and Aérospatiale are as follows. Those types which are still in production but were initiated by the two companies (such as the Ecureuil and BK.117) are detailed in the Aérospatiale and MBB sections.

Model	Notes
Tiger	Two-seat military attack helicopter with stepped cockpits, extensive armour plating, fixed tailwheel u/c, external stub wings each with dual hardpoints, nose-mounted chin 30-mm gun turret, large tailfin with three-blade tail rotor and two MTU/Turboméca/Rolls-Royce MTR.390 turboshafts with IR suppressors driving four-blade main rotor. Prot. F-ZWWW FF 27 Apl. 1991. 5 built.
NH.90	Medium-lift military helicopter for army and naval applications with 20-troop capacity, retractable tricycle u/c and two 2100 shp R-R-Turboméca RTM322-01/9 turboshafts driving a four-blade main rotor. Prot. F-ZWTH (c/n PT.1) FF 18 Dec. 1996. Second Prot. F-ZWTI (PT.2) FF Mar. 1997.
TTH-90	Production utility version of NH.90.
NFH-90	Production naval ASW and ASR version of NH.90.
EC-120 Colibri	Joint Aérospatiale/SAT/CATIC developed light 5-seat executive helicopter with streamlined fuselage and fenestron tail rotor, fixed skid u/c, 3-blade Spheriflex main rotor and one 504 shp Turboméca Arrius turboshaft. Prot. F-WWPA (c/n 01) FF 9 June 1995. Two further prototypes completed.
EC-120B	Production standard Colibri with Arrius 2F turboshaft.
EC-135T1	MBB Bo.108 with 7-seat cabin and new composite tailboom and 10-blade fenestron tail. Powered by two 696 shp Turboméca Arrius 2B turboshafts. 5511 lb TOGW Prot. D-HECX FF 15 Feb. 1994.
EC-135P1	EC-135 with two 732 shp Pratt & Whitney PW.206B turboshafts.
EC-155	Revised designation for Aérospatiale AS.365N4.
EC-635	Military version of EC-135 with composite armour and military equipment.

EUROPEAN
HELICOPTER
INDUSTRIES

INTERNATIONAL

With the anti-submarine Sea King becoming technologically dated, 1970s planning in the British Royal Navy resulted in a specification being considered by Westland Aircraft for a replacement. This materialised as the WG.34 project. A similar requirement from the Italian Navy had also been recognised and this led the British and Italian Governments to reach agreement for joint development of a new helicopter. This led to the establishment of European Helicopter Industries, which was formally constituted in June 1980.

Almost eight years of project definition and detailed design by Westland and its Italian partner, Agusta, passed before the first EH.101 (ZF641 c/n PP.1) took to the air on 9 October 1987. The EH.101 as it finally emerged was a large aircraft with a central cabin section capable of seating 30 passengers in its civil version, a retractable tricycle undercarriage which used external sponsons for the main units, and a five-blade main rotor which drew on the advanced rotor technology established by Westland's Yeovil factory. The three 1275 shp General Electric CT.7-2A turbines were mounted above the fuselage and the EH.101 had a conventional tail unit with a four-blade tail rotor.

The programme set by EHI provides for nine pre-production aircraft (c/n 50001 to 50009 – PP.1 to PP.9). Three non-flying airframes have been built for fatigue testing and avionics work together with a 'ground test vehicle'. Two of the pre-production aircraft (PP.8 and PP.9) have been used for civil certification and development.

The lengthy development cycle of the EH.101 was partly due to the fact that several different variants were planned. The Italian Navy requirement involves three versions consisting of eight machines equipped for ASW duties, four surveillance radar picket machines and four for maritime utility transport with a folding tail and rear loading ramp. The EH.101 can operate from frigate heli-decks and, with the folding tail, can be accommodated in the same sub-deck spaces as the Sea King. The Royal Navy will receive 44 Merlin HM.1s, the first of which (ZH821 c/n RN.01) was flown in March 1996 and was delivered on 27 May 1997. This is an ASW aircraft but the RAF will also receive 22 examples of the HC.3 utility version.

Canada was also expected to be a major customer with a requirement for up to 50 units but this was cancelled in the shakeup following the change of political regime. However, EHI has gained a 15 unit order for the AW.520 Cormorant, as a replacement for the Canadian Armed Forces fleet of Air-Sea Rescue Boeing CH-113s. EHI has proposed a further military EH.101 with stub wings and an enhanced propulsion system for AEW tasks and have in hand a possible replacement for the Sea King HC.4.

The EH.101 is now in full production at Westland's Yeovil factory and at the Agusta factories at Vergiate and Brindisi. The first commercial order has also been received for the civil Heliliner variant, which has large square windows and an additional port side door. This 30-seat verson received its U.K. certification in December 1994 and is fitted with 2000 shp CT7-6 engines. The first civil production EH.101 (CIV01) was rolled out by Agusta at the end of May 1997.

European Helicopter Industries EH.101 Merlin, ZF649 *(European Helicopter Industries)*

EH.101 Heliliner, G-OIOI *(Westland)*

FAIREY UNITED KINGDOM

In August 1945, The Fairey Aviation Co. Ltd was presented with proposals by Dr J.A. Bennett for the development of a compound autogyro-type aircraft. Fairey had spent the war years building the Fulmar, Barracuda and Firefly military aircraft and was embarking on the new GR.17/45 proposal which would become the Fairey Gannett anti-submarine aircraft. However, Bennett's proposal added an attractive new prospect of commercial business and Fairey established a Helicopter Department.

The FB-1 – which was later named the Gyrodyne – used a 520 h.p. Alvis Leonides engine buried in its rear fuselage to drive both the main three-blade rotor for lift and two tractor propellers mounted on pods at the tips of stub wings. The Gyrodyne's fuselage resembled that of a light aircraft with a cabin in the nose, a fixed tricycle undercarriage, twin tail fins and a rotor pylon mounted above the centre section between cabin and engine. The Gyrodyne prototype (G-AIKF c/n F.8465) first flew on 7 December 1947, followed by a second aircraft (G-AJJP/XJ389 c/n F.9420). Performance and stability were satisfactory and the prototype embarked on a number of speed record attempts. It was in the course of one of these that it crashed killing two of the Fairey test pilots.

The second Gyrodyne was then radically modified to become the Jet Gyrodyne. The existing tractor propellers were changed to pusher configuration with variable-pitch propellers and the Leonides engine was altered to drive two centrifugal compressors fitted inside the rotor pylon which fed compressed air to fuel-burning jet units at the tips of the lengthened two-blade rotor. In this form, the Jet Gyrodyne made its first transition flight on 1 March 1955. Subsequent testing of the aircraft laid the ground for Fairey's major project, the Rotodyne.

The Rotodyne was the first practical convertible helicopter which could be applied to commercial transport operations. With a capacious box fuselage for 23 passengers it used a fairly large low-aspect ratio wing to mount a pair of Napier Eland turboprops in standard engine nacelles to drive the Rotodyne in a horizontal plane. The large four-blade rotor used the tip jets developed on the Gyrodyne with power to the air compressors coming from the Eland engines. The Rotodyne had a retractable tricycle undercarriage and a twin fin tail unit and the first flight of XE521 (c/n F.9429), the prototype, took place on 6 November 1957, with the first transition flight in April 1958. The aircraft was revolutionary and much interest was paid by British European Airways, the RAF, New York Airways and Okanagan Helicopters. However, in February 1962, following the acquisition of Fairey by Westland, Government financial support was withdrawn and the Rotodyne project cancelled. There can be little doubt that this was one of the most short-sighted funding decisions of the post-war British political era.

One other project pursued by Fairey was the Ultra-light Helicopter. This was a response to British Army needs for a simple reconnaissance helicopter formulated in 1953. Fairey built six examples (c/n F.9423 to 9428), the first of which (XJ924) took to the air on 14 August 1955. The Ultra-light had a skid undercarriage and a main fuselage pod providing enclosed accommodation for a single pilot. Behind the pilot was a Turboméca Palouste turbine and a small tailboom with triple rudders. No tail rotor was necessary as the efflux from the turbine provided airflow for directional control over the tail unit. The Ultra-light's rotor was powered in the same way as that of the Jet Gyrodyne by tip propulsion units. As with many other projects, the Ultra-light elicited much interest and enthusiasm – but no orders. The project was finally abandoned in 1959.

As a part of Westland, Fairey's facilities at Hayes started to become involved in production of various new designs. The two pre-production Wasps were constructed at the new Fairy Aviation Division, followed by series manufacture both of the Wasp and the Scout which had been inherited in the Westland takeover of Saunders Roe. The Hayes factory was also involved in manufacturing work on the Westland Puma and some early Pumas carried Fairey construction numbers.

Fairey Jet Gyrodyne, XJ389

Fairey Rotodyne, XE521

99

FUJI   JAPAN

Fuji Heavy Industries (Fuji Jukogyo Kabushiki Kaisha) has its origins in the Nakajima company which was known for its substantial wartime aircraft production. Fuji was incorporated on 15 July 1953, and, once approval was given for the resumption of aircraft production, it reactivated a number of the former Nakajima facilities and took on licences from American companies to build aircraft. Its initial production models were the Beech B-45 Mentor (T-34) which was produced in some numbers for the newly constituted Japanese Air Self Defense Force (JASDF) and the Cessna L-19 Bird-Dog. These were followed by indigenous developments of the Mentor (LM-1 Nikko and KM-2 trainer), the Fuji FA-200 light aircraft and, more recently, major assemblies for Boeing airliners, the Lockheed P-3C and the Fokker 50.

In 1962, Fuji entered into a sub-licence agreement with Mitsui to build the Bell Model 204B. Earlier Bell models (the '47 series) had been built by Kawasaki under a sub-licence from Mitsui (who were the Japanese agent for Bell) but Kawasaki had moved into an arrangement with Boeing to build the Vertol 107. Due to the conflict of interest Mitsui nominated Fuji as the new sub-licensee to fulfil an initial production order for the Japanese Ground Self Defense Force (JGSDF). This involved the Model 204B gaining FAA certification, which was partially sponsored by Mitsui and awarded on 4 April 1963 (TC. H1SW). Fuji then completed a total of 90 examples of the UH-1B Iroquois which carried Fuji constructor numbers c/n MH-1 to MH-90.

Fuji also completed a batch of 35 commercial Model 204Bs (c/n CH-1 to CH-35) together with a further 22 Model 204B-2s (c/n CH-36 to CH-57) some of which were supplied to Bell in the United States. The Fuji-Bell 204s were identical to the Bell model except for the tail rotor being positioned on the starboard side of the tail fin instead of the port side. Fuji's Model 204B-2 was a unique variant introduced in 1973 with a slightly larger main rotor and improved service ceiling and altitude performance. This was the result of the installation of a 1400 shp Kawasaki-Lycoming KT5313B turboshaft engine, and a change to the tail rotor to make it turn clockwise.

The JGSDF also placed orders with Fuji over a period of years for 146 examples of the Bell 205 (UH-1H) which was designated HU-1H in military service. These Fuji-Bell 205s used the same starboard-set tail rotor with reversed direction and were fitted with a 1400 shp Kawasaki-Lycoming T53K-13B turbine engine. Fuji serials for these commenced at c/n 1H-1. They were followed by 70 units of the UH-1J (from c/n 1J-01). Fuji further developed the model 205 into the Advanced Model 205A-1 in cooperation with Bell, and the prototype of this variant (N19AL c/n 30166) first flew at Fort Worth on 23 April 1988. The Advanced A-1 variant featured the tapered composite rotor blades used on the Bell 212 and an 1800 shp T53-L-703 engine.

In 1968, Fuji researched the concept of a high-speed compound version of the Iroqouis. They built a test example of the Fuji-XMH which was a Bell 204B-1 (JA9009 c/n 3001) fitted with a 22-ft. span wing and enlarged horizontal tail surfaces. Following a first flight on 11 February 1970, the XMH was flown for three years in various configurations and provided promising results. However, Fuji decided not to continue with the programme and it was abandoned after some 57 test flights.

In 1979 the JGSDF took delivery of two Bell AH-1S HueyCobras for evaluation and this led to an order for 55 (later increased to 94) similar aircraft, powered by a Kawasaki-Lycoming T53-L-703 engine, being placed with Fuji. Helicopter production by Fuji has now largely ceased although further orders from the Japanese forces may result in the production lines being reopened.

Fuji-Bell 204B, JA9055

HILLER

USA

In 1942, Stanley Hiller Jr started to develop helicopters with coaxial rotor systems. It was Hiller's view that counter-rotating rotors was the ideal solution to the torque problem inherent in single-rotor helicopters, and his small company flew a prototype (the XH-44 Hillercopter) in 1944 which incorporated advanced control and operating systems. After joining with the Kaiser Company (which formed a Hiller Helicopter Division) the XH-44 was followed by the UH-4 Commuter – a two-seat personal helicopter with counter-rotating rotor blades on a common mast. In 1945 Stanley Hiller broke away from Kaiser and formed United Helicopters. This went on to build the J5 – an experimental single-seat helicopter flown by Hiller in 1946, which used a simplified rotor control system and a ducted airflow tail unit to control rotor torque.

United Helicopters (later Hiller Helicopters Inc.) abandoned the coaxial rotor principle and designed the Hiller 360 which was a more conventional helicopter with a single rotor and tail-mounted anti-torque propeller. It used the J5's rotor control system which allowed the pilot to operate the machine through a sub-rotor at right-angles to the main rotorblades controlled by the pilot via an overhead control handle. It embodied a fully enclosed three-seat cabin and a metal moncoque fuselage structure. Following further development the '360 adopted a pod and boom configuration with the engine exposed and the crew on a bench seat behind a fully glazed canopy.

Hiller Helicopters, which took over all activities in 1951, launched production of the UH-12 for the U.S. military forces. Used in Korea the H-23A was fitted with external medevac panniers, and Hiller 360s became established thereafter as the standard training helicopter for the U.S. military forces. As the HT Mk.1 (with four undercarriage legs) it was delivered to the Royal Navy as a training helicopter, and the type also became popular as crop sprayers with underslung chemical spray bars and a dual-skid undercarriage.

The company had also done research into ramjet tip rotor drive for helicopters with the experimental HJ-2 Hornet. This became the HJ-1 and Hiller delivered an evaluation batch of 14 to the U.S. Army, designated YH-32. They also looked at the concept of an ultra-light personal helicopter for use by individual soldiers, which could be dismantled and transported in the field. Thirteen examples of this XROE-1 Rotorcycle were built by Hiller. Saunders Roe in the U.K. were heavily involved in this programme and produced five of the Rotorcycles from Hiller components but with Saro transmissions. These were demonstrated in Europe and evaluated by the U.S. Marines but no production order was placed. An alternative concept for the U.S. Army was the VZ-1E 'Flying Platform' which used a ducted rotor system to raise a man-carrying 'saucer' off the ground.

The rather flat-fronted 'bug-eye' cockpit enclosure of the UH-12A and UH-12B gave way, in 1956, to a large rounded bubble canopy that gave the UH-12C increased cockpit space and much improved visibility. This was followed by the D and E models which were delivered in large numbers to the United States military forces and to the Royal Navy (16) and the Royal Canadian Air Force (25).

In 1960, Hiller Helicopters merged with Eltra Corporation (The Electric Autolite Company) and introduced the UH-12E4, which provided a two-foot extension to the existing cabin section so as to provide room for a single pilot seat ahead of the standard 3-place passenger bench seat. Existing UH-12Es could be retrofitted with this modification. Hiller also designed and built the prototype Model 1099 ('Ten99'), which was a utility helicopter with a square fuselage incorporating a rear-loading door and either six seats or a large cargo area.

In 1961, the U.S. Army issued a requirement for a four-seat light helicopter and Hiller submitted the Model 1100, which was selected for evaluation as the HO-5 (later OH-5A). Five OH-5As were delivered for evaluation, but the type was not selected – the winner being the Hughes OH-6A. The Model 1100 was nevertheless too good to abandon and Hiller started to put it into production for civil and overseas military customers.

At about this time, Fairchild Stratos entered into negotiations with Eltra and, on 5 May 1964, acquired Hiller Aircraft Co. In September of that year the corporate name was changed to Fairchild Hiller. Fairchild was already interested in V/STOL aircraft and had built a prototype of the M-224-1 experimental tilting wing aircraft for testing as the VZ-5 by the U.S. Army. When they took over, production of the UH-12 series was phased out in favour of development of the new FH-1100, and between 1966 and 1974 Fairchild Hiller built just under 250 of these helicopters.

Rights to the UH-12 were sold to Hiller Aviation of Porterville, California in 1973 and they restarted production of the UH-12E shortly afterwards. The UH-12 had also been the subject of a popular retrofit programme devised by Soloy Corporation and as such was first flown on 9 August 1973. This involved installation of a replacement 400 shp Allison 250-C20B turboshaft engine in the UH-12D and UH-12E and 180 aircraft were so converted, including ten UH-12E4s. Soloy also converted a substantial number (thought to be around 220) of Bell 47s.

Hiller Aviation also acquired rights to the FH-1100 and opened a new production line, but the company further changed hands with a sale to a Canadian investment house and then, in April 1984, its acquisition by Rogerson Aircraft Corporation. Under the name Hiller Helicopters, and then Rogerson Hiller, it produced plans for new variants of the FH-1100, and five examples of the RH-1100B Pegasus were completed between 1983 and 1986. In 1985 Rogerson also produced a prototype of the RH-1100M Hornet military

Fairchild Hiller FH-1100, N756F

derivative, but this did not progress further and in 1990 the company resumed production of the UH-12E.

By early 1993, Rogerson decided to dispose of the Hiller component and in July 1994 the Hiller family and a group of Asian investors reacquired the company, renaming it Hiller Aviation Corporation. In September 1995, the company also acquired the supplemental type certificates and conversion kits for the Soloy turbine conversions of the UH-12 and Bell 47. At the same time, the new management decided to abandon the UH-12E5 development which was in hand, but the UH-12E returned to production at Marina, California with output of an initial batch of 30 aircraft getting under way in mid-1996. Early deliveries are to be made to the Mexican Navy and Summit Helicopters Inc.

Production Details

Hiller prototypes generally had individual construction numbers as shown in the Table of Models. The serials for the small batch of HJ-1 Hornets are believed to be c/n 2001 to 2018 although this is unconfirmed. UH-12 serials started at c/n 100 and fell into the following batches:

Model	Serial Batch	Number Built	Notes
UH-12A	c/n 103 to 295 (excl. c/n 210)	192	Including military and civil production.
UH-12B	c/n 210 and c/n 296 to 748	454	Including military and civil production.
UH-12C	c/n 749 to 937, c/n 1035 and c/n 1037 to 1045	199	Civil production.
UH-12D	c/n 938 to 1034 (excl. 942 & 954), c/n 1046 to 1266, c/n 1271 to 1438, c/n 1036	485	H-23D production for US Army.
UH-12E4 (H-23F)	c/n 1267 to 1270	4	c/ns reallocated as c/n 2125 to 2128.
UH-12D	c/n 1271 to 1273	3	US Army H-23D.
UH-12C	c/n 1274 to 1826	553	US Army H-23G.
UH-12E	c/n 2001 to 2373	324	Military and civil production. 23 c/ns allocated to UH-12Cs and UH-12Ds on conversion to '12E. c/n 2309, 10, 11, 47, 48 and 2318 to 2338 not built.
UH-12L4	c/n 2500 to 2549	49	
UH-12E	c/n HA3001 to HA3083	83	Production by Hiller Aviation from spare parts, 1973 onwards. No US military aircraft. Incl. some UH-12E4.
UH-12E, UH-12E3	c/n 5001 to 5232 (current)	232	Production by Hiller Aviation/ Rogerson Hiller & Hiller Aircraft Corp.
UH-12E4	c/n HA4001	1	One aircraft built by Hiller Aviation.
YROE-1	c/n 1 to 13	13	c/n 4 to 13 built by Saro.

A number of UH-12s have been manufactured from spare parts (e.g. c/n J345 by Jensen Crop Dusters, WH6003 by World Helicopters, DLW3 by Evergreen).

The three Model 1100 prototypes were c/n 1 to 3, the OH-5A evaluation aircraft were c/n 4 to 8 and Fairchild-Hiller built FH-1100s had c/ns from 9 to 254. One new production FH-1100 from Hiller Aviation carried the c/n 2 and new production of the FH-1100 Pegasus by Rogerson Hiller was c/n 500 to 504.

Model Information

The different models produced by the Hiller companies over the years are:

Type No.	Name	Notes
XH-44		Experimental all-metal single-seat light helicopter with 90 h.p. Franklin engine, co-axial twin rotors & no tail rotor. Fixed t/w u/c. One Prot. NX30033 (c/n 500) FF 1944.
X2-235	Hillercopter	Developed version of UH-44. One built.
UH-4	Commuter	Two-seat all-metal helicopter with tricycle u/c and coaxial twin rotors. Prot. N67706 (c/n 1). Three built.
J-5		Single-seat experimental helicopter with open frame front mounting pilot and engine and metal cone tail with jet thrust duct. One built.
UH-5		Open frame experimental single-rotor helicopter with overhead control stick and engine mounted behind pilot. One Prot. N67707 (c/n 1) FF 1947.
HH-120	Hornet	Side-by-side two seat ultra-light helicopter with two Hiller ramjets attached to the ends of the rotor blades. No tail rotor. Fixed tricycle u/c. One Prot. N6728C (c/n 2).
HJ-1	Hornet	Developed HH-120 with fully enclosed fuselage and skid undercarriage. Prot. N8200H (c/n 1). 14 built.

Hiller 360 HTE-1, 128637 *(HGM Collection)*

HELICOPTERS AND ROTORCRAFT

Type No.	Name	Notes
	Sally	Open frame 3-seat helicopter with tip ramjets based on HJ-1. One only built.
1033	Rotorcycle	Single-seat personal collapsible-frame helicopter with tripod u/c, powered by one 45 h.p. Nelson H-63 engine. Designated XROE-1/YROE-1 for Marines evaluation.
360		Two-seat helicopter based on UH-5 of all-metal construction with fixed tricycle u/c, fully enclosed cabin and rear fuselage, overhead mounted control stick attached to Hiller rotor control, powered by one 175 h.p. Franklin 6V4-178-B32 engine. Prot. N68940.
UH-12		Developed '360 with framed 'bubble'-type cabin, no fuselage structure round engine, skid u/c and 175 h.p. Franklin 6V4-178-B33 engine. 2247 lb TOGW.
UH-12A	Raven	Production two-seat UH-12 with collective pitch ballast system and wooden rotor blades for civil and military customers. 2400 lb TOGW.
UH-12B		UH-12A with skid/wheel u/c, 200 h.p. Franklin 6V4-200-C33 engine and 2500 lb TOGW. USN HTE-2 and Royal Navy HT Mk.1 have wheel u/c.
UH-12C		UH-12B with moulded bubble canopy, 3 seats and metal rotor blades.
UH-12D		Military UH-12C with 250 h.p. Lyc. VO-435-A1C engine, new transmission system, 2750 lb. TOGW Prot. FF 3 Apl. 1956.
UH-12E		UH-12D with 305 h.p. Lyc. VO-540-A1A engine. OH-23G is 3-seat dual control trainer.
UH-12EL		UH-12E retro-fitted with Ham-Standard rotor stability augmentation system, stainless steel rotor blades and 3100 lb TOGW.
UH-12E3		Revised designation for Hiller Aircraft Corp. production UH-12E with 3 seats.
UH-12E3T		Revised designation for Hiller Aircraft Corp. 3-seat UH-12ET.
UH-12E4		UH-12E with inverted rear tail planes and lengthened cabin to accommodate pilot plus rear bench seat for 3 pax.
UH-12ET		UH-12E fitted with Soloy conversion to 400 shp Allison 250-C20B turboshaft.
UH-12E4T		UH-12E4 fitted with Soloy conversion to 400 shp Allison 250-C20B turboshaft.
UH-12E5		UH-12E4 fitted with five seats and 340 shp Lyc. VO-540 piston engine. Prot. flown but design not further developed.
UH-12E5T		Proposed turbine-powered UH-12E5 with Allison 250-C20B. Not built.
UH-12J-3		Unofficial designation for Soloy-converted UH-12E.
UH-12SL		UH-12E with supercharged Lyc. TIVO-540 engine and 'L' series rotor head with gyro-controlled stability augmentation system.

Type No.	Name	Notes
UH-12L		UH-12SL with unsupercharged VO-540 engine.
UH-12SL4		UH-12L with E4 four-seat cabin.
	Propelloplane X-18	Experimental X-18A research tilt-wing transport based on a YC-122 fuselage with pivoting wing mounting two 5850 shp T40-A-4 turboprops and a rear-mounted J-34 turbojet for pitch control. Prot. 57-3078 FF 24 Nov. 1959.
	C-142	Tilt-wing transport derived from X-18 and developed by Ling-Temco-Vought-Hiller-Ryan with four T64 engines.
1099	Ten99	Six-seat utility helicopter with box-shaped fuselage and tailboom powered by one 550 shp Pratt & Whitney PT6 turboshaft. Prot. N3776G FF 14 July 1961.
1100		Four-seat light military observation helicopter with low-set tailboom, skid undercarriage and powered by one 250 shp Allison T63 turboshaft. Prot. N81005 (c/n 1). FF 26 Jan. 1963. Designated OH-5A.
FH-1100		Developed civil version of OH-5A with five seats, Hiller 'L' rotor system and 317 shp Allison 250-C18 turboshaft.
RH-1100B	Pegasus	FH-1100 by Rogerson-Hiller with improved streamlined fuselage, larger rotor blades and one Allison 250-C20B turboshaft.

Much of Hiller's production over 50 years has been to military users. Information on the

Hiller YH-32 Hornet, 55-4963 *(HGM Collection)*

HELICOPTERS AND ROTORCRAFT

military designations for Hiller helicopters used by the United States forces and the British Royal Navy and Canadian Armed Forces are shown in the following table:

Model	Name	US Army	US Navy	Marine Corps	Royal Navy	RCAF	Total Delivered
UH-12A	Raven	YH-23 H-23A	HTE-1				123
UH-12B	Raven	H-23B OH-23B	HTE-2		HT Mk.1		308
UH-12C	Raven	H-23C OH-23C					145
UH-12D	Raven	H-23D OH-23D					348
UH-12E	Raven	H-23G OH-23G			HT Mk.2	CH-112 Nomad	834
UH-12E4	Raven	H-23F OH-23F					33
1100		YOH-5A					5
HJ-1	Hornet	YH-32	XHOE-1				14
1033	Rotorcycle			YROE-1			13

Hiller 1033 Rotorcycle YROE-1

KAMAN   USA

The search for solutions to the inherent stability and control problems of helicopters has taken many turns and one of the most unusual results came from Charles H. Kaman – founder of Kaman Corporation. Established in 1945 by the 26-year-old engineer with a war-chest of $2,000, the company developed a series of helicopters which embodied a design layout which is still unique but resulted in machines which were highly effective and maintained an enviable safety record.

Kaman's initial design focus concentrated on a 'servo-controlled rotor' system involving tabs fitted on the outer third of his helicopter's rotor blades, which could be controlled by the pilot to change the angle of attack of the blades. The first Kaman helicopter, the KSA-100, was a test unit which provided an effective starting point for the design development of the two-surface rotor control tab arrangement. From this point, Charles Kaman moved on to develop his answer to the torque problem in helicopters. The principle of the design was to have two rotors on closely-positioned pylons with angled rotors which would inter-mesh as they turned in opposing directions. This avoided the engineering complication of having two rotors on one mast (which Charles Hiller initially saw as a solution and was later adopted in production aircraft by Kamov), but still meant that a tail rotor was not required.

Kaman K-600, HH-43B Huskie, 62-4535

HELICOPTERS AND ROTORCRAFT

Despite many external pressures, not least from company investors, Charles Kaman's experimental K-125-A made its first flight in January 1947. It was a two-seat helicopter with a plywood-covered fuselage and a bubble canopy, which had two angled rotor mountings positioned behind the cockpit. The fuselage structure was manufactured for Kaman by Granville Bros Aircraft which had built the Gee Bee pre-war racers. The intermeshing rotors were driven by a Lycoming piston engine buried in the fuselage, and the designation of the helicopter was related to the horsepower rating of the engine.

Kaman's next version of the twin rotor concept was the K-190, which was a larger machine than the K-125-A with an open tubular frame fuselage providing an open forward platform for two or three occupants, and an engine installation in the central section driving twin intermeshing rotors with the now-familiar servo tabs. At the rear was a tubular structure on which was mounted a fixed fin – and on some aircraft a moveable rudder surface. The K-190, which gained its CAA type certificate on 15 April 1949, spawned the K-225, which started to gain military interest. The U.S. Air Force acquired one, which was designated H-22, and another was delivered to Elizabeth City, North Carolina for evaluation by the U.S. Coast Guard as the HK-1. The K-225 was a development machine which had some way to go before it could become a practical operational aircraft, but the military pilots who flew it found the Kaman machine to have exceptional stability. This led to the United States Navy working with the company to create a viable helicopter for shipboard support.

The U.S. Navy's requirements were met by Kaman heading in two different directions. The XHOK-1 was a four-seat version of the K-225 fitted with a 600 h.p. R-1340-48 engine – but still with the open-frame fuselage. Kaman then re-engineered the airframe with a full all-metal monocoque body structure which included a fully enclosed cabin, four-leg undercarriage, cladding for the twin pylons and a new tailboom structure which supported a large pair of rectangular tailfins. The first HOK-1 (Model K-600) was delivered to the U.S. Marine Corps on 18 April 1953, and it was certainly different from the

Kaman K-240 HTK-1, 128653 *(HGM Collection)*

other helicopters operated thus far by the American military forces. In addition to the Marine Corps, the U.S. Navy took a batch of 24 which were designated HUK-1.

The Navy also needed a training helicopter, and the stability characteristics shown by these designs prompted them to engage Kaman to design a smaller three-seat machine known as the HTK-1 (Model K-240). As with the HOK-1, this had a four-wheel undercarriage and a large Perspex-fronted cabin together with a tailboom carrying a cluster of three fins. Kaman received substantial orders for the new helicopters from the U.S. Navy and Marines, and then the U.S. Air Force took an interest. This led to an order for 18 H-43As which were based on the HOK-1 but had numerous changes including additional vertical tail surfaces. In many cases the engine of the H-43A, which was positioned below and behind the crew cabin, was left uncowled to improve cooling.

Kaman had been taking considerable interest in the possibility of turbine engines for helicopters. In December 1951, the original K-225 used for HOK-1 development was fitted with a Boeing 502 gas turbine and it became the world's first helicopter to fly with this type of powerplant. Further tests were carried out with turbine installations, including the first example of twin turboshaft engines on an HTK-1.

It was not surprising that the next move was to improve the H-43 Huskie by the installation of a 720 shp Lycoming T-53 turboshaft engine mounted on top of the fuselage. This resulted in much greater cabin volume by the release of space taken up by the previous piston engine. It also brought substantially better performance and made the Huskie into a very effective search-and-rescue helicopter. The U.S. Air Force acquired 200 examples of the HH-43B (K-600-3) which served during the 1960s. This model was also delivered to the air forces of Burma, Colombia, Thailand and Pakistan. A subsequent H-43F variant had a further increase in power and greater passenger capacity and a small batch was delivered to Iran.

With such success from the unconventional intermeshing twin rotor system it was highly surprising when, in 1956, the company did not adopt this form when designing its K-20 to meet a U.S. Navy requirement for a long-range search-and-rescue helicopter. The K-20 Seasprite was a very conventional helicopter with a single main rotor blade and tail

Kaman K-1125, N10029 *(via MS)*

stabilising rotor. Powered by a General Electric T58 turboshaft, the Seasprite was ordered in substantial numbers by the Navy. Initially, it used a single engine but most Seasprites were subsequently modified to twin-turbine configuration.

Kaman was involved in the extended 'LAMPS' competition (Light Airborne Multi-Purpose System) and the Seasprite was eventually selected as an interim solution to this anti-submarine requirement. In the event, the fleet of Seasprites underwent continuing modification to meet many naval requirements, the latest of which is an upgrade to Super Seasprite (SH-2G) configuration with twin T700 turboshaft engines. This provides the Seasprite with almost four-times the engine power of the original YHU2K-1 prototype. Existing surplus SH-2F airframes are being rebuilt to SH-2G standard and Kaman is starting to export the Super Seasprite with the first order coming from Egypt for 20 aircraft. Twelve examples of the SH-2G are also expected to be delivered to the Taiwanese Navy, and the Royal Australian Navy will receive 29 examples, designated SH-2G(A) for operation from ANZAC-class frigates.

Kaman Corporation grew over the years into a diversified engineering business, involved in substantial aviation parts subcontracting and in many fields outside aerospace ranging from industrial bearings to guitars. However, the core helicopter designs which started the company were shown still to be important when Charles Kaman announced the Model K-1200 'K-Max'. Stated to be the first commercial helicopter specifically designed for external vertical lift applications, the K-Max single-seater reverted to the system of inter-meshing twin rotors and continued the tradition of servo tabs for rotor pitch control. The K-Max 'Aerial Truck' is in current production and has been sold to customers such as Scott Paper and Louisiana Pacific Corporation for logging operations and is under evaluation by the U.S. Navy for 'VERTREP' cargo replenishment of ships under way.

Production details

The serial number batches used by Kaman are not fully documented, but the best information available is as follows:

Model	Serial Batches	Number Built	Notes
K-190A	c/n 2 and c/n 4 to 7	5	
K-225	c/n 8 to 14	7	c/ns not confirmed.
K-240	c/n 4-1 to 4-29	29	HTK-1.
K-600	not known	135	H-43A.
K-600-3/5	c/n 1 to 245 (unconfirmed)	245	H-43B and H-43F.
K-20	c/n 1 to 244 (unconfirmed)	244	Seasprite.
K-1200	c/n A94-0001 up	16	K-Max.

Model Information

Details of the various models designed and built by Kaman are:

Type No.	Name	Notes
K-125-A		Experimental two-seat helicopter with moulded plywood fuselage and cockpit with clear bubble canopy, fixed tricycle u/c, small tailplane with endplate fins, twin counter-rotating rotor pylons behind cockpit with two-blade rotors fitted with controllable servo tabs and one 125 h.p. Lycoming O-390-3 piston engine. Prot. N60377 (c/n 1) FF 15 Jan. 1947 at Windsor Locks, Ct.

Type No.	Name	Notes
K-190A		Open frame two-seat helicopter with single pilot seat and two-place rear bench. Fitted with a 190 h.p. Lycoming O-435-1 engine behind passenger section driving twin Kaman rotor pylons. Tail fin/rudder supported by open welded tube tail boom. Later aircraft fitted with enclosed cabin. Prot N 74105 (c/n 2). 5 built.
K-190B		Modified K-190A with three seats. One Prot. N74148 (c/n 3).
K-225		Open frame three-seat utility helicopter developed from K-190 with Kaman twin rotor system and provision for agricultural twin hoppers and dusting system. Powered by one 225 h.p. Lyc. O-435-A2 piston engine driving wooden main rotor blades. Prot. N404A (c/n 8). 7 built. One aircraft for USAF as H-22 (s/n 50-1271).
K-240	HTK-1	Three-seat U.S. Navy training helicopter based on K-225 with fully clad fuselage and tailboom structure, tailboom repositioned level with upper roof line, two (later three) large oval tailsurfaces, fixed four-leg u/c and one 245 h.p. Lyc. O-435-4 piston engine. Later designated TH-43E.
K-600	XHOK-1 (sic)	K-225 fitted with one 600 h.p. Pratt & Whitney R-1340-48 piston engine. One Prot. Bu.125466.
K-600	HOK-1 HUK-1	Four-seat support helicopter for US Marines with all-metal fuselage embodying high-set twin tailboom and twin vertical tailfins (later changed to three fins), four-leg u/c and Kaman counter-meshing rotor system driven by one 600 h.p. Pratt & Whitney R-1340-48 piston engine. Also known as the K-3. Later designated OH-43D. Navy version designated HUK-1 (UH-43C).
K-600	H-43A Huskie	USAF version of HOK-1 for rescue duties with four tailfins and minor equipment changes.

Kaman K-Max, N131KA *(Kaman)*

HELICOPTERS AND ROTORCRAFT

Type No.	Name	Notes
K-600-3	HH-43B Huskie	Re-engineered H-43 with 860 shp Lyc. T53-L-1A turboshaft repositioned above fuselage and longer cabin with rear entry hatch to accommodate up to 8 pax and 2 crew.
K-600-4		Proposed H-43 with Blackburn-Turboméca Twin Turmo 600 turboshaft.
K-600-5	HH-43F	H-43B powered by one 825 shp T53-L-11A turboshaft with reduced diameter main rotor blades and capacity for 11 pax and 2 crew.
K-700		Proposed rescue helicopter for USAF based on K-1125 with two PT6A turboshafts, streamlined fuselage and large tail fin. Not built.
K-800	Seacat	Naval armed helicopter with Seasprite-type fuselage, stub wings, cruciform tail with pusher prop and twin turbine engines. Not built.
K-16B		V-Stol research aircraft based on Grumman Goose fuselage with tilting wing and two General Electric T58-GE-2A turboprop engines. One Prot. Bu. 04351 (N1523V).
K-17		Experimental open cockpit two-seat helicopter with metal fuselage skid u/c, tail boom with small tail rotor surrounded by protective shroud. Fitted with single main rotor with internal ducting for compressed ducted jet flow provided by a 400 shp Blackburn-Turboméca Turmo turbine. One Prot. N268B (c/n 1) FF 1958.
KSA-100	Aercab	Foldable single-seat emergency aircrew escape autogyro known as Kaman SAVER with telescoping rotor blades and Williams Research WR-19 turbofan engine. Prot. N6256 FF 29 Dec. 1971.
K-1125	Huskie III	Medium civil transport helicopter using K-600 components but with enlarged fuselage and main cabin to accommodate 12 pax, single vertical fin on single tailboom, small horizontal tailplane, fibreglass main rotor blades and two Boeing YT-60 (later 770 shp Pratt & Whitney PT6B-11) turboshafts. One Prot. N10029 (c/n 122). FF Aug. 1962.
K-20	Seasprite YHU2K-1	Long-range naval search & rescue helicopter with 2 crew and max 12 seats or stretchers or equipment, retractable tailwheel u/c, conventional tail unit with fin and starboard-side tailplane, 3-blade tail rotor, single four-blade main rotor with servo tabs driven by one 875 shp General Electric T58-GE-6 turboshaft positioned on top of fuselage. Prot. YSH-3A Bu.147202 (c/n 1) FF 2 Jul. 1959. Later designated YUH-2A.
K-20	Seasprite UH-2A	Production Seasprite with 1250 shp T58-GE-8 turboshaft, autopilot and autostabiliser, external winch etc. Initially HU2K-1.
K-20	UH-2	Experimental compound helicopter for U.S. Army with short-span wings, additional GE YJ85 turbojet engine on starboard fuselage and other mods for high speed flight. Prot. Bu.147978.
K-20	Seasprite UH-2B	UH-2A for VFR operations only. Some later fitted with IFR instrumentation. Initially HU2K-1U.

Type No.	Name	Notes
K-20	Seasprite UH-2C	UH-2A and UH-2B converted with two 1250 shp. GE T58-GE-8B turboshafts. Prot Bu.147981.
K-20	Seasprite HH-2C	Converted UH-2A gunship with under-nose 7.62 mm minigun, two side-mounted miniguns and armour plating, dual mainwheels, 4-blade tail rotor, 12500 lb TOGW. Six conversions.
K-20	Seasprite NUH-2C	Experimental UH-2C with stub wings carrying two Sperry Sparrow III missiles. One aircraft Bu.147981.
K-20	Seasprite HH-2D	HH-2C without armour plating and weapons for rescue missions. 70 conversions of UH-2A and UH-2B.
K-20	Seasprite SH-2D	Anti-submarine LAMPS-I version with LN66 search radar in chin radome, ASQ-81 towed MAD, provision for external Mk.44/46 ASW homing torpedoes and external sonobuoy launcher etc. 20 SH-2s converted. Prot. Bu.147981 FF 16 Mar. 1971.
K-20	Seasprite YSH-2E	Two experimental advanced LAMPS conversions of HH-2D with additional large under-nose radome for APS-122 radar.
K-20	Seasprite SH-2F	Modified SH-2D with new Kaman-101 titanium rotor hub and extended-life blades, tailwheel repositioned forward, strengthened u/c, two 1350 shp T58-GE-8F turboshafts and improved Marconi LN66P radar. 85 conversions plus 54 new-build aircraft.
K-20	Super Seasprite SH-2G	SH-2F fitted with two 1723 shp General Electric T700-GE-401 turboshafts in enlarged external pods driving redesigned composite rotor blades. Prot. Bu.161653 converted from SH-2F. FF April 1985.
K-1200	K-Max	Single-seat aerial crane helicopter with twin intermeshing two-blade composite main rotors with servo tab pitch control, no tail rotor, vertical fin/rudder and tailplane with endplates, fixed tricycle u/c with surface spreader plates. Powered by one 1,500 shp Allied Signal T3517A-1 turboshaft. Prot. N3182T (c/n A94-0001) FF 23 Dec. 1991.

Kaman K-225, 125446 *(HGM Collection)*

Kaman HU2K-1 Seasprite, 150167 *(Kaman)*

KAMOV   SOVIET UNION

The Kamov OKB was established in 1945 by Nikolai Ilyich Kamov who had started his aviation career in flying boat design under Grigorovich. Kamov moved into autogyro development in 1930, joining N.K. Skrzhinskii in the design of a gyroplane based on an Avro 504 fuselage. This led to a series of experimental gyrocopters which were eventually abandoned in favour of the development of true helicopters.

Kamov's OKB was tasked with research into counter-rotating rotor systems for helicopters, and several experimental open-platform machines with pontoon landing gear were built to test the new rotor mechanisms. For these Ka-8 and Ka-10 designs, Kamov engineered an effective method of mounting two rotors on one mast – each rotor being independently driven. The rotors counter-rotated so that the helicopter had a neutral torque reaction and therefore no need for a stabilising tail propeller.

The Kamov system was first applied to a production helicopter in the two-seat Ka-15 which entered flight testing in 1952. This neat little machine had a fully enclosed fuselage and bubble cockpit canopy and was ordered in some numbers by the Soviet Navy (AV-MF) during the early 1950s. In military service, it had external hardpoints to carry depth charges, but the Ka-15 was also used for a variety of civil functions including medical evacuation and crop spraying. In 1958 this machine set a number of new helicopter closed-circuit speed records. Kamov subsequently produced a larger version, the Ka-18, which had a four-seat cabin and was employed in small numbers by Aeroflot.

In the late 1950s, the Kamov bureau experimented with the huge Vintokryl compound helicopter. In basic layout it was a conventional high wing aircraft but it was fitted with a lift rotor operating at each wingtip together with normal propellers for forward propulsion. In many ways, this was a development of a concept tested on Ivan Bratukhin's Omega helicopters of the mid-1940s. The Ka-22 gained a world record for rotary wing aircraft in 1961, achieving a top speed of 228 m.p.h. but it did not go into production.

Kamov's links with the navy had been strongly forged and in 1960 the coaxial rotor design was used on the Ka-25 'Hormone' anti-submarine helicopter. The elimination of the long tail boom required by helicopters with a tail propeller meant that the Ka-25 could have a relatively large capacity fuselage but, by using folding rotor blades, fit comfortably onto carrier deck lifts. Many variants of the Ka-25 were produced for the AV-MF covering various anti-submarine warfare tasks, electronic surveillance and countermeasures, search and rescue, on-board transport and the role of an over-the-horizon missile targeting platform.

In 1973, Nikolai Kamov died and his bureau lived on under S. Mikheyev. The Ka-25 grew in size and capability with increasing power and a bewildering array of external stores, antennae, radomes and sensors. This was succeeded by the Ka-27, which was externally similar but was actually a completely new helicopter with a much larger fuselage and the new Isotov TV3 turboshaft engine. The Ka-27 was exported to several overseas users including India and Yugoslavia. The Ka-27 was a naval helicopter but it formed the basis for the enlarged Ka-29 assault transport version capable of carrying 16 troops. The Ka-27 also had an equivalent Ka-32 civil transport version which has served widely with Aeroflot and other Russian air carriers including Vladivostok Air, Hevi-Lift and Nefteyugansk. Examples have also been sold to the USA, Colombia and Papua New Guinea, and the Ka-32 was used for a wide range of tasks including Arctic ice reconnaissance. It is marketed internationally by the Aviazapchast agency.

The main civil application for the Kamov rotor system was on the remarkable little Ka-26. Originally flown in 1965, the Ka-26 has a two-seat pilot's compartment pod in the nose and a detachable passenger compartment behind. Above the passenger section is a stub wing mounting two podded piston engines which drive a coaxial rotor. The design is completed with a twin-boomed tail unit and fixed four-leg undercarriage. The Ka-26 is highly versatile. With the passenger pod removed it can operate as a flying crane, and separate modules can be added to equip it for crop spraying, fire fighting or seismographic survey. This helicopter has had considerable commercial success with more than 180 examples exported to other Warsaw Pact countries and elsewhere. Large numbers were sold to Hungary and also to East Germany and Romania for agricultural use. The main manufacturing plant is now the Kumertau Aviation Product Enterprise (KUMAPP).

The latest design from the Kamov Bureau is the single-seat Ka-50 'Hokum' which resulted from a 1975 requirement for a close support attack aircraft for the Soviet Ground Forces. The Ka-50 is half fixed-wing aircraft and half helicopter with a complex armoured fuselage, short span wings and a fin and rudder with conventional control surfaces. This is all topped off with a high-speed coaxial rotor assembly. The Ka-50 is equipped with fixed nose armament and the pilot has an ejector seat which, when activated, triggers explosive bolts to blow off the rotors. It has not been acquired by CIS forces to date but is being actively marketed to western governments. Kamov is also working on a side-by-side two-seat Ka-52 version which is seen as giving more flexibility in battlefield situations.

Kamov Ka-25

HELICOPTERS AND ROTORCRAFT

Production Details

Serial numbers for the early Kamov helicopters and the purely military models are unknown but are assumed to follow the 'normal' Soviet system. The Ka-26 uses a seven-digit number (e.g. 7101701) consisting of the year built (e.g. 71), Batch Number (e.g. 017) and serial number in the batch (e.g. 01). The highest known serial number is c/n 7806508. The Ka-32 has a four-digit serial which is believed to consist of a two-digit batch number and two-digit serial number in the batch. Known Ka-32 serials fall in the range c/n 5504 to c/n 9009 and most batches appear to be of ten aircraft although individual serials up to 26 are known to have been issued.

Model Information

All known models designed by the Kamov OKB are as follows:

Type No.	NATO Codename	Approx. No. built	Notes
Ka-Skr-1		1	Pre-war autogyro designed by Kamov and Skrzhinskii.
Ka-Skr-2		1	Developed Ka-Skr-1 with improved powerplant.
Ka-8		3	Experimental open single-seat helicopter with pontoon landing gear and two three-blade rotors mounted on same rotor shaft and counter-rotating to eliminate torque effect. Powered by one 45 h.p. M-76 piston engine. Prot. FF 1947.
Ka-10	Hat	4	Enlarged version of Ka-8 with small strut-braced tail unit and 55 h.p. Ivchenko AI-4V piston engine. Prot. FF Sept. 1949.
Ka-10M	Hat	8	Ka-10 with twin fin tail, built for coastal patrol.
Ka-15	Hen	200+	Two-seat helicopter with fully enclosed fuselage, twin fin tail unit, Ka-10M coaxial rotor system, cabin with fully glazed canopy and four-leg u/c. Powered by one 225 h.p. Ivchenko AI-14V engine. For Soviet Navy (AV-MF). Prot. FF 1952.
Ka-15M	Hen		Civil model for Aeroflot. Some fitted with external chemical tanks and spraybars for agricultural operations.
Ka-15S	Hen		Medical evacuation version with external stretchers.
Ka-18	Hog	n/a	Ka-15 with lengthened fuselage to provide four-seat cabin, stepped windshield, enlarged fins and 275 h.p. Ivchenko AI-14VF piston engine. Prot. FF 1957.
Ka-20	Harp	n/a	Anti-submarine helicopter with box-shaped fuselage and short tailboom mounting three-fin tail unit, fixed four-leg u/c, twin three-blade coaxial rotors and two Glushenkov GTD-3F turboshaft engines mounted above cabin. 16535 lb TOGW. Prot. FF 1960.

Type No.	NATO Codename	Approx. No. built	Notes
Ka-22	Hoop	1	'Vintokryl'. Large experimental 80-seat transport helicopter with aircraft type fuselage and tail unit, fixed high wing with engine module at each wingtip driving a four-blade rotor and a tractor propeller, fixed tricycle u/c. Powered by two 5620 shp Ivchenko TB-2 turboshafts. Prot. FF 20 Apl. 1960.
Ka-25PL	Hormone-A	260	Production ASW version of Ka-20 with under-nose radome, dipping sonar under rear fuselage, belly weapons bay for two torpedoes or depth charges, ESM sensor fairing on top of tailboom and two 900 shp Glushenkov GTD-3F turboshafts.
Ka-25K	Hormone-B	190	Airborne missile control version with additional fuel, no weapons bay, enlarged nose radome, retractable u/c and advanced avionics and communications suite. Also said to be designated Ka-25T.
Ka-25K		1	Early designation given to civil development of Ka-25 with 12-passenger cabin and chin-mounted observation turret for control of underslung loads. Powered by two 900 shp Glushenkov turboshafts. Prot. SSSR-21110.
Ka-25BSh	Hormone-A		Minesweeping variant of Ka-25PL without sonar.
Ka-25PS	Hormone-C		SAR model of Ka-25 without weapons bay, fitted witn rescue hoist, provision for long range tanks, internal stretcher fittings or 12 passenger seats for COD role.

Kamov Ka-29

Type No.	NATO Codename	Approx. No. built	Notes
Ka-26	Hoodlum	900	Light multi-role helicopter with front crew pod and six-seat cabin or detachable 6-seat passenger module, twin boom tail unit with twin fins, stub wing mounting u/c legs and two Vedeneyev M-14V-26 piston engine pods driving twin three-blade coaxial rotors. Prot. FF 1965. Sometimes fitted with agricultural spraybars or geophysical survey ring emission unit.
Ka-27	Helix		New helicopter broadly based on Ka-25 for AV-MF with redesigned broader chord rotor blades, strengthened transmissions and u/c, two tail fins and two 2170 shp TV3-117BK turboshafts, increased fuel and 27775 lb. TOGW. Prot. FF Dec. 1974.
Ka-27PL	Helix-A	90	Ka-27 for anti-submarine missions with extended cockpit with additional windows, enlarged belly weapons bay for four torpedoes and upgraded electronics suite.
Ka-27PS	Helix-D		ASR version of Ka-27 without weapons bay, rescue winch, external fuel tanks, searchlight and other rescue equipment.
Ka-28	Helix-A		Ka-27PL for export customers with 2170 shp TV3-117BK turboshafts.
Ka-29RLD	Helix-B		Ka-27 with redesigned bulged three-seat cockpit section with flatter three-panel armoured glass windscreen for AV-MF use as electronic surveillance platform with extending belly-mounted radar antenna. Later Ka-31.

Kamov Ka-32T, RA-31099

Type No.	NATO Codename	Approx. No. built	Notes
Ka-29TB	Helix-B		Naval assault transport variant of Ka-29 with wider cockpit section, 16-troop cabin, modified chin radar, external weapons pylons with four hardpoints.
Ka-31			Radar post version of Ka-29 with extendable ventral radar array. Formerly Ka-9RLD.
Ka-32A			Civil transport version of Ka-27 certificate to FAR-29/33 with 16 passenger seats and provision for lifting underslung loads. Powered by two 2190 shp Klimov TV3-117V turboshafts.
Ka-32A-1			Civil Ka-27 for firefighting operations.
Ka-32C			Ka-32 for maritime SAR, medevac and support operations.
Ka-32K			Ka-32 for heavylift operations with retracting observation gondola under rear fuselage.
Ka-32S	Helix-C		Naval version of Ka-32 with high level avionics and SAR equipment.
Ka-32T	Helix-C		Ka-32 utility model for civil or military use with stripped down equipment and avionics.
Ka-50	Hokum	12+	'Werewolf' or 'Black Shark'. Single-seat attack helicopter with aircraft-type fuselage and fin/tailplane, retractable tricycle u/c. Fitted with short span wings with four strongpoints carrying tube-launched AT-X-16/9M121 Vikhr-M laser guided missiles, 80mm rocket packs etc. and tip-mounted ECM pods. Powered by twin Klimov TV3-117VK turboshafts mounted behind cockpit driving three-blade coaxial main rotors. Prot. (V-80) FF 27 Jul. 1982.
Ka-50N	Hokum	1	All-weather attack version of Ka-50 with Shkval-V sighting system and nose-mounted FLIR.
Ka-52 Alligator	Hokum	1	Ka-50 with wider fuselage and redesigned side-by side two-seat cockpit section. FF 25 Jun. 1997
Ka-62		1	Medium multi-purpose helicopter with 14-passenger cabin, retractable tailwheel u/c, fenestron tail powered by two RKMB RD-600, Glushenkov TVD-155 or Turboméca RTM322 turboshafts.
Ka-126	Hoodlum-B	13	Ka-26 with engine pods removed from stub wings, fitted with one Mars Kobcyenko TVO-100 turboshaft engine positioned on top of fuselage, modified rotor blades, new fuel system. Prot. CCCP-01963 FF Oct. 1988. Also built in Romania.

Type No.	NATO Codename	Approx. No. built	Notes
Ka-128		1	Ka-126 with 722 shp Turboméca Arriel 1D1 turboshaft.
Ka-226		1	Ka-126 with two 420 shp Allison 250-C20B turboshafts, deeper and wider two-seat cockpit with large windshield and nose, reshaped tail fins, modified transmission, enlarged cabin section with larger windows. Prot. FF 1994.

Kamov Ka-50

Kamov Ka-226

KAWASAKI   JAPAN

The present-day Kawasaki Heavy Industries is involved in a wide range of manufacturing including heavy sea-going bulk carriers, electric locomotives, chemical production plants and a wide range of engineering and construction products. Kawasaki Aircraft Co. had been established in 1937 and built a range of military aircraft during World War II. Following reorganisation in March 1954, it became the Kawasaki Kokuki Kogyo KK and then joined the Kawasaki Heavy Industries Group in April 1969.

Kawasaki had recommenced aviation operations after the war, firstly with the overhaul of military aircraft and then with license production of new aircraft for the expanding Japanese Self Defense Forces. These included Lockheed T-33 trainers and P-2 Neptunes. Kawasaki has also become a major producer of helicopters and is unusual in having entered licence agreements with several manufacturerers – Bell, Boeing-Vertol, Hughes/McDonnell Douglas and MBB.

In 1952, the company took out an agreement with Mitsui & Co. (the Japanese licensee for Bell Helicopter Corp.) to build the Model 47 helicopter for the Japanese forces and for commercial customers. The first Kawasaki-built Bell 47 flew on 1 November 1952, and they built 24 Model 47Ds (some of which were later converted to 47G standard), 180 Model 47G-2s and a batch of 33 Model 47G-2As. These were mainly sold to the JASDF and JGSDF but a fair number also entered the Japanese civil fleet.

The company also produced their own variant of the Model 47 – titled KH-4. This was based on the Model 47G-3B (and, indeed, four 47Gs were converted to KH-4 standard). The KH-4 used the same engine as the Model 47G but had a new enclosed cabin with solid doors. Other changes included higher fuel capacity, a new control system and redesigned instrument layout – and a higher useful load. The KH-4 could accommodate four people – the pilot in front and three passengers on a rear bench seat. In some ways it mirrored the modifications introduced by Agusta in their A-115 and Hiller in the UH12E-4. The KH-4 was a successful model for Kawasaki, and a final production total of 211 was produced including a batch of 19 aircraft for the JGSDF and a number for the Thai Air Force.

The next alliance developed by Kawasaki was with the Vertol Division of the Boeing Company. Boeing-Vertol had been producing the Model 107 tandem-rotor medium transport helicopter and Kawasaki entered into an agreement which would allow it to build the type to meet the needs of the JASDF. A total of 39 was ordered by the JASDF over a period of fiscal years with the first aircraft flying in May 1962, and Fuji also built 60 for the JGSDF and nine for the JMSDF. These naval aircraft were used both for transport and as minesweepers. Subsequently, in 1965, Boeing granted Kawasaki exclusive manufacturing rights to the Vertol 107, and a separate FAA type certificate was issued in November 1965.

The KV-107 also sold in some numbers to domestic civil operators and 31 were exported outside Japan. These included sales of eight to Sweden and three to Thailand together with 16 mission-specific variants to the Saudi Arabian Government. All later production units were the KV.107-IIA version which was developed by Kawasaki, and fitted with higher powered CT7 turboshafts which brought improved operating performance to the aircraft. A total of 160 KV-107s was completed and production ended in February 1990.

Further modernisation of the JGSDF prompted Kawasaki to join forces with Hughes which was supplying the OH-6 to the United States Army. A JGSDF requirement for a multi-role unit-level helicopter resulted in Kawasaki setting up a production line for the Hughes 500M Defender (known as the OH-6J), and later the 500D with the larger five-blade rotor and faired rotor head which was designated OH-6D in Japanese military service. These were generally identical to the US-built equivalent versions. The JGSDF and JMSDF received a total of 120 of the OH-6J followed by 62 of the OH-6D. Kawasaki also put the Model 369HS (Model 500C) into production for civil users and, later, the Model 369D. These aircraft were marketed for a wide variety of roles including crop spraying, aeromedical work and police and fire support services.

With extensive production experience under its belt, Kawasaki moved forward into a joint design and manufacturing venture with Messerschmitt-Bölkow-Blohm. They had already been developing a helicopter designated KH.7 and elements of this went into the new BK-117 medium-weight helicopter. The BK-117 used the dynamic system of the Bo.105 and MBB took responsibility for programme management and development of the main rotor, tail and tail rotor, engine housing, hydraulic system, mechanical controls and sections of the fuselage floor and landing gear. Kawasaki was in charge of the main rotor transmission, the airframe, fuel and electrical systems and interior trim and equipment.

Following German certification on 9 December 1982, and JCAB certification on 17 December of that year the BK-117 went into production with parallel German and Japanese production lines. A single source system is used so that individual parts and assemblies are manufactured in Germany or Japan according to responsibility, but final assembly is separately carried out in Donauworth and Gifu. The Japanese-built

Kawasaki KH-4, JA7377 *(via PRK)*

prototype first flew in August 1979, with Japanese certification being awarded on 17 December 1982. To date, Kawasaki has built 110 examples of the A-3, B-1 and B-4 versions of the BK-117.

Yet another licence agreement emerged for Kawasaki in 1984 when the JASDF and JGSDF selected the Boeing-Vertol CH-47 Chinook as their tactical airlift helicopter. This was to act as a higher capacity replacement for the KV-107. The new licence agreement covered a Japanese-configured CH-47J version of the U.S. Army's CH-47D with a carrying capacity of three crew and 55 troops. Boeing-Vertol delivered three evaluation CH-47Ds for operational testing prior to full production commencing. Powered by a pair of Mitsubishi-Lycoming T55-K-712 turboshafts, initial orders were for 14 CH-47Js for the JASDF and 31 for the JGSDF, and first deliveries were made by Kawasaki in 1986.

In 1996, Kawasaki started flight testing the OH-1 'Kongata Kansoko' – or light observation helicopter. The naming of this machine is belied by its appearance which follows the classic lines of the Eurocopter Tiger and Denel Rooivalk. It is a two-seater with a stepped cockpit, fenestron tail and strongpoints fitted to small stub wings. It seems likely that Kawasaki will ultimately be selected to deliver the definitive version of the OH-1 to the Japanese Ground Forces for anti-tank operations.

Production Details

Model	Serial Batch	Number Built	Notes
KB-47D-1	c/n 1001 to 1024	24	Some converted to Model 47G.
KB-47G-2	c/n 101 to 280	180	
KB-47G-2A	c/n 501 to 533	33	
KH-4	c/n 2000 to 2210	211	
500M	c/n 6301 to 6420	120	OH-6J. Data unconfirmed.
500D	c/n 6421 to 6599	210	OH-6D. Data unconfirmed.
369HS	c/n 6601 to 6649	49	Model 500C for civil sale.
369D	c/n 6701 to 6708	8	Civil sale.
KV.107	c/n 4001 to 4160	160	
BK-117	c/n 1001 to 1111	111	
KV.CH-47J	c/n 5001 to 5051	51	c/ns unconfirmed.
OH-1	c/n 32001 to 32004	4	Prototypes.

Model Information

Details of all Kawasaki helicopter types to date are as follows:

Type No.	Name	Notes
K-Bell 47D-1		Kawasaki version of Bell 47D. Some converted to KB-47G.
K-Bell 47G-2		Kawasaki version of Bell 47G-2.
K-Bell 47G-2A		Kawasaki version of Bell 47G-2A.
KH-4		Kawasaki-Bell 47G-3B with lengthened partially enclosed cabin providing front pilot seat and rear 3-place bench seat, increased useful load, redesigned control system. Prot. JA7340 (c/n 2000). FF Aug. 1962.

Type No.	Name	Notes
KV.107-II-1		Licence-built Boeing-Vertol 107 twin rotor medium transport helicopter powered by two 1250 shp IHI-GE CT58-110 turboshafts. Standard utility model for civil or military users.
KV.107-II-2		Airline model with 25 passenger seats and rear baggage section under tail.
KV.107-II-3	RH-46	JMSDF Naval mine countermeasures variant with long-range tanks and external winch.
KV.107-II-4	CH-46	JGSDF tactical 26-troop transport variant with strengthened cabin floor and loading ramp.
KV.107-II-5		Long range search & rescue variant for JASDF with external long range tanks, rescue winch, domed windows, searchlights and enhanced navigation aids. Swedish HKP-4c and Canadian CH-113. Swedish aircraft upgraded to two Rolls-Royce Gnome H.1200 turboshafts after delivery.
KV.107-II-7 KV.107-II-8		Civil executive transport variants with 6/11 seats.
KV.107-II-9		Proposed aeromedical variant.
KV.107-IIA-3		KV.107-II-3 with 1400 shp General Electric CT58-140-1 turboshafts. Prot. JA9509 (c/n 4013) FF 3 Apl. 1968.
KV.107-IIA-4		KV.107-II-4 with 1400 shp General Electric CT58-140-1 turboshafts.
KV.107-IIA-5		KV.107-II-5 with 1400 shp General Electric CT58-140-1 turboshafts. 8 aircraft delivered to Sweden fitted with Rolls-Royce Gnome H.1200 turboshafts.
KV.107-IIA-17		Specialised long range passenger/medical version with two cabin sections. One delivered to Tokyo police.
KV.107-IIA-SM1		Four firefighting KV.107 for Saudi Arabian Govt.
KV.107-IIA-SM2		Four aeromedical KV.107 for Saudi Arabian Govt.
KV.107-IIA-SM3		Two deluxe transport KV.107 for Saudi Arabian Govt.
KV.107-IIA-SM4		Three air ambulance KV.107 for Saudi Arabian Govt.
BK.117		Medium transport helicopter jointly developed by Kawasaki and MBB with engine module above cabin section and rear clamshell doors allowing through cargo access to cabin. Max 11-seat capacity. Equipped with skid u/c, conventional boom & tail rotor with tailplane and large endplate fins. Powered by two 550 shp Lycoming LTS 101-650B-1 turboshafts. Kawasaki Prot. JQ-0003 (c/n P3) FF 10 Aug. 1979.
BK.117 A-1		Production BK.117 with 550 shp LTS-101-650B-1 engines and 6283 lb TOGW.
BK.117 A-3		BK.117 A-1 with 7055 lb TOGW and increased useful load, new stability augmentation system and enlarged redesigned tail rotor.
BK 117 A-4		BK.117 A-3 with increased fuel capacity, improved transmission and new automatic flight control system.

Type No.	Name	Notes
BK.117 B-1		BK.117 A-3 with two 592 shp LTS-101-750B-1 engine and 7055 lb TOGW.
K-H.369HM	OH-6J	Kawasaki-built Hughes 500M for JGSDF and JMSDF.
K-H.369D	OH-6D	Kawasaki-built Hughes 500D for JGSDF and JMSDF.
K-H.369HS		Kawasaki-built version of Hughes 500D for civil sale.
K-H.369D		Civil version of K-H.369D.
KV.CH-47J	CH-47J	Kawasaki-built version of Boeing-Vertol CH-47D Chinook.
OH-1	OH-1	Light two-seat observation and attack helicopter with stepped cockpits, tailplane and fin and rudder incorporating buried 'fenestron' tail rotor, twin 884 shp Mitsubishi XTS1-10 turboshafts driving four-blade main rotor and fixed tailwheel u/c. First of four Prots. s/n 32001 FF 6 Aug. 1996.

Kawasaki OH-1

Kawasaki-Vertol KV.107-IIA-17, JA9511

MBB   GERMANY

In 1947, Dr Ludwig Bölkow formed the Ingenieurbau Bölkow and ten years later this became the Bölkow Entwicklungen K.G. The company embarked on a wide range of aviation activities and became particularly well known for the Kl.107 and Kl.207 light aircraft and the Bö.208 Junior and Bö.209 Monsun which followed. However, Dr Bölkow also became deeply interested in rotorcraft and initially developed a static trainer (the Bö.102 Heli-Trainer) which embodied all essential elements of a conventional helicopter, but was mounted on an articulated gantry to allow a student controlled experience of helicopter systems. This machine was sold in some numbers to the West German military forces.

The Heli-Trainer required little modification to become a flying helicopter and Bölkow did construct one example of the Bö.103. However, the main role of the Bö.103 was to experiment with new rotor concepts and the prototype was fitted with a single-blade fibreglass rotor counterbalanced by a short extension and balance weight on the other side of the rotor head. This was mirrored in the tail rotor. Bölkow's research led to development of rigid-hub rotor systems, and contracts were placed by the German Defence Ministry for the Bö.46 research helicopter which was built to test a high-speed rotor designed by Hans Derschmidt. This system consisted of a large star-shaped rigid hub with relatively short, hinged, fibreglass blades that went a long way toward resolving the compressibility and tip-stall problems of rotors turning at very high speeds. This programme was abandoned in 1964 – but not before Bölkow had learned much which would be of value in developing its production helicopter models.

Bölkow's next development was the light two-seat Bö.104 which was to use both the revolutionary NSU-Wankel rotary engine and also a hingeless GRP main rotor. In the event, the company determined that a larger helicopter was more commercially viable and they discontinued work on the Bö.104 in favour of the four/five seat Bö.105.

Design of the Bö.105 started in July 1962. It featured several revolutionary concepts, the most notable of which was the 'System Bölkow' hingeless rigid rotor system with its titanium head and four reinforced composite blades. The Bö.105 was also the first 4/5-seat aircraft to be designed from the outset with twin turbine engines, and the structure provided a fully usable fuselage pod with rear clamshell loading doors that allowed the loading of bulky items such as medical stretchers throughout the whole cabin length. The prototype Bö.105 was destroyed in resonance tests, and the first flying prototype took to the air in February 1967, with German certification being achieved in October 1970.

On 6 June 1968, Bölkow-Entwicklungen KG merged with Messerschmitt AG to form Messerschmitt-Bölkow GmbH. This was followed by a further merger with Hamburger Flugzeugbau in May 1969, to create Messerschmitt-Bölkow-Blohm (MBB) which became the largest German aerospace company. MBB marketed the Bö.105 widely and gained initial orders from the German Army for 279 examples and from the Luftwaffe for 20. Large numbers of aircraft went to other governmental organisations in Germany including the police forces of Bavaria, Nordrhein-Westfalen and Niedersachsen, and the Bundesgrenzschutz and ADAC-Katastrophenschutz. Exclusive sales rights were granted to Boeing-Vertol for the United States together with a production licence option although this was eventually replaced by a wholly-owned marketing company, MBB Helicopter Corporation. Ultimately, in December 1983, MBB signed an agreement with Fleet Industries in Canada for the Bö.105LS to be built in a new factory at Fort Erie. The first Canadian-built aircraft flew in 1986 and this factory became the manufacturing point for the 'LS model and a completion centre for North American Bö.105s and BK.117s.

Production licences were also entered into with PT Nurtanio in 1984 for production of the Bö.105 and for joint development of a four-seat helicopter designated NB-109. This did not, in the event, materialise, but Nurtanio built over 60 examples of the Bö.105, initially from German-supplied kits and then progressively through local fabrication. Further aircraft were built in the Philippines by PADC, and Bö.105s for the Spanish and Iraqi military forces were assembled by CASA in Spain. The Bö.105 sold strongly to civil operators and was particularly popular for police work and for medical emergency services because of its rugged construction and through-loading capability. It was also sold to the Mexican Navy and other users for anti-drug patrol.

With the Bö.105 successfully established in the market, MBB looked to a larger companion helicopter. In discussions with Kawasaki Heavy Industries in Japan it was decided jointly to develop a new 11-seat helicopter. Design and production of specific segments was shared between the two companies. Kawasaki was responsible for the fuselage, electrical systems and main transmission while MBB dealt with the main and tail rotors, flight controls, tail boom, hydraulics and systems integration.

The BK-117 development team started work in early 1977 and quickly refined the design, which had a main fuselage pod with rear-opening clamshell doors, and a pair of Lycoming LTS101 turboshafts set above the cabin and driving a four-blade main rotor. The rotor head was virtually identical to that of the Bö.105 and the tail boom was also based on the structure used in the earlier helicopter. The first prototype (D-HBKA) was flown in Germany on 13 June 1979, with Kawasaki's first aircraft following two months later. Two static test airframes were also built and German LBA certification to FAR Part 29 equivalent standard was granted on 9 December 1982. The BK-117 has been progressively developed with several increases in gross weight and changes in engine power. It has found a particular market with the emergency services for medical rescue work where its large through-cabin makes loading of stretchers particularly easy. MBB has also tried to market military versions of the BK-117 but has yet to be successful in this area.

MBB BK-117, N160BK *(MBB)*

HELICOPTERS AND ROTORCRAFT

On 1 January 1992, MBB joined with Aérospatiale to form Eurocopter. The activities of MBB, known as Eurocopter Deutschland, under this new alliance are described under the Eurocopter section.

Production details

Model	Serial Batch	Number Built	Notes
Bö.105	S.1 to S.928 up	926	Also prototypes c/n V-1 to V-7. Some c/ns (e.g. S.911 to S.914 are spare/replacement fuselage pods only).
Bö.105			Assembly by PADC: c/n S-81 & 82, c/n S-93 & 94, c/n S-99 & 100, c/n S-142 to 145, c/n S-161 to 170, c/n S-181 to 185, c/n S-226 to 230, c/n S-233 to 235.
Bö.105LS	c/n 2001 to 2016	16	Built by MBB at Donauworth (German main production line).
Bö.105LSA3	c/n 2017 to 2050	34	Built by MBB Helicopter Canada at Fort Erie, Ontario.
Bö.105M	c/n 5001 to 5075	75	Military for German Army.
Bö.105P	c/n 6001 to 6212	212	Military for German Army.
Bö.105CB	c/n N001 to N121		Nurtanio serial numbers for Indonesian production. Aircraft also allocated MBB serials in S series.
BK.117	c/n 7001 to 7521	521	Also prototypes P.1 to P.4 (inc. P.1 and P.4 ground test airframes) and pre-production c/n S-01.

MBB Bö.105C, D-HMUD *(MBB)*

Model Information

Details of all MBB helicopter models are as follows:

Type No.	Notes
Bö.102 Heli-Trainer	Single-seat light non-flying training helicopter with ground-mounted gantry, open frame fuselage and light tubular tail boom structure, semi-enclosed cockpit, skid u/c and one 40 h.p. ILO piston engine mounted behind cabin.
Bö.103A	Flying version of Bö.102 with open cockpit, experimental GRP rigid rotor system and one 82 h.p. Agusta GA.70/V piston engine. One Prot D-HECA FF 9 Sep. 1961.
Bö.104	Proposed 2-seat light helicopter with two 120 h.p. NSU-Wankel rotary engines driving a rigid three-blade rotor. Not built.
Bö.46	All-metal research helicopter with two seat cockpit incorporating glazed observer nose, skid u/c and one 800 shp Turboméca Turmo IIIB turboshaft driving Derschmidt five-blade rigid high-speed rotor system. Prot. Bö.46-V1 D-9514 (c/n V1) FF 30 Jan. 1964. Three built.
Bö.105V	4/5-seat light helicopter of all-metal monocoque construction with four-blade rigid rotor system, round-section fuselage with 4 cabin doors incorporating rear cargo door and cargo area beneath engine installation, light alloy tailboom with small fixed tailplane. 4410 lb TOGW. Powered by two Allison 250-C18 turboshafts. Prot. (c/n V-1). destroyed in ground resonance tests. First flying prot D-HECA (C/n V-2). FF 16 Feb. 1967. Third prototype flown with two 375 shp MAN Turbo 6022-701-A3 turboshafts.
Bö.105A	Production version of Bö.105V with deeper fuselage and more enclosed cabin structure, modified skids, endplate fins. 4629 lb TOGW. Powered by two 317 shp Allison 250-C18 turboshafts (MAN-Turbo 6022 turboshafts initially offered as an option but then abandoned), First a/c D-HAPE (c/n V-4) FF 1 May 1969.
Bö.105ATH	Bö.105M for Spanish army with HOT missiles.
Bö.105B	Third Prototype (c/n V-3) Powered by two MAN-Turbo 6022B turboshafts.
Bö.105C	Bö.105 powered by two 400 shp Allison 250-C20 turboshafts. 5070 lb TOGW. Includes 33 built from kits by PADC in Philippines.
Bö.105CB	Bö.105C powered by two 420 shp Allison 250-C20B turboshafts and fitted with strengthened rotor gearing.
Bö.105CBS	Bö.105CB with 10-inch fuselage stretch at rear of cabin and extra small rear side windows. Swedish Army version Hkp.9B.
Bö.105CBS-2	Bö.105CBS with improved transmission and max 5512 lb TOGW.
Bö.105C-2	Bö.105C with improved transmission and max 5512 lb TOGW.
Bö.105CB-2	Bö.105CB with improved transmission and max 5512 lb TOGW.
Bö.105CS-2	Bö.105C-2 with Bö.105S fuselage stretch etc.
Bö.105CBS Super Five	Bö. 105CBS with new main rotor blades providing greater thrust capacity and upgraded main gearbox.
Bö.105D	Bö.105CB certificated to U.K. CAA standards with minor mods. Single-pilot IFR approved.
Bö.105DB	Bö.105D powered by two 420 shp Allison 250-C20B turboshafts and fitted with strengthened rotor gearing.

Type No.	Notes
Bö.105DBS-4	Bö.105DB with Bo.105S fuselage stretch etc.
Bö.105GSH	Spanish army version with 20mm Rheinmetall cannon.
Bö.105L	Bö.105C with two 550 shp Allison 250-C28C turboshafts and reinforced transmission. Prot. D-HDMV FF March, 1979.
Bö.105LOH	Spanish Army observation version.
Bö.105LS	Bö.105L with Bo.105S fuselage stretch. Prot. D-HDNM FF 23 Oct, 1981.
Bö.105LS A-1	Bö.105LS with 4-club seating to give max 6-seat capacity, improved electrical system etc. 5291 lb TOGW.
Bö.105LS A-3	Bö.105LS with 5732 lb TOGW and minor strengthening for hot and high operations. Mostly built by MBB Helicopters Canada Ltd.
Bö.105LS B-1	Bö.105LS with Pratt & Whitney PW.205B engines. Prot. C-FMCL FF 1988.
Bö.105M	Military version of Bö.105.
Bö.105S	Generic designation for Bö.105 with 10-inch fuselage stretch at rear of cabin and extra small rear side windows. Some standard aircraft converted to 'S' configuration.
Bö.105HGH	Experimental high-speed test helicopter with Bö.105 fuselage with additional ventral body fairing, four-leg u/c, high-speed faired rotor head etc. Prot. D-HAPE (c/n V-4).
Bö.105M VBH	Bö.105M for German Army. Some modified to BSH-1 standard with G.D. Stinger air-to-air missiles for anti-helicopter support missions.
Bö.105P PAH-1	PAH-1 anti-tank helicopter for German Army. Prot. D-HAPE/9832 (c/n V-4). Many aircraft upgraded to KWS standard with Allison C20R-3 turboshafts and new rotor blades.

Bölkow Bö.106, D-HDCI *(MBB)*

Type No.	Notes
Bö.106	Bö.105 with wider main cabin module and two additional (total 7) seats. Powered by two 420 shp Allison 250-C20B turboshafts. Prot D-HDCI (c/n S.84) FF 25 Sept. 1973.
Bö.108	7-seat helicopter developed from Bö.105 with redesigned streamlined nose, enlarged tail incorporating new endplate fins, FVW bearingless hingeless rotor and two Allison 250-C20R turboshafts. 5291 lb TOGW. Prot. D-HBOX (c/n VT-001). FF 15 Oct. 1988. Second prototype has longer fuselage, wider cabin, 5513 lb TOGW and two Turboméca TM.319-1B turboshafts. Developed into EC-135.
BN.109	Projected 4-seat helicopter based on scaled-down Bö.105 developed by MBB and Nurtanio, powered by one Porsche piston engine. Not built.
BK.117	Medium transport helicopter jointly developed by MBB and Kawasaki with engine module above cabin section and rear clamshell doors allowing through cargo access to cabin. Max 11-seat capacity. Equipped with skid u/c, conventional boom & tail rotor with tailplane and large endplate fins. Powered by two 550 shp Lycoming LTS 101-650B-1 turboshafts. Prot. D-HBKA (c/n P.2). FF 13 June 1979.
BK.117 A-1	Production BK.117 with 550 shp LTS-101-650B-1 engines and 6283 lb TOGW.
BK.117 A-3	BK.117 A-1 with 7055 lb TOGW and increased useful load, new stability augmentation system and enlarged redesigned tail rotor.
BK.117 A-3M	Proposed military version of A-3 with raised skids, machine-gun turret below cockpit, external pylons for eight Euromissile HOT-2 missiles and roof-mounted targeting sight.
BK 117 A-4	BK.117 A-3 with increased fuel capacity, improved transmission and new automatic flight control system.
BK.117 B-1	BK.117 A-3 with two 592 shp LTS-101-750B-1 engine and 7055 lb TOGW. BK.117B-2 has 7,385 lb TOGW.
BK.117 C-1	BK.117 B-1 with Turboméca Arriel 1E turboshafts. First tested on F-WMBB (c/n 7007).

Bölkow Bö.108, D-HBOX *(MBB)*

McDONNELL DOUGLAS,
HUGHES AND SCHWEIZER   USA

McDonnell Douglas is now well known for its range of Hughes-designed military and executive helicopters. However, McDonnell's interest in rotary wing flight goes back to 1944 when it acquired an interest in Platt Le Page Aircraft. Platt Le Page had been working on helicopter projects under Army Air Corps funding since 1938, basing this development on the counter-rotating twin rotor concepts pioneered by Focke-Achgelis in Germany. The XR-1 which few in 1941 had the layout of a conventional fixed wing aircraft with three blade rotors at each wingtip. As it turned out, this design exhibited insoluble control and vibration characteristics and was abandoned in 1946. McDonnell continued its interest in the dual rotor layout with its own XHJD-1 design for the U.S. Navy, but this proved to be less advanced than other competing designs and was eventually discontinued.

Other helicopter concepts were explored by the company in the 1940s. Personal helicopters for battlefield surveilance enjoyed a period of favour and McDonnell devised the XH-20 'Little Henry' which was a simple frame helicopter with a triangulated overhead structure mounting a two-blade tip-jet driven rotor. This was followed by the Model 79 'Big Henry' which was a larger machine, but both designs suffered from excessive fuel consumption and a high noise level which resulted in their failing to reach production.

In 1951, McDonnell embarked on a new project for the U.S. Army – the XV-1. This was an ambitious convertiplane design aimed at combining the forward speed and stability of a fixed wing aircraft with the vertical takeoff advantages of the helicopter. The all-metal XV-1 had a four-seat cabin, slightly swept wings, twin tailbooms and a central pylon carrying the Continental piston engine with an advanced three-blade rotor driven by compressed air ducted to the tips. The engine also drove a pusher propeller mounted at the rear of the fuselage pod. Much testing took place and many lessons were learned, but the XV-1 was not found to offer much benefit over less complex helicopters and it was abandoned in 1957. McDonnell also tried to use the ducted rotor concept on the small Model 120 crane helicopter but this was also terminated due to a lack of interest from potential military or civil users.

Whilst these experiments were discouraging, McDonnell Douglas (as it had become following the merger of the two companies on 28 April 1967) had a strongly established belief in helicopters. In 1984, therefore, it decided to acquire Hughes Helicopters Inc. and this formed the basis of a new Helicopter Division which became McDonnell Douglas Helicopters in January 1986.

The famous Howard Hughes had become involved in helicopter development when his

Hughes Tool Co. acquired the experimental XH-17 flying crane project from Kellett. Hughes' team at Culver City, California set up a helicopter department with a nucleus of Kellett engineers and completed the proof of concept airframe in late 1949. The helicopter stood thirty feet off the ground on four massive legs which would straddle the underslung load. It was fitted with a Waco CG-15 glider cockpit section, twin General Electric turbines and an enormous two-blade rotor with pressure jet tip propulsion. The XH-17 flew in October 1952, but was eventually allowed to lapse – largely because of its very high fuel consumption. Ten years later, Hughes undertook a further U.S. Army funded investigation into pressure-jet powered rotors, and built the Model 385 (XV-9) experimental helicopter. This machine, which first flew on 5 November 1964, used the nose of a Hughes 369, an H-34 undercarriage and various other components from other aircraft. It was powered by two General Electric YT64 gas generators fitted on pods, which produced hot exhaust gas that was piped to multi-vane efflux units at the tips of the three rotor blades.

During 1955, the Hughes interest in helicopters resulted in the purchase of rights to the McCulloch MC-4 light tandem rotor machine. This did not go into production but Hughes used the simplified rotor design pioneered by the MC-4's designer, D.K. Jovanovich, on a new light two-seat helicopter – the Model 269. As originally conceived, the 269 was built around a rectangular firewall bulkhead with a bubble canopy and cockpit floor attached to the front, the 180 horsepower Lycoming fitted to the back, and a triangulated tubular strut tail unit carrying a small stabilising rotor; a skid undercarriage hung below the structure.

The 269 prototype flew in October 1956, but the production Model 269A embodied numerous changes. In particular, the tail assembly was changed to a single tube boom with strut bracing, the cockpit was deeper and more streamlined and a small tailplane was added on the starboard side of the boom. Hughes quickly interested the U.S. Army in the 269A and built a test batch of five YHO-2 observation helicopters which were well received by the military evaluators. However, it was four years before an Army production order was placed – and then it was for the TH-55A Osage dual control version, which became the standard basic training helicopter with almost 800 examples being delivered.

In the meantime, the Hughes 269A was achieving success in the civil market with optional carburetted or fuel injected versions of the Lycoming HO-360 engine and with single or

Hughes 369D, N501G

dual controls. It was succeeded by the Model 300 (269B) which could seat three, and had a small increase in power. A number of Model 300s were constructed by BredaNardi in Italy (as described in the Agusta section). Eventually, in November 1983, Hughes subcontracted all production of the Model 300 to Schweizer Aircraft of Elmira in up-state New York, and Schweizer purchased all rights to the 269 series in November 1986. The Model 269 in its many variants has been exported widely to countries as far apart as New Zealand, Norway, Liberia, Hungary, Japan and Argentina.

Under Schweizer, the 269 has sustained steady sales – particularly for agricultural operations and law enforcement. Several specialised variants have been produced by Schweizer including the Sky Knight for police duties and the TH.300C dual control version sold to Turkey and other overseas military users. Schweizer also used the 269 airframe as the basis for its contender in the 1990 Army competition for a TH-55 replacement. The Schweizer 330 has an enlarged cabin, seating four, and a fully-clad fuselage and faired-in tailboom with a larger tail unit. The main change, however, is the move to a 200 shp Allison 250 turboshaft engine. As it turned out, Schweizer did not win the U.S. Army competition, but the '330 is in production for civil customers and is built at Elmira next to several versions of the Model 300.

The light observation Helicopter (LOH) competition announced by the U.S. Army in 1960 resulted in final proposals from Bell and Fairchild Hiller, with Hughes being included in the short list at the last moment. The Hughes proposal was for a compact helicopter with what is best described as an egg-shaped fuselage with a tapered tailboom and four-blade semi-rigid rotor. Designed by Mal Harned (who later conceived the Gates Twin-Jet Helicopter) the Model 369 (YOH-6A) was powered by an Allison 250 turboshaft, and five prototypes were built and evaluated at Fort Rucker in 1965. The YOH-6A was smaller than its competitors but its performance, ease of maintenance and the ruggedness of its construction resulted in Hughes being awarded the production contract – much to the annoyance of Fairchild Hiller. Above all, it had a very competitive price and it was evident when the OH-6A went into production that Hughes would earn little or no profit on the contract.

The definitive OH-6A embodied a number of changes over the prototypes, notably the replacement of the tapered monocoque tailboom with a slimmer unit mounting a three-finned tail. The U.S. Army ordered 714 OH-6A 'Cayuses' (subsequently increased to

McDonnell Douglas MD.600N, N92007

1420) which were delivered between 1966 and 1970. This was in time for the Cayuse to be deployed to Vietnam where it was used widely for armed support of the larger UH-1 transports, and for observation and artillery marking. The OH-6A was fitted with external weapons, most commonly including a 7.62mm XM-27E gun pod mounted under the left-hand cabin door.

While the Cayuse was progressing through its military evaluation, Hughes was also working on the civil Model 500, which was announced in the spring of 1965. Four prototypes were built and the Model 500 (or 369A to quote its official factory and certificated number) received its type certificate on 24 August 1966. The civil model sold well, even though it had a somewhat smaller cabin than the competing Bell Jet Ranger. Its strengths were in having a higher maximum speed and greater range than the Bell aircraft.

The Model 500 was progressively improved with increasingly powerful variants of the Allison 250 turboshaft engine. The 500D, introduced in 1976, had a modified T-tail, and the 500E was distinguished by a reshaped fuselage pod with a slightly pointed nose. The '500 was also built under licence in Italy by BredaNardi who delivered a substantial number to the Italian para-military Guardia di Finanza and a couple to the Maltese Armed Forces. Military versions of all the later models were offered – particularly the 500MD Defender which was an unarmed scout or general purpose machine for export sale. Its offensive version, the Scout Defender, had armour plating and multiple external weapons hardpoints. Defenders have been delivered to a number of countries including the Philippines, Colombia and Mexico.

In the mid-1980s, McDonnell Douglas sought ways of replacing the traditional tail rotor with a more efficient and less vulnerable anti-torque system. This resulted in the NOTAR ('no tail rotor') which involved replacing the existing tailboom with a larger constant-section tail section into which is ducted pressurised air which is then ejected sideways from the end of the boom to counteract the turning effect of the main rotor. This system reduces the danger of the tail rotor striking a ground object on takeoff or landing and is expected to be used on all future McDonnell Douglas civil helicopters. The prototype MD.530N (N530NT) was first flown in December 1989. This was, essentially, a Model 530K with the NOTAR boom. As the Model 520N (the 369 designations were dropped at this point) it went into production and was subsequently joined by the Model 600N,

McDonnell Douglas MD.900, N9016W

which has an enlarged fuselage with three rows of seats, and was certificated in the summer of 1997.

During 1972, Hughes had become involved in a Request for Proposals (RFP) for the U.S. Army for an advanced attack helicopter. The new helicopter was to be a two-seater armed with a 30-mm cannon and anti-tank missiles, with easy maintainability in the field and maximum battle damage resistance. The Hughes Model 77 emerged as one of two finalists and two flying prototypes were built. The YAH-64A had a tandem cockpit with flat-plate glass, a slim fuselage, prominent fin and tailplane (mounted on the fin tip initially but subsequently lowered to boom level) and stub wings to carry the required ordnance.

The fly-off took place in 1976 and the YAH-64A emerged the winner over Bell's YAH-63A. Production commenced at San Diego and Mesa, Arizona in 1983, and at the time of takeover by McDonnell Douglas in the following year a steady stream of Apaches was reaching the Army to fulfil a production order that eventually totalled 937 aircraft. The company is currently developing the AH-64D Longbow Apache which introduces a mast-mounted Westinghouse Longbow radar, increased power and more sophisticated avionics. McDonnell Douglas will remanufacture 232 of the U.S. Army's AH-64As to this configuration.

The most recent introduction by McDonnell Douglas is the MD-900 Explorer. It was clear that, although the Model 500 continued to gain orders its cabin volume was sometimes considered too small, which made it compare unfavourably with the Bell 430 or the Ecureuil. McDonnell Douglas applied its NOTAR system to a more capacious helicopter with a six-seat main cabin and two-crew forward compartment. The MDX – later designated MD-900 Explorer – is produced through a complex system of profit sharing subcontractors, and the first prototype was flown in December 1992. The first MD-900s were delivered to customers in the summer of 1995. With the acquisition of McDonnell Douglas by Boeing, all current models are now marketed under the Boeing name.

Production Details

The early Hughes system of allocating construction numbers was complicated because it incorporated an initial sequence of two or three numbers indicating the month and year built – followed by a sequential serial number. The first production aircraft was 29001,

McDonnell Douglas AH-56A Apache

indicating that it was built in February 1959, with a serial number 001. The last unit to use this system was a Model 269C, c/n 811074 – which was built in August 1971, with a serial number 1074. Each new model started a new serial sequence from c/n 0001. It was also intended that the Hughes 369 from c/n 1079 would use an alphanumeric system with one of 16 suffix letters after each serial number. Thus, the serial sequence would be c/n 1079A, 1079B, 1079C etc. to c/n 1079Y and then c/n 1080A to 1080Y. There is no evidence that this system was actually adopted. McDonnell Douglas altered the system to eliminate the date prefix and to add a letter to indicate the model (e.g. Model 369D c/n 1205D). The more recent McDonnell Douglas types have adopted a two-letter prefix to the individual serial number although the Model 900 merely has its type number in front of the serial (e.g. 900-00026). Schweizer continued the existing sequence of serial numbers for the Model 269 when it took over full responsibility for the type, but added an 'S' prefix. The serial batches issued are as follows:

Model	Serial Batch	Number Built	Notes
269A	c/n 0001 to 0314 (shown with date prefix as c/n 29-0001 to 123-0314)	314	First two or three numbers indicate month & year built.
269A	c/n 0315 to 1109	795	With date prefix. TH-55 Osage.
269A-1	c/n 0001 to 0040	40	With date prefix.
269B	c/n 0001 to 0461	461	With date prefix.
269C	c/n 0001 to 1074	74	With date prefix.
269C	c/n 1075 to 1165	91	No date prefix.
269C	c/n S1166 to S1727	562	Schweizer production.
269C-1	c/n 0001 to 0038+	38	No date prefix.
269D	c/n 0001 to 0057+	57	No date prefix.
369A, 369H	c/n 0001 to 1435	1435	With date prefix.
369 (OH-6)	c/n 0001 to 1445	1445	

Hughes 269C, G-BAUK

Model	Serial Batch	Number Built	Notes
KH369HS	c/n 6601 to 6649	49	Kawasaki production.
KH369D	c/n 6701 to 6708	8	Kawasaki production.
369HE	c/n 0101E to 0215E	115	With date prefix.
369HS	c/n 0001S to 0873S	873	With date prefix.
369HM	c/n 0001M up		
369D	c/n 0001D to 1099D	99	With date prefix except c/n 1068, 1087 and 1095.
369D	c/n 1100D to 1226D	126	No date prefix.
369E	c/n 0001E to 0536E	529	No date prefix. McDD production from c/n 0190.
369F & FF	c/n 0003F to 0123F	121	No date prefix. McDD production from c/n 0052 (369FF).
520N	c/n LN001 to LN081+	81	
600N	c/n RN001 to RN033+	33	
MD-900	c/n 900-00001 to 00129+	129	
AH.64A	c/n PV.01 to PV.815	815	

Model List

The designations allocated to the Hughes designs are confusing and in some cases there is inconsistency in the way in which they have been allocated. The certificated design numbers for the two models are 269 and 369 with appropriate suffixes to identify changes to the basic type. However, all the models have also been given marketing designations. Thus, the Model 269B was marketed as the Hughes 300. The 369 was marketed with designations in the 500 series (e.g. 500D, 530F, 500M etc.). More recently, the '369' type number has been dropped and new variants are certificated under their marketing designations (e.g. the Model 600N). The following table attempts to detail all designations which have been used:

Type No.	Marketing Designation	Notes
269	269	Hughes-designed side-by-side 2-seat light helicopter with framed bubble fuselage pod, braced tubular rear boom structure with small tailplane, skid u/c, 3-blade rotor and 180 h.p. Lyc. O-360-C2B piston engine mounted uncowled behind pod. Prot. N80P (c/n 001 – later 990001) FF 2 Oct. 1956. 3 built.
269A	269	Production 269 with single tube tailboom, starboard-mounted tailplane, twin fuel tanks and 160 h.p. Lyc. O-360-C2D or 180 h.p. O-360-B1A engine. 1550 lb TOGW but inc. to 1670 lb from c/n 0315. Military YHO-2 and later TH-55A. 35 built as TH-55J by Kawasaki for JGSDF.
269A-1	269	269A with 180 h.p. HIO-360-B1A engine, 1670 lb TOGW and 30-gal fuel capacity.
269B	300	269A with three seats and 180 h.p. HIO-360-A1A engine.
269C	300C Sky Knight	269B with 190 h.p. HIO-360-D1A engine and 2050 lb TOGW. Built by Hughes and Schweizer.
269C	TH-300C	2-seat dual control military training version of 300C.

Type No.	Marketing Designation	Notes
269C-1	300CB	Schweizer built 2-seat dual-control trainer with reduced 1750 lb TOGW, 180 hp Lyc. GHO-360-C1A , increased fuel, no fuel pump and smaller tail fin.
269D	330 Sky Knight	Schweizer-built 3/4 seat light helicopter derived from 300 with 15-inch wider cabin, faired in tail section, tail fin and tailplane with finlets, pointed nose, 2200 lb TOGW and 420 shp Allison 250-C20W turboshaft engine. Prot. N330TT FF 1988. Contender in U.S. Army NTH competition.
269D	330SP	Model 330 with increased-area rotor blades, larger rotor hub, increased TOGW, increased range and max speed.
NH-300C	NH-300C	Model 300C built by BredaNardi.
369	YOH-6A	Four-seat light observation helicopter with, 4-blade rotor, egg-shaped fuselage pod, fixed skid u/c and tapered tailboom with two tail surfaces. Powered by one 282 shp Allison T63A-5A turboshaft. Named 'Cayuse'. Prot. 62-4212 FF 27 Feb. 1963.
369A	500	Five-seat civil version of OH-6A with increased fuel and 4-blade rotor powered by one 317 shp Allison 250-C18A turboshaft. Prot N9000F FF 13 Sept. 1966. Also built under licence by BredaNardi, RACA and Kawasaki.
369A	500U	Utility version of Model 500.
369H	OH-6A Cayuse	Production version of 369 for U.S. Army with 317 shp Allison 250 T63-A-5A turbine, slimmer tailboom, three tail surfaces, strengthened u/c.
369H	OH-6B Cayuse	250 examples of OH-6A modified with 420 shp Allison 250 T63-A-720, infrared engine suppression, FLIR sensor and upgraded avionics for ANG use.
369H	EH-6B	Four electronic surveillance versions converted from OH-6A with 400 shp Allison 250-C20 engine.
369H	MH-6B	23 Special forces attack conversions of OH-6A with Allison 250-C20 engine, external weapons mountings for two

Platt LePage XR-1, 42-6581 *(HGM Collection)*

| | | 7.62mm miniguns, FLIR sensor etc. |
| 369H | AH-6C | 15 conversions of OH-6A similar to MH-6B with additional external capacity for rockets or anti-tank missiles. |

Type No.	Marketing Designation	Notes
369HE	500	Production version of 369H with Allison 250-C20 engine.
369HS	500C	369HE with 400 shp Allison 250-C20B to provide improved hot & high performance.
369D	500D	500C with 420 shp Allison 250-C20B engine and five-blade rotor with domed rotor fairing, T-tail with small endplates and 4-blade tail rotor. Also built by BredaNardi, RACA , Korean Air and Kawasaki.
369D	OH-6D	Model 500D built by Kawasaki for Japanese military use.
369D	EH-6E	Three Model 500D for US Army electronic special missions aircraft with IR suppression and advanced avionics.
369E	500E	500D with more pointed nose, 3000 lb TOGW and larger tail fins. Prot.FF 28 Jan. 1982. Also built by BredaNardi and Korean Air.
369F	530F	500E for hot & high operations with 650 shp Allison 250-C30 turboshaft, larger diameter main rotor and 3750 lb TOGW. Prot. FF 22 Oct. 1982.
369F	AH-6G	AH-6F with 650 shp Allison 250-C30 engine.
369FF	530F	530F with upgraded drive system.
NH-500M		Nardi-built military version primarily for use of Guardia di Finanza.
369M		Alternative designation for OH-6A and all military versions of Model 369.
369HM	500M	Export military version of OH-6A.
369MD	500MD Scout	Export military 500D with armour-plating in cockpit area, infra-red suppression equipment, improved cockpit, extra ventral fin, 420 shp Allison 250-C20B turboshaft, mission equipment control system, modular quick-change external weapons points and optional mast-mounted target-acquisition sight module. Also Nardi-built NH-500MD.
369MD	500MD Defender	500D for export military users for general liaison and training.
369MD	MH-6E	500MD for US Special Forces. Some upgraded to MH-6H with new engine.
369MD	AH-6F	MH-6E with additional external hardpoints for Stinger air-to-air missiles, TOW missiles or Hughes Chain Gang cannon and mast-mounted sight.
500N	OH-6 NOTAR	OH-6 with enlarged tailboom containing NOTAR ducted thrust tail control system and braced V-tail surfaces. Prot. 12917 FF 17 Dec. 1981.
500N	520N	Production 500N with tailplane and twin fins. Prot. N520NT FF 1 May 1990.
	520K	500 with longer main rotor and larger 4-blade tail rotor, lengthened tailboom, increased lifting capacity and Allison 250-C30 turboshaft.
	520L	MD.500E with larger diameter rotor and extended tailboom, powered by one Allison 250-C20R.

	530N	520N with 650 shp Allison 250-C30 turboshaft. Prot. N530NT FF 29 Dec. 1989.
Type No.	**Marketing Designation**	**Notes**
369FF	530MG Defender	500MD with 650 shp Allison 250-C30 turboshaft and pointed nose contour.
600N	600N	520N with 30-inch stretched 7/8 seat fuselage with three seat rows, left-hand pilot position, FADEC fuel control, six doors, extra side windows, longer tailboom, enlarged tailfins, NOTAR, powered by one 808 shp Allison 250-C47M turboshaft driving six-blade main rotor. Prot. N630N FF 22 Nov. 1994.
	630N	Initial designation for 600N.
MD-900	Explorer	Eight-seat executive helicopter with six-place club-seated cabin, streamlined fuselage with NOTAR boom, five-blade main rotor driven by two 629 shp. Pratt & Whitney PW206B turboshafts, fixed skid u/c and tailplane with twin fins. Prot. N900MD FF 18 Dec. 1992.
MD-902	Explorer	MD-900 with improved Pratt & Whitney PW206E engines, improved air inlets, modified NOTAR inlet design and altered stabiliser control system. Prot. N9224U FF 5 Sept. 1997.
H-77	AH-64A Apache	Tandem two-seat attack helicopter with fixed tailwheel u/c, slim tailboom with vertical fin mounting four-blade tailrotor and two 1696 shp. GE T700-GE-701 turbines fitted in external pods and driving four-blade main rotor. Prot. 73-22247 (c/n AV.1) FF 30 Sept. 1975.
AH-64D	Longbow	AH-64A equipped with Longbow multi-targeting radar/missile system with radar unit in mast mounted pod, enlarged fuselage side fairings and 1800 shp GE T700-GE-701C engines. Prot. 90-0324 FF 15 April 1992.

Schweizer 330PD, N357PD *(Schweizer)*

MIL

SOVIET UNION

For many years, the Mil OKB had virtually exclusive control of Soviet helicopter development. Dr Mikhail Leontyevitch Mil was a pre-war protege of Nikolai Kamov. He headed the experimental helicopter section of the TsAGI (Central Soviet Institute for Aviation Hydrodynamics) during World War II, and subsequently set up his own design bureau to develop helicopters following his experience with Kamov's pre-war autogyros. It should be explained that, under the Soviet system, the design bureau (OKB) was responsible for design and development of new aircraft types to specifications raised by military planners or by Aeroflot within Kremlin economic plans. Once a design reached production stage it was passed on to separately controlled production factories to be built to quantity targets established centrally. Therefore, Mil must be regarded in a somewhat different light from the integrated designing and building organisations of western manufacturers.

The first design from the Mil OKB, the four-seat GM-1, was extraordinarily advanced for its day, with a pod and boom fuselage and all-metal monocoque construction that would not seem out of place in the 1990s. Despite the destruction of the first two GM-1s during flight testing, the design was refined into the production Mi-1 and put into large scale production for the Soviet armed forces. Between 1950 and 1965 several thousand Mi-1s were built in Soviet factories and at PZL-Swidnik in Poland – which took over production responsibility in 1955. Mi-1s served in the USSR until the mid-1980s. The design was subsequently enlarged and developed into the turbine powered Mi-2 and built at PZL-Swidnik with over 2000 examples being exported back from Poland to the Soviet Union.

Mil's second design was the Mi-4, which was required by the Soviet Army as a 14-troop general purpose helicopter to give greater capacity than was available with the Mi-1. The Mi-4, which resulted from a planning directive issued in 1951, first appeared in late 1952, and was externally very similar to an enlarged Sikorsky S-55 with the same arrangement of a nose-mounted piston engine in an angled installation with an articulated drive to a four-blade rotor. As with the S-55, the crew compartment was above the engine and the main passenger compartment below and behind the nose section. Small vehicles and military equipment could be loaded through rear clamshell doors. Over 3000 military and civil Mi-4s were built, with many exported to Warsaw Pact countries and a large batch of licence-built Z-5s being produced in China between 1959 and 1965.

The Mi-4P was used for passenger routes, entering service with Aeroflot in 1958 and operating as a passenger transport, fire fighting helicopter and general utility machine in the remotest parts of the Soviet Union. Aeroflot's passenger services operated between central Moscow and the airports at Vnukovo and Sheremetyevo, and Royal Nepal Airlines also used a pair of Mi-4s. A few Mi-4s were fitted with spray bars for agricultural operations.

Most Aeroflot machines had square windows rather than the portholes of the military variants, and were sometimes fitted with spats on all four wheels. Export Mi-4s went to over 30 countries including Cuba, Indonesia, Yemen, India and Algeria.

In many ways, the Soviet Union saw more potential for the helicopter during the 1950s than was accepted in the West. This led to the development of ever larger machines such as the Mi-6 which first flew in 1957. This huge helicopter was capable of carrying up to 90 troops, and used a pair of Soloviev D-25V turbines to drive a mighty five-bladed main rotor. The Mi-6 was not only used for military transport but also by Aeroflot for cargo carrying, fire fighting, aeromedical work and passenger transport – particularly in Siberia. Some 800 examples were built between 1959 and 1980 but most were out of service by the early 1990s. It became recognised that the Mi-6 had a poor payload in relation to its empty weight and it was eventually replaced by the Mi-26.

The Mi-6 was also important because it led to the Mi-10 crane helicopter. This machine had what is best described as a flattened Mi-6 fuselage with the same engines, rotor blades, tail and transmission system. It stood high off the ground on four multi-strutted legs that allowed the Mi-10 to straddle loads, which were then winched up to lie under the fuselage. The winching system incorporated an unusual arrangement of lifting arms that caught the four corners of the load in order to raise them upwards. The Mi-10K variant had a much shorter undercarriage and a second crew station which faced backwards and allowed precision control by the second pilot for crane operations.

Mikhail Mil died in 1970 and the OKB continued under his name, headed by Mirat Tsichenko, developing further revolutionary aircraft including their largest machine – the extraordinary V-12. The V-12 had a fuselage and tail unit more akin to a fixed wing transport and was lifted by two Mi-6 rotors mounted at the ends of outrigger wings. A pair of D-25VF turbines was fitted at the tip of each wing to power the rotors. With the crew perched in a cockpit above the nose the V-12 had an unobstructed cabin capable of carrying 120 passengers. Unfortunately, testing of the V-12 started with a disastrous heavy landing and the Mil team experienced major stability difficulties with the two remaining prototypes. The performance of the V-12 never matched that of Mil's other large transport helicopters and it was eventually abandoned.

In the early 1960s a replacement was sought for the Mi-4, and Mil OKB used many of its systems and main rotor in the design of the V-8 which became possibly its most successful helicopter. The Mi-8 had a larger, almost circular-section, fuselage with a flight deck in the extreme nose, and two Isotov TV2 turboshafts mounted on top of the fuselage so as to give a fully usable interior space. Initial versions of the Mi-8 were for civil transportation and had large rectangular cabin windows. For military troop carrying the Mi-8 had

Mil Mi-1, CCCP-17411 *(DR)*

porthole windows and rear clamshell doors to allow easy loading of equipment. Later, the Mi-8 was given offensive armament on large strut-braced external mountings. Equipment on these armed versions included six Sagger anti-tank missiles or four 16-tube rocket launching pods, and nose-mounted machine-guns or cannon. A naval derivative, the Mi-14, had a boat type hull for water landings and was fitted with ASW equipment, or with the necessary winches and other equipment for a search-and-rescue role. It is thought that the factories at Kazan and Ulan Ude together produced more than 15000 of the Mi-8 and its Mi-17 derivative which is aimed at export customers.

The Mi-8 also spawned the Mi-24 gunship helicopter which gained notoriety for its operations in Afghanistan. Widely exported to the Warsaw Pact countries, the Mi-24 uses the TV3 engines, transmission and rotor of the Mi-17 on a new fuselage, with stub wings carrying rockets and other offensive armament. As a gunship it was unusual in having a separate cabin capable of carrying eight troops. In the early Mi-24A the pilot sat behind the armament operator and had relatively poor forward vision but the later Mi-24D provided a raised rear seating position for the pilot and a bubble nose for the weapons position. Several variants of the Mi-24 were built by the Rostvertol factory with varying armament specifications.

Mil subsequently extended the gunship concept for the Mi-28, using Mi-24 dynamic systems attached to a new slim fuselage, and the first of these prototypes was flown in November 1982. Compared with its Western equivalent, the AH-64A Apache, the Mi-28 is considerably heavier with a more powerful engine and more than double the ordnance capacity. The Mi-28, which has an unusual scissor-type tail rotor and a high degree of armour and battle damage resistance, has undergone protracted development. It is under consideration for the Swedish Army, but it has been announced that the Ka-50 rather than the Mi-28 will be the new attack helicopter for the Russian army. The Mi-28 is built at the Rostvertol factory at Rostov-on-Don.

Mil's replacement for the heavy transport Mi-6 was the Mi-26 – a large but agile and elegant machine capable of a wide range of roles from passenger and freight transport to flying crane work. Two new Lotaryev D-136 free turbine engines were used and, in the design style which had become generally accepted, these sat on top of the fuselage and powered an eight-bladed rotor. Unlike the Mi-6, the Mi-26 was not fitted with an auxiliary wing but achieved better overall performance and a much improved load-carrying capability than those of its predecessor. Production commenced in 1980 and it is thought that approximately 550 examples have been completed. A batch of 20 was delivered to the Indian Air Force, and more than a dozen Mi-26s of the Ukraine Air Force and other operators have been active in Bosnia, wearing United Nations colours.

With changing times in the Soviet Union, Mil directed its attentions to more commercial projects and the two factories (Ulan Ude and Kazan) which had responsibility for production of the helicopters increasingly assumed a commercial independence and developed their own products. Mil has particularly focused on the light civil market and has designed a piston-engined four-seat helicopter – the Mi-34. With a layout similar to Aérospatiale's Ecureuil but a smaller cabin, this helicopter is aimed at Western customers and was designed from the outset to use a Textron-Lycoming TIO-540 piston engine, although

Mil Mi-10K, CCCP-04102

Mil Mi-14

aircraft for domestic use would be fitted with twin VAZ-430 rotary engines. Mil now considers that the most potential lies in the Mi-34A which has been upgraded to turbine power with an Allison 250 engine. This is now being promoted by a new entity – MI Light Helicopters.

The Mil OKB is also working on a range of other new designs, including the Mi-38 (an EH-101 sized machine) the prototypes of which are now being constructed at Kazan with cooperation from Eurocopter, the Mi-40 enlarged development of the Mi-28 and the very light three-seat Mi-52. Kazan Helicopters is also building the prototype ANSAT light utility helicopter and has completed one ground test example. All these projects are, however, dependent on market openings, but scarce funding is the source of chronic stagnation in the Russian aerospace industry.

Production Details

Serial numbers for Mil helicopters are issued by the factory assigned to produce the particular model. They follow the 'modular batch' system used by Soviet industry but the breakdown of the system varies greatly for different helicopter types. It even changes within the production history of an individual model. No information is available for the Mi-1 and Mi-4 and details of the Mi-2 are contained in the section on PZL-Swidnik. The serials for military models Mi-12, Mi-14 and Mi-24 are also unavailable. Some information on the other types is incomplete (and sometimes conflcting) with some serial batches following no clear system, but the serial numbers are best described as follows:

Model	C/n example	Serial – Part 1	Serial – Part 2	Notes
Mi-2				See PZL-Swidnik
Mi-6	7683507	Yr.built (1 or 2 digits) – e.g. 5=1965, 10=1960 plus Factory Code 68.	Batch No. (2 digits from 00 to 43) and serial no. (2 digits from 01 to 10).	Used from 1959 to 1969. Part 1 not used on civil aircraft.
Mi-6	715503	Yr.built (2 digits) – e.g. 71=1971.	Batch No. (2 digits from 48 to 73) and serial no. (2 digits from 01 to 10).	Used from 1970 to 1974. Part 1 not used on civil aircraft.
Mi-6	0453		Batch No. (2 digits from 01 to 21) and serial no. (2 digits).	From 1974. Serial system not fully understood.
Mi-8	1532		Batch No. (2 digits from 01 to 87) and serial no. (2 digits from 01 to 99).	Kazan (GAZ-9) built 1967 to 1980. Batch sizes variable.
Mi-8	9732809	Factory No. 9 plus year built (e.g.73 = 1973).	Batch No. (2 digits from 03 to 93) and serial no. (2 digits from 01 to 99).	Ulan Ude (GAZ-99) built 1070-1981. Serials integrated with Kazan production.
Mi-8PPA Mi-9	7612		Batch No. (2 digits from 75 to 88) and serial no. (2 digits from 01 up).	Ulan Ude-built. Batch sizes variable.
Mi-8MT Mi-8MTV	94448		System unknown. Serial range 93343 to 96876.	Kazan-built from 1981.
Mi-10	2266		4-digit serial between 2161 and 2299.	
Mi-26	34001212475	All aircraft are prefixed with 340012	5-digit serial in range 12084 to 12504 and 26208 up (Mi-26TC).	

In addition, many Mil helicopters have export serial numbers, normally with five or six digits or letters, arranged in batches, but the system is not currently understood.

Model Information

Details of all Mil models are given in the following table. Initial design designations were normally given a 'V' prefix (e.g. V-8) and these were changed to the 'Mi-' prefix once the type moved into production at the assigned manufacturing plant.

Type No.	NATO Codename	Notes
Mi-1	Hare	Four-seat light military and civil helicopter of pod & boom layout with fixed tricycle u/c with one AI-26V piston engine driving three-blade main rotor and tail rotor. Prot. FF Sept. 1948.
Mi-1T	Hare	Mi-1 with improved radio, fluid de-icing and three seats.
Mi-1U	Hare	Dual-control trainer version of Mi-1T.
SM-1	Hoplite	Mi-1 built by PZL-Swidnik.
Mi-2	Hare	Extensively redesigned Mi-1 with twin Isotov GTD-350 turboshafts fitted above fuselage pod and lengthened main cabin to accommodate six pax. plus two crew. Built by PZL.
Mi-4	Hound	12-passenger military & civil transport helicopter with nose-mounted ASh-82V piston engine driving 4-blade main rotor, 2-crew cabin above main passenger compartment, monocoque tailboom with fin mounting 3-blade tail rotor, 4-leg main u/c. Prot. FF May 1952. Approx. 3200 of all variants built.
Mi-4A	Hound	Military assault version with fixed armament.
Mi-4KP	Hound	Military airborne command post.
Mi-4L	Hound	6-passenger version with VIP deluxe cabin.
Mi-4M	Hound	Attack version with gun turret under nose, external rocket packs and electronic jamming equipment.
Mi-4P	Hound	Civil version for Aeroflot with square cabin windows, wheel spats and 10-passenger cabin with toilet and baggage section.

Mil Mi-26T, RA-29109

Type No.	NATO Codename	Notes
Mi-4PLO	Hound-B	Naval anti-submarine version with ventral observer station, chin-mounted radar, dipping sonar, external ASW bombs and sonobuoys and MAD.
Mi-4PS	Hound	VIP 'Salon' model with 4 passenger seats.
Mi-4Skh	Hound	High-altitude version also used for agricultural operations with external spraybars or under-fuselage duster hopper or for fire fighting with underslung fire suppression module.
Mi-4T	Hound	Military transport version with under-fuselage observation position, cargo floor and window-mounted gun positions.
Harbin Z-5		Chinese licence-built version of Mi-4 powered by one HS7 piston engine. Production included 86 passenger version, 7 agricultural, 13 rescue and 2 aerial survey. Prot. FF 14 Dec. 1958. 545 built.
Harbin Z-6		Harbin Z-5 with stretched forward cabin section, cockpit repositioned in nose and powered by one WZ5 turboshaft engine mounted on top of fuselage. 11 built.
Mi-6	Hook	Heavy transport helicopter with streamlined 90-seat fuselage incorporating rear clamshell doors and conventional tailboom and fin, small shoulder-mounted wings, fixed tricycle u/c, glazed nose with aimer's panel, provision for externally-mounted fuel tanks and powered by two 5500 shp Soloviev D.25V turbines mounted on top of fuselage driving five-blade main rotor. Prot. FF Sept. 1957. Approx. 800 built.
Mi-6A	Hook	Civil version for Aeroflot with up to 65 seats or equipped for cargo operations.
Mi-6P	Hook	Fire suppression model without wings and fitted with underslung water dispenser or cabin tanks with external nozzles.
Mi-6R	Hook	Military command post with extensive communications electronics.

Mil Mi-28

Type No.	NATO Codename	Notes
Mi-6S	Hook	Ambulance version with 40-stretcher capacity.
Mi-6T	Hook	Military assault transport with nose-mounted machine-gun.
V-7		Experimental 4-seat light helicopter with egg-shaped fuselage, skid u/c, thin triangulated tail boom structure, powered by two AI-7 tip-mounted ramjets. One Prot. FF 1959.
V-8 Mi-8	Hip	Medium tactical assault helicopter with round-section fuselage with square windows and incorporating 2-seat cockpit in nose, Mi-4 tailboom with port-side mounted 3-blade tail rotor, Mi-4 main rotor and transmission, fixed tricycle u/c and one 2700 shp Soloviev AI-24V turbine mounted on top of fuselage. Subsequently fitted with 5-blade rotor and two 1400 shp Isotov TV2-117 engines. Prot. FF 1961. Approx. 9000 built.
Mi-8P	Hip-C	Production civil V-8 with 28 passenger seats, wheel spats, improved soundproofing, square cabin windows and cargo floor.
Mi-8PS		Civil VIP 'Salon' model with 7, 9 or 11-seat interior.
Mi-8PP	Hip-K	Special missions military model with porthole windows, communication interception and jamming equipment and numerous external antennae including 24 four-blade aerials.
Mi-8S	Hip-C	Mi-8P with VIP 11-passenger interior. Also known as Mi-8PS.
Mi-8SMV	Hip-J	Military border surveillance model with external sensors.
Mi-8T	Hip-C	Standard 24-seat military and civil utility transport with round porthole windows, cargo floor, integral winch, optional external fuel tanks, provision for external rocket pods or guns.

Mil Mi-2, SP-WXS

Type No.	NATO Codename	Notes
Mi-8TB	Hip-E	Armed version of Mi-8T with nose-mounted gun, external strut-braced pylon outboard of main u/c for anti-tank missiles and rocket pods (up to 192 rockets) etc.
Mi-8TB	Hip-F	Export version of Mi-8TB with AT-3 Sagger missiles.
Mi-8TBK	Hip	Mi-8T with minor changes to external armament fit.
Mi-8TG	Hip	Mi-8T fitted with TV2-117TG multi-fuel engines (for kerosene, LPG etc.) with external LPG tanks.
Mi-8VZPU	Hip-D	Airborne command post variant with external box housings, special comms equipment and related antennae.
Mi-8M	Hip	See Mi-17.
Mi-8MA	Hip	Mi-8 equipped for Arctic operations.
Mi-8MB	Hip	Medical evacuation version of Mi-8.
Mi-8MT	Hip-H	Military Mi-17 equipped as Mi-8T. Various sub-designations for Russian military versions (e.g. Mi-8MTU, Mi-8MTPB etc.).
Mi-8AMT	Hip	Mi-8MT with TV3-117VM engines for hot and high operations.
Mi-8AMTSh	Hip	Ulan Ude-built Mi-8 attack helicopter with nose radar and external mountings for SHTURM-V air-to-ground rockets and IGLA-V air-guided missiles and external armour plating in cockpit area.
Mi-8MTV-GA	Hip	Kazan-built civil transport version of Mi-8 with square windows etc.
Mi-8MTV-1	Hip	Civil version for high-altitude operations.
Mi-8MTV-2	Hip	Mi-8MTV with minor modifications.
Mi-8MTV-3	Hip	Multi-use 30-troop military Mi-8MTV with cabin armour protection, nose mounted machine-gun, external strut-braced ordnance pylons for bombs or rocket launchers, countermeasures dispensers, infra-red exhaust shields etc.

Mil Mi-24V, 0710 *(Czech AF)*

Type No.	NATO Codename	Notes
Mi-9	Hip-G	Mi-8 fitted as airborne command relay platform.
V-10 Mi-10	Harke	Large flying crane helicopter based on Mi-6 with reduced depth 28-passenger fuselage, cockpit in nose with extensive glazing, multi-strutted four-leg u/c, external fuel tanks, powered by two Soloviev D-25V turboshafts driving five-blade main rotor with Mi-6 transmission. Prot. FF 1960. Approx. 80 built.
Mi-10R	Harke	Production V-10 with installed system for attaching underslung loads and turbine APU. Some believed converted from Mi-6.
Mi-10K	Harke	Mi-10R with shorter u/c, narrow tail fin, modified cockpit and gondola fitted with dual controls.
V-12	Homer	Very large experimental passenger helicopter with 120-seat fuselage incorporating rear clamshell doors, side-by-side rotor system comprising large reverese taper wings with tip-mounted dual engine pods and two five-blade rotors, tricycle u/c with multi-strutted main units, aircraft-type fin and tailplane. Powered by four 6500 shp Soloviev D-25VF turboshafts. Prot. FF 1968. 3 built.
V-14	Haze	Development of Mi-8 for naval operations with boat hull, no rear loading doors, u/c retracting into external pods. Powered by two TV2-117A turboshafts. Prot. FF Sept. 1969.
Mi-14PL	Haze	Production ASW version of V-14 with chin mounted radar, rear fuselage weapons bay with depth charges and torpedoes.
Mi-14PLM	Haze-A	Mi-14PL with TV3-117MT engines and changes to installation of detection equipment.

Mil Mi-34A

Type No.	NATO Codename	Notes
Mi-14PS	Haze-C	SAR version of Mi-14PL with enlarged cabin door, searchlights, rescue hoist etc.
Mi-14BT	Haze-B	Mi-14 fitted to tow minesweeping float with tow operator's position in rear fuselage and external winch system in fairing.
Mi-17	Hip-H	Modified Mi-8 (initially Mi-8M) with Mi-14 dynamic systems, tail rotor on starboard side and two TV3-117MT turboshafts. Designed for export customers. Prot. FF 1976.
Mi-17PP	Hip-H	Mi-17 with communications interception and jamming equipment similar to Mi-8PPA.
Mi-17TB	Hip-H	Mi-17 with external weapons similar to Mi-8TB.
Mi-17-1		Mi-17 for civil operations with chin-mounted radar, lower boom mounted antenna fairing, improved soundproofing, square windows, 24-pax seating and two 2200 shp TV3-117VM engines.
Mi-17-1VA		Mobile hospital variant for disaster support.
Mi-17-1V		Export version of Mi-8MTV. Mi-17-1VA is aeromedical version.
Mi-17M		Rescue version of Mi-8MTV with revised cabin doors etc.
Mi-17MD		Mi-17M with 40-troop capacity, cabin doors both sides and pointed radar nose.
Mi-17P		24-seat civil passenger Mi-17 with square cabin windows, additional soundproofing etc.
Mi-17PI		Electronic jamming version of Mi-17. Also Mi-17PG.
Mi-17Z-2		Electronic intelligence gathering version for Czech AF with external circular electronic pods.
Mi-171		Ulan Ude-built export version of Mi-8AMT.
Mi-172		Export version of Mi-8MTV.

Mil Mi-4, 511 *(Polish AF)*

Type No.	NATO Codename	Notes
Mi-18		Initial designation for Mi-8.
Mi-18		Mi-17 with 3-ft fuselage extension, retractable undercarriage and modified cabin doors.
Mi-22	Hook-C	Mi-6 for military communication relay duties.
Mi-24	Hind	Mlitary attack helicopter with passenger cabin for eight troops, Mi-8 dynamic system, tandem two-seat nose crew compartment, retractable tricycle u/c, anhedralled stub wings for multiple armament fit, powered by two Soloviev TV2 turboshafts.
Mi-24A	Hind-A	Production Mi-24 with flat-panel cockpit transparencies, starboard tail rotor, nose 12.7mm weapons station and four external stores points.
Mi-24D	Hind-D	Mi-24 with stepped cockpit giving improved vision for pilot in rear seat, modified gunsight and chin gun mounting, larger cabin door window, port tail rotor and improved armour.
Mi-24DU		Unarmed dual-control trainer version of Mi-24D.
Mi-24F		Mi-24D with TV3-117MT engines with inlet filters and infra-red suppression fairings.
Mi-24G		Mi-24D with large external gun mounted on lower forward fuselage.
Mi-24H		Mi-24 for Poland with modified offensive weapons fit.
Mi-24K	Hind-G2	Reconnaissance version with externally mounted camera and video downloading capability.
Mi-24P	Hind-F	Mi-24F with chin turret replaced by sensor and 9A623K cannon externally mounted on starboard side. Mi-24PS for police operations.
Mi-24U	Hind-C	Unarmed trainer version of Hind-A.

Mil Mi-6

Type No.	NATO Codename	Notes
Mi-24V	Hind-E	Mi-24F with nose light, external rocket pods, new pilot HUD.
Mi-24VP		Mi-24V with 23-mm cannon in nose turret.
Mi-25	Hind	Mi-24 for export without high classification systems.
V-26 Mi-26	Halo	Heavylift helicopter designed as Mi-12 replacement with streamlined pod/boom fuselage, 4-seat nose flightdeck, main cabin with three porthole windows each side and rear clamshell doors with loading ramp, fixed tricycle u/c. Powered by two D-136 turboshafts driving 8-blade composite main rotor. Prot. FF 14 Dec. 1977. Appx. 540 built.
Mi-26A		Production military V-26 with 100-troop capacity and advanced rotor system and auto-hover.
Mi-26M		Improved Mi-26A with upgraded engines, 'glass' cockpit, new rotor blades and upgraded avionics.
Mi-26MS		Medical evacuation version of Mi-26A.
Mi-26P		High-density passenger transport with 96 seats.
Mi-26T		Civil cargo version of Mi-26A.
Mi-26TM		Crane version of Mi-26A with under-nose second pilot position and auto stabilisation for use with underslung loads.
Mi-26TZ		Flying tanker version with internal fuel pods.
Mi-28A	Havoc	Two-seat gunship helicopter with stepped cockpits, slim tailboom with large fin and assymetric four-blade tail rotor, fixed tailwheel u/c, stub wings with tip electronics pods and chaff dispenser and four hardpoints, chin-mounted gun turret, powered by two externally mounted 2,200 shp TV3-117VMA turboshafts driving 5-blade main rotor. Prot. FF 10 Nov. 1982. 4 built to date.

Mil Mi-8

Type No.	NATO Codename	Notes
Mi-28N	Havoc	Night attack version of Mi-28A with mast-mounted FLIR, chin turret with 2A42 30-mm cannon, external mounting for 16 Ataka missiles and 40 S-8 rockets or two GSh-23 guns. Sole Prot. FF 14 Nov. 1996.
Mi-34	Hermit	Light four-seat heicopter with streamlined fuselage/boom, T-tail, fixed skid u/c and powered by one M-14.V26 piston engine mounted behind cabin driving 4-blade composite rotor. Prot. FF 1986.
Mi-34A	Hermit	Export version of Mi-34 with Allison 250-C20R turboshaft, increased gross weight, upgraded transmission and modified low-maintenance rotor head.
Mi-34C	Hermit	Production Mi-34 version with 325 h.p. M-14B26B piston engine.
Mi-34P	Hermit	Mi-34 for export with Lycoming TIO-540-J2B piston engine.
Mi-34VAZ	Hermit	Mi-34A fitted with two VAZ-430 rotary piston engines.
Mi-35	Hind	Mi-24V for export sale.
Mi-35D	Hind	Mi-24 with transmission from Mi-28.
Mi-35M	Hind	Mi-24 with Mi-28 dynamic system, rotor blades and hub, fixed u/c, redesigned stub wings to carry Ataka and IGLA-V missiles and two 2250 shp TV3-117VMA turboshafts.
Mi-35P	Hind	Mi-24P for export sale.
Mi-38		Kazan-designed medium lift helicopter to replace Mi-17 with larger capacity cabin, advanced flight deck, retractable tricycle u/c, 6-blade main rotor and powered by two TV7-117V turboshafts. To fly in 1999.
Mi-40		Proposed Mi-28 with enlarged fuselage containing cabin for eight troops, modified u/c in sponsons incorporating weapons hardpoints and additional lower fuselage barbette.
Mi-52		Proposed three-seat light helicopter.
Mi-54		Proposed 10-seat executive/utility helicopter similar to Agusta 109.
ANSAT		Kazan-designed utility helicopter project with 9-seat capacity and twin Klimov/Pratt & Whitney PK206C turboshafts.

ANSAT mockup *(P. Foster)*

MITSUBISHI   JAPAN

When the Peace Treaty with Japan was concluded in 1952, companies such as Mitsubishi Heavy Industries (the Mitsubishi Jokogyo Kabishiki Kaisha) were able to return to aircraft production. Famous for the wartime A6M Zero, Mitsubishi started off with over-haul of military aircraft such as the USAF F-86 Sabres based in Japan at that time, and then moved on to production of Sabres for the emerging Japanese Air Self Defense Force (JASDF), and to the Mu-2 turboprop business aircraft and the Mu-3 Diamond executive jet.

Early in the post-war development period, Mitsubishi overhauled the U.S. Air Force's Sikorsky S-55 helicopters and this led to a licence being granted by Sikorsky for produc-tion of the type for the Japanese military forces and the developing civil market. A small batch of Sikorsky-built aircraft was delivered initially and then Mitsubishi produced a total of 45 units of the S-55C (including 17 for the JASDF, 14 for the JGSDF and 10 for the JMSDF) which were delivered between December 1958, and January 1962. The first aircraft was delivered to the JASDF as s/n 81-4705 and the production aircraft carried Mitsubishi serial numbers c/n M55-001 to M55-045.

Mitsubishi had established a good relationship with Sikorsky and took up a further licence to build the Sikorsky S-62. This suited the needs of the JASDF and the JMSDF for search and rescue, and also had civil applications. The first S-62J (JA 9005 c/n M62-001) first flew in 1962, and Mitsubishi started military S-62J deliveries in August 1963. They eventually completed 25 aircraft (c/n M62-001 to M62-025) including two to the Philippines, one to Thailand and five Japanese commercial orders.

With the S-62J reaching retirement age, the natural follow-on to the S-62 programme was Sikorsky's Sea King. The last S-62J departed in 1983 but substantial numbers of Sea Kings had been procured by the JMSDF to replace them. Production commenced in 1964 and the Navy initially acquired a small batch of six S-61As (and one S-61A-1) two of which were allocated as support aircraft for the Japanese Antarctic Expedition. Mitsubishi also built three S-61s for commercial users, and 11 examples of the S-61AH which was similar to the standard S-61A, but fitted with rescue equipment for long-range SAR missions from bases at Hachinohe, Atsugi, Iwo Jima and Kanoya.

The main production, however, was the HSS-2 (an identity based on the initial designa-tion allocated by the U.S. Navy). The 55 HSS-2s built were almost identical to the U.S. Navy Sea King, sonar-equipped for anti-submarine operations. A further 28 HSS-2As (S-61B-1) incorporated upgraded electronics including station-keeping radar. JMSDF Sea Kings were attached to the destroyer fleet where appropriate and operated from naval shore bases. These initial Sea Kings were subsequently replaced, from 1979 onwards, with 84 examples of the HSS-2B. This differed from the earlier version in having considerably better anti-submarine capability with improved sonar and radars, magnetic anomaly detector and additional sonobuoy storage and ejectors. Total production of the S-61 by Mitsubishi was 185 aircraft (with c/ns M61-001 to M61-185).

The newest licence production programme to come to Mitsubishi is of the Sikorsky S-70B-3. The ubiquitous S-70/UH-60 was seen as the natural successor to the HSS-2, and two units of the S-70A-12 were supplied in kit form by Sikorsky prior to Mitsubishi production of 18 UH-60Js for the JMSDF, and eight for the JASDF. The programme was then extended to take in a specialised anti-submarine version for the JMSDF based on the S-70B-3 Seahawk, and the first of a total requirement for 80 aircraft was delivered in 1991. In JMSDF service, the S-70B is designated SH-60J.

The most recent Mitsubishi-originated helicopter programme is the MH.2000. This 7/12 seat commercial helicopter (JQ6003) was first known as the Mitsubishi RP-1 and first flew in July 1996, followed by a second machine (JQ6004). Japanese certification was awarded in August 1997. The MH.2000 has its engine module and dynamic system positioned behind the cabin section to keep the sound level in the passenger compartment to a minimum. Power is provided by a pair of 800 shp Mitsubishi MGS-100 turboshafts and the MH.2000 is fitted with a tail fenestron similar to that on the Aérospatiale Dauphin.

Mitsubushi MH.2000

PZL-SWIDNIK   POLAND

Following World War II, the Polish aircraft industry, which had been strong and innovative during the mid-war years, was reorganised. From 1949 onwards the nationalised industry became known as WSK (Wytwornia Sprzetu Komunikacyjnego – or Transport Manufacturing Works) as the overall identity for separate subsidiaries which carried the old name – PZL ('Panstwowe Zaklady Lotnicze'). Marketing of all aircraft and products was handled by PEZETEL – Foreign Trade Enterprise Ltd.

Design and manufacture of helicopters was established in a separate subsidiary known as PZL-Swidnik (also sometimes referred to as the WSK Pulawski Works). Much experimentation with helicopters took place in the 1950s, particularly with the designs of Bronislaw Zurakowski but these did not materialise as viable production models. Accordingly when operations commenced in 1951 at a brand-new factory in Swidnik (located to the east of Warsaw), commercial activities were concentrated on sub-contract manufacture of MiG-15 components for the PZL-Mielec plant. However, in 1955 it was decided to transfer production responsibility from the Soviet Union to Poland for the Mil Mi-1 light helicopter and this was allocated to the Swidnik factory.

The first Polish-built Mi-1 was flown in 1956 and over 1500 were delivered to the Soviet Union. PZL referred to this as the SM-1 and subsequently, in 1959, the PZL design team under Jerzy Tyrcha developed it into the SM-2, which featured a completely redesigned forward fuselage and enlarged cabin area with capacity for internal carriage of stretchers in the ambulance role. PZL-Swidnik completed its production of 1680 examples of the SM-1 and SM-2 in 1965.

In January 1964, a new licence agreement was signed which brought the Mil Mi-2 to the Swidnik production line. The Mi-2 was based on the Mi-1 but the entire engine installation was revised with a pair of Isotov turboshaft engines positioned above the main fuselage. This provided an uninterrupted cabin section which gave great flexibility for a wide range of military and civil roles and improved the load-carrying abilities of the Mi-1 by virtue of the higher power and lower weight of the new engines. The Mi-2 was developed by the Mikhail L. Mil Bureau, and the V-2 prototype was flown and tested in Russia, but production was immediately allocated to PZL-Swidnik under the Soviet policy of devolving manufacturing to specialist plants in Warsaw Pact countries.

The Mi-2, which could carry eight passengers and one crew, was widely exported, with many going to other satellite countries and to the Soviet Union. Twenty-five different configurations were identified by PZL including training, passenger transport, agricultural, ambulance, search and rescue, photo-mapping, fire-fighting etc. Out of the production of 5080 examples, large numbers were used in military roles, with various options available for externally-mounted armament or additional fuel capacity.

The Mi-2 was widely used as an agricultural aircraft, with large externally-mounted hoppers and spraybars. PZL further modified the Mi-2 as the PZL Kania by installing higher-powered Allison 250-C20 turboshafts, and this resulted in improved fuel consumption, a higher gross weight with one extra passenger seat and longer range. It was intended that the Kania would be sold as the 'Taurus' in the United States through an agreement with Spitfire Helicopters, but this came to nothing and only a handful of Kanias have been completed.

PZL-Swidnik are currently concentrating on production of the W-3 Sokol. This helicopter is an entirely new design by PZL's design team under Stanislaw Kaminski, and while it is externally similar to the Kania it is a larger helicopter with capacity for two crew and twelve passengers. Aimed at the full range of civil and military applications, the Sokol has been delivered in quantity to the Polish military forces (40 examples) and to Myanmar (12), Korea (3) and the German Border Police (6). On 31 May 1993, it became the first Eastern bloc helicopter to be awarded FAA certification.

Several military versions of the Sokol have been tested, including the W-3WB Huzar which PZL has developed in association with Denel in South Africa. No orders have been obtained for the W-3WB but a simplified version has been ordered by the Polish Air Force. Now under test is the SW-4 light six-seater which is targeted at the market currently dominated by the Eurocopter Ecureuil. However, PZL-Swidnik continues to be short of development funds and certification of the SW-4 is still some way off.

Production Details

PZL-Swidnik serial numbers are a combination of several fields with digits indicating the model type, batch and serial number within the batch. In addition some models (e.g. the Mi-2) have further digits indicating the month and year of manufacture. Details are as follows:

Model	c/n Example	Field 1 Model Type (2 digits)	Field 2 Batch (2 digits)	Field 3 Unit no in batch (2 digits)	Field 4 Month built (2 digits)	Field 5 Year built (1 digit)
Mi-1						
Mi-2	552025101 (Prototypes ZD0101113 to ZD0106)	51=transport 52=agriculture 53=passenger 54=trainer 55=rescue 56=military 57=photo/rec 58=military VIP	From 01 to 112	Variable with normally 50 aircraft in each batch	01 (January) to 12 (December)	From 6 (1966) to 2 (1992)
Sokol	310308	30=prototypes 31=civil transport 32=medical 36=Polish military 37=export civil 39=Anakonda	From 01 to 07 further batches as production continues	Variable with normally 20 aircraft in each batch	Not used	Not used
Kania	900202	90= Kania	From 01 to 03	Max 5 aircraft per batch	Not used	Not used
SW-4	600104	60= SW-4	Batch 01	01 to 04	Not used	Not used

Model Information

Details of models built by PZL-Swidnik are as follows:

Type No.	Notes
JK-1 Trzmiel	Single-seat open frame ultra-light helicopter with two rotor-tip mounted Wojcicki pulse-jets. Prot. FF 28 June 1957. 2 built.
BZ-1 Gil	Two-seat light helicopter designed by Bronislaw Zurakowski, with enclosed fuselage, open cockpit, fixed tricycle u/c and one 105 h.p. Walter Mikron 4-III piston engine. One Prot. SP-GIL FF 4 April 1950.
BZ-4 Zuk	Four-seat helicopter with single main rotor, main fuselage/ cabin section, open frame rear boom structure, fixed four-wheel u/c and one 320 h.p. Narkiewicz WN-4 piston engine located behind cabin. Prot. FF 10 Feb. 1959. 2 built.
SM-1	Polish-built Mil Mi-1T helicopter. Prot. FF Sept. 1956. 1680 built.
SM-1S	Ambulance version of SM-1.
SM-1SZ	Dual-control training version of SM-1.
SM-1W	SM-1 fitted with 575 h.p. AI-26V (LiT-3) piston engine. 5300 lb TOGW. FF 1960.
SM-1WS	Medical version of SM-1W with external stretcher panniers both sides.
SM-1WZ	Crop-spraying version of SM-1W with external hoppers.
SM-1WSZ	Dual-control training version of SM-1W.
SM-1Z	Crop-spraying version of SM-1.
SM-1	SM-1 fitted with experimental variable incidence wings. FF 24 Mar. 1971.
SM-2	Five-seat development of SM-1W with modified forward fuselage including nose hatch for stretcher loading and increased 4166 lb gross weight. Prot. S2-0002 FF 18 Nov. 1959.
Mi-2	Developed 8/9-seat version of Mil Mi-1 with two 400 shp PZL-Isotov GTD-350 turboshaft engines mounted on top of fuselage, and cabin extended rearwards into former engine compartment. New nose contour, larger tail fin and tailplane, metal tail rotor, tricycle u/c with twin nosewheels and optional external extra fuel tanks. First flight of Polish-built aircraft 4 Nov. 1965. 5080 built.

PZL SM-2, 3004 *(Polish AF)*

Type No.	Notes
Mi-2B	Mi-2 with redesigned electrical system and upgraded avionics.
Mi-2M	Mi-2 with wider ten-seat cabin, retractable nosewheel and two 450 shp PZL Isotov GTD-350 turboshafts. 8157 lb TOGW. Prot. SP-PSK FF 1 Jul. 1974. Not put into production. 4 built.
Mi-2R	Rescue version of Mi-2 with external winch and stretcher capacity.
Mi-2RM	Naval version of Mi-2.
Mi-2T	Military trainer version of Mi-2.
Mi-2URN	Gunship version of Mi-2 with two external MARS2-16 rocket launchers, 23-mm cannon and interior-mounted machine-guns.
Mi-2URP	Anti-tank version with four externally mounted AT-3 Sagger missiles.
Mi-2US	Gunship version with two external 7.62mm gun pods, 23mm cannon and interior-mounted machine-guns.
SM-4 Latka	Three-seat helicopter with enclosed cabin, open-frame rear fuselage, skid u/c, GRP main rotor and one 180 h.p. Narkiewicz WN-6S piston engine mounted at an angle behind cabin section. Prot. FF 1962.
SW-4	4/5 seat civil helicopter of conventional streamlined appearance with all-metal monocoque fuselage, single three-blade main rotor, skid u/c, tail fin and small tailplane with endplate fins. Powered by one 450 shp Allison 250-C20R turboshaft. Alternative powerplant is 615 shp P&W PW200/9. 3086 lb TOGW. 5 built.
W-3 Sokol	Fourteen-seat all-metal monocoque medium helicopter resembling enlarged Kania for civil or military use with fixed tricycle u/c and two 1000 shp PZL-10W turboshafts driving a new design four-blade main rotor. Prot. FF 16 Nov. 1979. 100 built to date.
W-3A Sokol Falcon	W-3 with modifed electrical and hydraulic stystems, larger main u/c wheels and improved avionics. Certificated for single-pilot operation. Prot. SP-PSK (c/n 360420).

PZL Sokol, 420 *(Polish AF)*

Type No.	Notes
W-3 Huzar	Attack version of W-3 with 23mm cannon and four external stores pylons for rockets and other ordnance.
W-3WB Huzar	Armed support version of W-3 with chin cannon installation, two external MARS-2 rocket pods, and two ZT-35 rocket launcher pods.
W-3RM Anakonda	Sokol for offshore search and rescue with external winch, six external flotation bags and sealed fuselage.
Kania	Mi-2 fitted with recontoured nose, composite main rotor blades and two 420 shp Allison 250-C20B turboshafts. 7826 lb TOGW. Prot. SP-PSA FF 3 June 1979. 8 built to date.

PZL SW-4

PZL Kania, SP-SSA

ROBINSON HELICOPTERS   USA

Many manufacturers have produced prototypes of the 'ultimate personal helicopter' but only one man, Frank Robinson, has really made the promise come true. Robinson was a highly experienced helicopter engineer with over 16 years' service with companies such as Bell, Kaman and Cessna when he resigned from Hughes Helicopters in June 1973.

He saw a real niche for a two-seat piston-engined personal helicopter which would sell at a price within the reach of the average private pilot. The result was the R.22 which flew in August 1975, and Frank Robinson raised a few eyebrows with claims that he would sell 500 R.22s annually. The R.22 was certainly successful and Robinson Helicopter Co. almost achieved their target with production from their Torrance, California factory exceeding 400 in 1992.

The R.22 is a basic 'pod and boom' light helicopter with side-by-side seating for two and the engine positioned in an open cowling below and behind the cabin driving a two-blade main rotor and conventional tail anti-torque propeller. The prototype differed little from the production model except in its powerplant. First tests were made with a 115 h.p. Lycoming O-235 engine, but this was soon upgraded to a 124 h.p. O-320. R.22s are fitted with a central T-shaped control column which can be fitted with single or dual controls. The training market was not initially seen as being the principal target for the R.22 but as it turned out this became the main role for the R.22 for some while.

The R.22 has become the world's dominant light piston helicopter achieving a number of world class records for speed, distance and altitude. Deliveries started in 1980 and achieved an 80% share of the piston helicopter market in the following year. Volume sales to an expanded and less experienced market did have the shortcoming of a higher accident rate, although the R.22 proved to be highly reliable with low costs of operation. Several safety reviews were carried out by the FAA but the R.22 was cleared on each occasion. Nevertheless, Robinson has introduced company-promoted safety programmes to reduce accident rates.

It has also progressively improved the specification and has introduced kits to equip the aircraft for a wide range of utility roles including water operations with large pontoon floats. There is also a specific law enforcement version and an IFR Trainer with an enlarged instrument panel. Aircraft have been acquired for applications such as cattle herding, traffic watch, agricultural spraying and aerial photography. The new R.22 models with increasing power output have been titled 'Alpha', 'Beta' etc. R.22s have been exported widely, with the United Kingdom and Australia being important destinations. Military deliveries have also been made with an order for 40 for Argentina, and a batch of ten aircraft delivered as trainers to the Turkish Army.

With the success of the R.22, customers started to demand a larger version and Frank Robinson designed the four-seat R.44 Astro. The prototype started flight testing at Torrance in mid-1990. The R.44 followed the same general layout as the R.22 with the engine and rotor mast behind the cabin pod to make maximum use of the passenger space and ensure that there was no need for a power-train bulkhead between front and rear seats. Most importantly, it could be sold at under $250,000 and offered four-seat capacity at a much lower cost than the competing turbine helicopters. High speed performance clearly fell short of the Jet Ranger and Ecureuil but the Robinson filled a very significant market niche.

Robinson R.22HP, G-BSEK

Robinson R.44, G-OCCB

HELICOPTERS AND ROTORCRAFT

Serial numbers of Robinsons follow Frank Robinson's philosophy and are straight-forward and uncomplicated. The basic R.22 started with the prototype at c/n 0001 and finished at c/n 0199. c/n 200 to approximately 0350 were R.22HP and the R.22 Alpha ran from c/n 0350 to 0500. The Beta was introduced at c/n 501 and R.22 serials have now reached approximately c/n 2620. Aircraft built as Mariners have an 'M' suffix to their serial (e.g. c/n 2481M). The R.44 started at c/n 0001 and has now reached approximately c/n 0300.

Model Information

In detail, the models built by Robinson Helicopter Co. are as follows:

Type No.	Name	Number Built	Notes
R.22		199	Side-by-side two seat light helicopter with pod & boom fuselage, rotor pylon behind cabin, fin and starboard-side tailplane, skid u/c and one 124 hp Lycoming O-320-A2B piston engine mounted behind cockpit driving two-blade main rotor via belt drive. 1300 lb TOGW. Prot. N67010 (c/n 0001) FF 28 Aug. 1975.
R.22HP		151	R.22 fitted with O-320-B2C engine, longer skids and additional weights on rotor tips.
R.22	Alpha	151	R.22HP with 1370 lb TOGW, relocated battery and tail boom angled upwards. Special IFR training and police variants available.
R.22	Beta	2120	R.22 with uprated 131 hp O-320-B2C engine, enlarged instrument panel, modified cabin heating, rotor brake.
R.22	Beta-II		R.22 with 180 h.p. Lycoming O-360 engine, throttle governor, revised carburettor heat system.
R.22	Mariner		R.22 Beta fitted with pontoon floats and additional ground-handling wheels.
R.44	Astro	300	Four-seat helicopter based on R.22 design principles with fully enclosed cabin section, skid u/c, tubular tailboom with fin and starboard tailplane, powered by one 260 h.p. Textron Lycoming O-540 piston engine driving two-blade main rotor . Prot. N44RH (c/n 0001) FF 31 Mar. 1990.
R.44	Clipper		R.44 with twin pontoon floats and corrosion proofing for water operations.

SAUNDERS ROE   UNITED KINGDOM

In the 1930s, the Glasgow company, G. & J. Weir Ltd built a number of autogyros as a licensee of the Cierva Autogiro Company. Weir's Managing Director, James Weir, was an enthusiastic promotor of the idea of rotary wing flight and was also the Chairman of Cierva. Licensed production led to experiments with a small helicopter, the Weir W-5, which used a side-by-side twin rotor layout similar to that of the German Focke Achgelis Fa.61. It flew successfully in June 1938, and was certainly the first British helicopter and also well in advance of Igor Sikorsky's VS-300. The single seat W-4 was succeeded by the larger two-seat W-5 and the three-seat W-6, but further work was halted by the onset of war.

It was not long, however, before James Weir aroused the interest of the Ministry of Aircraft Production in a new military helicopter and the reconstituted Cierva company set to work at Thames Ditton in Surrey. Three projects were launched and each proceeded towards a different conclusion. The first machine, the W-9, was designed with a number of radical features for controlling helicopters including a linkage of the throttle mechanism to the rotor pitch control, elimination of the tail rotor and a rotor hub layout which was based on a universal joint to facilitate tilting of the hub. The W-9 had a single three-blade rotor, fixed tailwheel undercarriage and a two-seat enclosed cabin in the nose. The tail section was a long tapered metal tube with a directional control vent at the end to eject engine exhaust and so derive thrust to offset rotor torque. The W-9 prototype first flew in late 1944, but crashed in 1946 and was abandoned.

At the same time, Cierva was also working on a cargo helicopter which could also do crop spraying. The W-11 Air Horse was built by Cunliffe Owen at Southampton and was unique in having two outrigger rotors plus a third rotor pylon above the nose. Equipped with a multi-strutted fixed undercarriage, it was a curious and, for the times, futuristic machine. It was certainly the world's largest helicopter when it flew in 1948. The all-metal fuselage had a rear clamshell door to load freight and the two crew sat under a glazed canopy above the forward fuselage. The prototype was tested and modified during 1949, but crashed and was totally destroyed on 13 June 1950, with the consequence that further development was abandoned and the second prototype was never flown.

Cierva's third helicopter was the small two-seat W-14 Skeeter. This machine was less radical than its predecessors. It had an enclosed cabin with a 100 h.p. Jameson FF-1 piston engine installed in the centre section behind, and a triangular-section tailboom with a three-blade tail rotor. It was fitted with a wood and fabric three-blade main rotor. While it flew fairly satisfactorily, the Skeeter 1 suffered from the extreme unreliability and over-heating of the Jameson engine. In the Skeeter 2 which followed in 1949, a transversely-mounted 145 h.p. Gipsy Major 10 engine was installed together with a main rotor of increased diameter. This second machine had a more streamlined cabin pod and a completely new slim tapered tubular tailboom. However, the designers of the Skeeter were plagued by ground resonance problems which caused the destruction of the Skeeter 2 in June 1950.

Despite these problems, Cierva did receive an order from the Ministry of Supply for two service evaluation machines designated Skeeter 3. Unfortunately, the pressure caused by the crash of the first Air Horse and the company's dwindling finances resulted in Cierva being taken over by Saunders Roe Ltd on 22 January 1951. The two Skeeter 3s were built and then passed for testing by the A & AEE at Boscombe Down. There followed a period of considerable modification to the undercarriage and rotor head and the engine power was increased by installation of a 180 h.p. Blackburn Bombardier 702 engine. Saunders Roe also built a single Skeeter 4 for Royal Navy evaluation. Eventually, the ground resonance problems which had dogged the project from the outset were resolved through modifications both to the rotor blade dampers and to the undercarriage.

There then followed further evaluation with another batch of four Skeeters including one T.11 trainer and three AOP.10 army cooperation aircraft. Again, this gave rise to further changes but in May 1956, the company received the first of a series of orders for the Skeeter AOP Mk. 12 for the British Army, powered by a 215 h.p. Gipsy Major engine. Sixty-four examples were delivered between May 1958 and July 1960, and they served with the Army Air Corps as observation and training machines, but were finally withdrawn from service in 1968 because of reliability problems. Several civil Skeeters were constructed, but the other main customer was the German Heeresflieger which received six Mk. 50 aircraft, and the Bundesmarine which had four Mk. 51s. These were delivered to Germany in 1958, but had a short service life and were sold to Portugal in 1961. It seems that they were stored and never used by the Portuguese Air Force.

In 1957, Saunders Roe (Saro) was approached by the Paris-based Helicop-Air which was the European agent for the Hiller 1033 Rotorcycle. Hiller had flown the first two prototypes of the Rotorcycle single-seat collapsible helicopter, but it was thought that manufacture in Europe would be less expensive than production in the United States. Saro assembled the first Rotorcycle and flew it in October 1959, and followed this with a further nine aircraft of which five were YROE-1s for the U.S. Marine Corps and the balance for civil sale in Europe. The Rotorcycle was demonstrated extensively and appeared at the Paris Air Show but no sales were forthcoming and Saro ceased building this unusual machine.

Saunders Roe had been involved in many projects other than helicopters during this period, but industry rationalisation resulted in the company being absorbed by Westland in August 1959. Saunders Roe had been working on plans for a completely new light heli-

Cierva W.11 Air Horse, G-ALCV *(via MS)*

copter designated P.531. This was intended as a turbine-powered replacement for the Skeeter, with greater carrying capacity. Detailed design work commenced in late 1957 and a prototype P.531 was constructed at Saunders Roe's Eastleigh factory. Externally, it looked like a scaled-up Skeeter with a wider four-seat cabin with four doors, and a fixed four-leg undercarriage. The Blackburn-Turboméca Turmo engine was fitted on a flat decking immediately behind the cabin driving a four-blade rotor system similar to that of the Skeeter.

Saro constructed two prototypes of the P.531 (G-APNU and G-APNV) and flew the first of these on 20 July 1958, with a further two military P.531-0 prototypes following. The fifth aircraft was designated P.531-2 and it had a longer six-seat cabin section, a raked windscreen, skid undercarriage and a Blackburn Nimbus engine. In this form it was ready for production and Saro was awarded an initial contract for eight aircraft, designated Sprite AH.1 (later changed to Scout AH.1) for the Army Air Corps. Following the takeover by Westland, further orders were placed for the Scout, which were constructed at the Fairey plant at Hayes, Middlesex, and the P.531 design went on to be developed into the naval Wasp variant which joined the Scout on the production line in 1963.

Production Details

Details of Skeeters and the P.531 prototypes are shown in the following table. The initial 'W' numbers relate back to the Weir period of Cierva. Saro used a series of numbers prefixed SR (of which SR901 to SR903 were the Princess flying boats). The main Skeeter production used a serial number sequence which was also used for other separate components and therefore some gaps occurred. Details of production of the Scout and Wasp are included under the Westland chapter.

Model	Serial Batch	Number Built	Notes
Skeeter 1	W.14/1 to W.14/5	1	Prototype G-AJCJ.
Skeeter 2	W.14/2	1	Second Prot. G-ALUF.
Skeeter 3 and 4	W.14/3 to W.14/5	3	
Skeeter 5, 6 and 7	SR904 to SR907	4	Saro-type c/ns.
Skeeter AOP.10/T.11	S2.3012, 3036, 3051, 3070	4	
Skeeter AOP.12	S2.5061 to S2.5120 S2.7145 to S2.7161	64	Excluding c/n 5081, 5091, 5111 and German units.
Skeeter 50	S2/5061, 5062, 5063, 5073, 5077, 5082	6	For West German Army.
Skeeter 51	S2/5065, 5070, 5083, 5092	4	For West German Navy.
Saro-Hiller YROE-1	S2.7588, S2.7592 to S2.7596	10	Plus four unknown c/ns. Hiller c/ns 3 to 12.
P.531 and P.531-0	S2.5267 and S2.5268	2	G-APNU and PNV.
P.531 Mk.2	S2.5311 and S2.5312	2	G-APVL and PVM.

Model Information

Type/Name	Notes
W.9	Cierva-designed experimental two-seat all-metal helicopter with fixed tailwheel u/c, ducted efflux tail control system and one 205 h.p. Gipsy Six piston engine driving three-blade rotor. Prot. PX203 FF Oct.1944.

HELICOPTERS AND ROTORCRAFT

Type/Name	Notes
W.11 Air Horse	Large all-metal cargo helicopter with twin outriggers and forward support structure carrying three 3-blade rotors. Powered by one 1620 h.p. Rolls-Royce Merlin 24 engine. Prot. G-ALCV/VZ724 FF 7 Dec. 1948.
W.14 Skeeter 1	Two-seat light helicopter with fixed tricycle u/c, triangular-section tailboom powered by one 110 h.p. Jameson FF-1 piston engine located in mid section. Prot G-AJCJ (c/n W.14/1) FF. 10 Oct.1948.
W.14 Skeeter 2	Developed Skeeter 1 with more compact fuselage pod, tapered tubular tailboom, revised u/c and powered by one 145 h.p. D.H. Gipsy Major 10 engine. Prot. G-ALUF (c/n W.14/2) FF 20 Oct.1949.
P.501 Skeeter 3	Skeeter 2 with improved rotor head and undercarriage, increased gross weight and Gipsy Major 8 engine. Two built, WF112 and WF113.
Skeeter 3b	Skeeter 3s re-engined with 180 h.p. Blackburn Bombardier 702 engine.
Skeeter 4	Skeeter 3b for Royal Navy evaluation. Prot WF114 FF 15 Apl. 1952.
Skeeter 5	Civil version of Skeeter 4 with steel rotor shaft, improved rotor bearings, blade dampers and modified u/c. Prot G-AMTZ (c/n SR.907). FF May, 1953. One built. Later converted to Skeeter 6.
Skeeter 6	Skeeter 5 with 200 h.p. Gipsy Major 200 engine and dual controls. Prot G-ANMG (c/n SR.904) FF 26 May 1955. Also G-ANMH (c/n SR.905).
Skeeter 7	Skeeter 6 with 215 h.p. Gipsy Major 215. Prot. G-ANMI (c/n SR.906) FF 23 June 1954.
Skeeter 8	Civil version of Skeeter 7. One aircraft only G-APOI (c/n S2/5081).
Skeeter AOP.10	Skeeter 6 to military AOP specification with Gipsy Major 200. Three built for service test (XK480 to XK482).
Skeeter T.11	Skeeter AOP.10 with dual controls for RAF training evaluation. One aircraft XK479 (c/n S2/3012).
Skeeter AOP.12	Production AOP variant for Army Air Corps with 215 h.p. Gipsy Major 215.
Skeeter 50	Skeeter AOP.12 for West German AF. 4 built.
Skeeter 51	Skeeter AOP.12 for West German Navy. 4 built.
P.531	5-seat light military helicopter with single 4-blade main rotor and fixed 4-leg u/c. Powered by one 400 shp Blackburn-Turboméca Turmo 603 turboshaft positioned aft of cabin. Prot. G-APNU (c/n S2.5267) FF 20 Jul. 1958. Prototypes designated Mk.0 and Mk.1. See Westland chapter.
Hiller 1033 YROE-1	Single-seat collapsible personal helicopter powered by a 45 h.p. Nelson engine. 10 built under licence from Hiller.

Saunders Roe Skeeter AOP.12, XL738

SIKORSKY AIRCRAFT   USA

Igor Sikorsky can justifiably be regarded as the creator of the whole concept of modern helicopters even though advanced machines had been built in Germany and Britain during the early 1930s. Already a leading aircraft designer and helicopter experimenter in Russia, he escaped the Russian Revolution and established Sikorsky Aero Engineering Corporation in March 1923, in the United States. The following two decades saw Sikorsky become a subsidiary of United Aircraft and Transport Corporation and develop a range of magnificent flying boats. But Igor Sikorsky's dream was to create a practical helicopter and on 14 September 1939, he lifted off the ground in the Vought-Sikorsky VS-300, which was the world's first direct-lift aircraft.

The genius of Igor Sikorsky was that the basic layout of the VS-300 set the standard on which all subsequent helicopters have been created. The VS-300 was a rudimentary craft of welded tube with a simple three-wheeled undercarriage, and it changed in configuration before almost every flight. The first untethered flight was made on 13 May 1940, and a year later Igor Sikorsky set a world helicopter endurance record of 1 hour 32 minutes. Successful experimentation led to an order from the U.S. Army Air Corps for an experimental machine – the XR-4 which was the VS-300 with twice the power – and this rapidly proved to the U.S. military the potential of the helicopter, particularly for rescue and liaison tasks.

Sikorsky was separated from Vought on 1 January 1943, and the tube and fabric R-4 training helicopter went into production at new premises in Bridgeport, Connecticut. The R-4 was not only important in being the first real production helicopter accepted by the American forces, but also because it introduced the standard layout of main rotor and tail anti-torque propeller. The R-4 also used a three-control system of rudder pedals (to control the tail propeller), cyclic pitch handle (to alter the angle of the main rotor) and collective pitch lever to achieve control in the vertical plane. This became the standard method of control used by virtually all helicopters designed subsequently.

In truth, the R-4 had severe limitations in terms of manouvrability and lifting ability, but it did prove the flight capability of helicopters. It was followed by the R-5 and R-6, which adopted all-metal monocoque construction and increasingly sophisticated systems. The R-6 Hoverfly II was a two-seat streamlined derivative of the R-4. It pioneered several new construction concepts with substantial sections of magnesium in the structure, a moulded fibreglass forward fuselage, moulded Plexiglass bubble windshield and a tailwheel undercarriage, but it was underpowered with its 180 h.p. engine and suffered from breakages of its three rotor blades. However, the larger R-5, which had a longer cabin section accommodating a pilot in the nose and observer/winch-operator on a rear seat, had a much more powerful 450 h.p. Pratt & Whitney R-985 engine. It soon demonstrated its ability to be a serious search-and-rescue machine which could reach an accident more quickly than an air-sea rescue launch, and could hover and pick up the downed aircrew while fixed wing rescue aircraft such as the B-17H could only drop rafts or light boats.

The R-5 was soon refined into one of Sikorsky's most famous helicopters – the S-51 Dragonfly. This had a wider cabin than the R-5, a three-place bench seat for passengers, a tricycle undercarriage and more power. The main customer for the S-51 was the United States Navy (HO3S), but the largest production total came from Westland which completed a large batch of military and civil S-51s and further developed it into the Westland Widgeon.

As the helicopter became accepted as a valuable tool rather than a rather wierd oddity, there was demand for ever more power and capability. Sikorsky built a small number of S-52 four-seat helicopters, but the next large volume development was the S-55, which was designed in 1948 to meet a U.S. Army requirement for a ten-passenger utility transport. This design, which had a classic fuselage-pod and tailboom layout, established the principle of separating the crew compartment, the engine installation and the main cabin. The engine was buried in the nose below and ahead of the crew compartment, with an angled drive shaft which ran through the lower part of the cockpit to the main rotor mast.

The S-55 (H-19 Chickasaw) was adopted by the USAF, USN, US Army, Marine Corps and US Coast Guard, and became the standard utility helicopter from 1951 until the early 1970s. The S-55 was delivered in time to become one of the key rotary-wing aircraft in the Korean war. It was certificated in March 1952, and sold to civil operators, including New York Airways which used it on scheduled mail services, British European Airways and the Belgian airline, Sabena, which operated a Brussels passenger shuttle. It was also built under licence in France by Sud Aviation (as the 'Elephant Joyeux'), in Japan by Mitsubishi and in Britain by Westland as the Whirlwind and Gnome Whirlwind. After service with the U.S. forces, many H-19s were refurbished and fitted with turbine power-plants for logging and other utility operations, and a significant number of these machines still give excellent service.

A further advance in capacity came with the S-58 which started off as an anti-submarine helicopter for the U.S. Navy. The cockpit and engine section were similar to that of the

Agusta Sikorsky ASH-3D, MM5003N *(Sikorsky)*

S-55, but the S-58 had a continuous fuselage with a separate vertical fin carrying the tail rotor rather than a pod and boom layout. This provided increased capacity for 16 troops in the army version – and, not surprisingly, the power was almost doubled compared with the H-19. The S-58 was the first Sikorsky helicopter to be built in a new 850,000 sq.ft. factory at Stratford, Connecticut which the company opened in October 1955. During the mid-1950s the H-34 took over as the standard utility helicopter for all the American services and, again, they were built in France and Britain under licence. As with the S-55, the S-58 became a candidate for turbine conversion with examples of all the military variants being modified by many companies such as Carson Helicopters, Orlando Helicopter Airways, Air Asia and Utility Helicopters Inc. Some of the piston-engined version had flown with Chicago Helicopter Airways, and the turbine models have operated successfully in the passenger services from the New York heliports to Kennedy Airport and other destinations.

By 1953, helicopters had demonstrated that they were an essential part of the military equation. The US Marines put out a requirement for a large assault transport helicopter which could carry light vehicles or up to 36 equipped troops. Sikorsky's answer was the S-56 which was eventually delivered primarily for Army use. It was still a single-rotor helicopter, albeit with a huge five-blade main rotor, but it needed twin 2100 h.p. radial engines which were positioned on stub wings that also carried the retractable main undercarriage units. The S-56 (H-37 Mojave) had a crew compartment mounted in the nose above clamshell nose doors which allowed loading of all the necessary military equipment. Over 150 were built by Sikorsky and delivered between 1956 and 1961, and the design formed the basis for the Westminster which was developed by Westland. The H-37 served faithfully in Vietnam even though more modern turbine-engined helicopters were becoming available by that time. The dynamic components of the S-56 were also used to develop the S-60 Skycrane and its derivative the S-64, which operated in some numbers with the U.S. Army into the 1990s. The S-64 continues to be the ultimate heavy-lift helicopter produced in the West and it still serves with companies such as Evergreen for logging and other major tasks.

The next project to reach production was the S-62, and it introduced an interesting new concept – the amphibious helicopter. Using many established components from the S-55, the S-62 had a planing boat hull with outrigger floats attached to the forward fuselage, and was powered by a single General Electric turboshaft positioned on top of the main cabin section and driving a three blade main rotor. The S-62 did not find favour with the main U.S. military agencies, but it was adopted by the U.S. Coast Guard who acquired 99 examples. These entered service in 1963 and were eventually retired in 1989. The S-62

Sikorsky R-4 Hoverfly, 43-46514 *(via MJH)*

was sold to a number of civilian users including export customers in South Africa, Canada and Thailand, and a small batch was also completed under licence in Japan by Mitsubishi.

The general concept of the S-62 led to the S-61 which was perhaps the most versatile airframe to emerge from Sikorsky. This started as the S-61B, designed as the HSS-2 (later H-3) for anti-submarine operations with the U.S. Navy. Like the S-62, the S-61 had a boat hull and outrigger floats, but it was a larger helicopter with two turbine engines linked through an overrunning clutch system driving a single large five-bladed main rotor. The rotor blades were designed for power folding for carrier stowage, and incorporated a unique spar pressurisation system for detecting fatigue cracking. Like the S-62, the crew compartment was in the nose, and the H-3 had an unobstructed cabin section due to the positioning of the engines on the fuselage roof.

Sikorsky produced a range of different variants of the S-61 using the standard nose and fuselage centre section together with the power pod – but incorporating additional stretch segments ahead of and behind the engines and, in the case of the S-61R, a new rear fuselage with a slimmer tail boom and a rear-loading ramp. The civil S-61L was ordered by Los Angeles Airways and had a non-amphibious hull and a fixed strutted undercarriage. The later S-61N was a stretched passenger-carrying version which had the full water landing capability and was used extensively by BEA Helicopters and Bristow Helicopters on offshore oil operations in the North Sea. In an apparent reversal of design philosophy, a number of S-61Ns have been rebuilt by Helipro Corporation as the S-61 Short. This involves removal of a 50-inch plug from the forward fuselage in order to improve lifting capability, and six conversions have been completed to date.

A few passenger-carrying VIP versions of the basic Sea King were also produced, including VH-3As for American presidential use, but the main volume production of the S-61 was for the U.S. forces. In 1961 the Vietnam conflict was escalating and the H-3 went into full scale production to meet a wide range of tasks. It was used for minesweeping (RH-3A), tactical rescue of downed aircrew (HH-3A) and anti-submarine warfare. The USAF acquired the S-61R as the CH-3C and CH-3E long-range tactical transports, and the HH-3E 'Jolly Green Giant' rescue helicopter which was equipped with a large air refuelling boom and armoured panels. The similar HH-3F Pelican was delivered to the US Coast Guard with internal capacity for 15 stretchers, and Agusta also built this version for SAR missions for the Italian Navy. Variants of the S-61 continued in production at Stratford until 1980. Export models were sold to Malaysia, Brazil, Argentina and Iran and, again, Westland constructed a large number of Sea Kings for use by the British,

Sikorsky R-6A *(HGM Collection)*

German, Norwegian and Indian forces. The Japanese Maritime Self Defence force also bought Mitsubishi-produced SH-3As.

The quest for ever larger military transports took Sikorsky into its largest current production helicopter – the S-65 which was, again, intended to meet a Marines requirement for an assault helicopter capable of carrying 38 equipped troops. This employed much of the design philosophy of the S-61R combined with the dynamic components of the S-64 Tarhe although it no longer featured a sealed boat hull. Named CH-53 Sea Stallion the new helicopter had its two General Electric T64 turbines mounted in pods on either side of the main rotor pylon and had external sponsons containing fuel but which could also mount external stores including supplementary long-range tanks. As with the Pelican/Jolly Green Giant, the CH-53 had a rear ramp with an automated loading system allowing rapid access for two jeeps or a 105mm howitzer. The H-53 was also used by the USAF and by the US Navy which fitted a batch of RH-53As for mine sweeping and countermeasures.

The S-65 has continued to grow and the CH-53E Super Stallion is a later model which is fitted with three T64 engines and a mighty seven-blade main rotor that allows the helicopter to lift up to 16 tons of payload. A multi-mission mines countermeasures version for the US Navy is known as the MH-53E Sea Dragon and is equipped for towing an AMCM sled. Export variants of this series are designated S-80E and S-80M respectively, and the initial examples have been sold to Japan.

On 1 May 1974, Sikorsky Aircraft became a subsidiary of the newly established holding company, United Technologies Corp. At about this time the company was developing its current major product – the S-70. In 1972 the U.S. Army had launched the UTTAS (Utility Tactical Transport Aircraft System) competition, and Sikorsky's submission emerged as the winner after a competitive evaluation against the Boeing-Vertol YUH-61A. The first Sikorsky UH-60A Black Hawk was delivered in April 1979, and the type has become the standard tactical helicopter transport for the US military forces. It has also been developed into a comprehensive range of special purpose aircraft for search and rescue, medical evacuation and covert operations. This includes the NightHawk, which has been designed for the U.S. Air Force with advanced avionics, a refuelling probe and additional fuel tanks to replace the HH-3A for the rescue of downed airmen behind enemy lines.

A number of overseas air arms have been supplied with the S-70 through U.S. military

Sikorsky S-51 HO3S-1, 122508 HGM Collection)

appropriations, and other specific variants have been supplied under direct purchase to a variety of foreign customers. The Sea Hawk is a dedicated naval anti-submarine version which has a modified undercarriage to allow it to operate off frigates and destroyers. It is being manufactured in Japan by Mitsubishi and the first production unit was delivered in 1991. In 1987, Westland in the U.K. flew an experimental S-70C (the civil variant) which they intended to build commercially, but anticipated orders did not materialise and the prototype was exported to the United States.

Sikorsky's current executive helicopter is the S-76, which was first flown in 1977 and fulfils the need of business operators for a high-speed machine with ample cabin capacity for VIP seating layouts. The S-76, like other Sikorsky products, has been through a programme of progressive product development which has included increases in useful load, and improved variants of the Allison 250 turboshaft engines and related transmission systems. Sikorsky has also offered the S-76 with alternative Turboméca Arriel engines, and has developed military variants of the S-76 – although no hostile military variants have been ordered to date. The S-76 serves in various support role configurations including search-and-rescue and medevac. Military users include the Spanish Air Force, Chilean Army, Royal Hong Kong Auxiliary Air Force and Honduran Air Force, and the S-76 will be built in Korea for the South Korean Army.

The company has embarked on a number of advanced programmes for the future including the S-76 Shadow development aircraft with an additional nose-mounted cockpit for the LHX advanced light helicopter programme, and the S-75. The S-75 ACAP demonstrator has been built to test composite airframes for helicopters under a research project for the U.S. Army. For the future, Sikorsky is pressing ahead with the S-92 Helibus medium-lift helicopter, which is targeted at civil and military customers and will replace the S-61 in many transport applications – particularly for oil support tasks. This is being developed by a consortium which includes Mitsubishi, CATIC, Embraer, AIDC and Gamesa. It has also teamed with Boeing in the development of the RAH-66 Comanche reconnaissance/attack helicopter.

Sikorsky S-52, NC92823 *(HGM Collection)*

Production details

Each Sikorsky design has had its own individual serial batch with the type number prefix and a sequential number starting at 01 or 001. The batches allocated were as follows:

Model	Serial Batch	Number Built	Notes
S-51	c/n 51.01 to 51.294	294	Does not include Westland-built Dragonfly.
S-52	c/n 52.001 to 52.095	95	
S-53	c/n 53.001 to 53.003	3	c/n information unconfirmed.
S-54	c/n 54.001	1	
S-55	c/n 55.001 to 55.1281	1281	Does not include 45 Mitsubishi-built S-55C, Sud-built S-55 and Westland-built Whirlwind.
S-56	c/n 56.001 to 56.155	155	
S-58	c/n 58.001 to 58.1821	1821	Does not include Sud-built H-34.
S-59	c/n 59.001 to 59.002	2	
S-60	c/n 60.001	1	
S-61	c/n 61.001 to 61.827	827	Does not include 185 Mitsubishi-built S-61 and Agusta-built AS-61A-4, HH-3F and AS-61N1.
S-62	c/n 62.001 to 62.145	145	Does not include 25 Mitsubishi S-62J.
S-64	c/n 64.001 to 64.105	105	
S-65	c/n 65.001 to 65.670	670	
S-65	c/n V65.001 to V65.110	110	CH.53G built by VFW-Fokker.
S-67	c/n 67.001	1	
S-69	c/n 69.001 to 69.003	3	
S-70	c/n 70.001 to 70.1783	1783	Does not include Mitsubishi-built H-60J.
S-72	c/n 72.001 to 72.002	2	
S-75	c/n 75.001	1	
S-76	c/n 76.001 to 76.0480	480	Current.

Model Information

In general terms, Sikorsky allocates the -A suffix in its designations to land-based military helicopters, -B to naval versions and -C to civil variants. However, many of the U.S. military variants do not have a specific Sikorsky designation. In detail, the helicopters developed by Sikorsky are as follows:

Type No.	Designation	Notes
VS.316A S-48	R-4 H-4B HNS-1 Hoverfly I	Side by side-two-seat helicopter of tube & metal/fabric construction with fixed tailwheel u/c. Powered by one 185 hp Warner R-550-1 piston engine mounted behind cockpit. Prot. 41-18847 FF 14 Jan. 1942. 145 built.
VS.372	R-5 H-5 Dragonfly	Tandem-two-seat helicopter constructed of metal tube with moulded plywood skinning developed from R-6 with tailwheel u/c. Powered by one 450 hp P&W R985 Wasp Junior engine. Prot. 42-28236 FF 18 Aug. 1943. 76 built.

Type No.	Designation	Notes
VS.316B	R-6 Hoverfly	Developed R-4 with moulded fuselage, tricycle u/c and 225 h.p. Lyc. O-435-7 engine. Prot. 43-47955 FF15 Oct. 1943. 247 built.
S-51	H-5 HO2S HO3S Dragonfly	Four-seat 'pod & boom' type helicopter based on H-5 with tricycle u/c, metal fuselage and wood/fabric (later metal) rotor blades. Powered by one 450 hp P&W R985 Wasp Junior. Prot. N92800 FF 16 Feb. 1946.
S-52-1		Two-seat all-metal 'pod & boom' type helicopter with fixed tricycle u/c powered by a 178 hp Franklin engine. 1900 lb TOGW. Prot. NC92823 (c/n 52.001) FF 12 Feb. 1947. 4 built.
S-52-2	H-18 H-39	Three/four-seat version of S52-1 with longer cabin section, four-wheel u/c and 245 h.p. Franklin 6V6-245-B16F engine. 2700 lb TOGW. Prot. 49-2888. Two a/c converted to S-59. 4 built.
S-52-3	HO5S	USN and USCG version of S-52-2 with 245 hp Lyc. O-245-1 engine, fuel and electrical system changes and inverted-V ventral stabiliser. One aircraft fitted with Ford Taurus V-8 engine and recontoured nose in 1989.
S-52-5		S-52-3 fitted with 320 shp Turboméca Artouste II turboshaft Prot. FF 24 Jul. 1953. See S-59.
S-53	XHJS-1	Four-seat military helicopter similar to S-51 with tricycle u/c, small tail rotor pylon, tailplane and powered by one 525 h.p. Continental R-975-34 engine. Prot. Bu. 30368 FF 22 Sept. 1947. 3 built.
S-54		Believed to have been a tandem twin-rotor project. Not built.
S-55	YH-19 Chickasaw	Military 12-seat utility helicopter of 'pod & boom' layout with fixed 4-wheel u/c and straight tailboom, narrow vertical fin and inverted-V tail surfaces. Powered by one 550 shp P&W R-1340-S3H2 piston engine. Prot. FF 10 Nov. 1949.
S-55	H-19A	Production miltary S-55.

Sikorsky S-55 UH-19B, 52-7553

Type No.	Designation	Notes
S-55A		Commercial S-55 with 700 shp Wright R-1300-3 engine, bent tail boom, broad vertical fin, horizontal tailplane and hydro-mechanical clutch system.
S-55B	CH-19E HRS-3 Chickasaw	Production military S-55 with 600 h.p. R-1340-57 engine. See table for military designations.
S-55C		Nine-seat commercial S-55 with bent tailboom, 550 h.p. Pratt & Whitney R-1340-S1H2 engine and 7200 lb TOGW.
S-55D	H-19B	Military version of S-55A.
S-55E		Unofficial designation for civilianised CH-19E.
S-55F		Unofficial designation for civilianised UH-19F.
S-55G		Unofficial designation for civilianised HH-19G.
S-55-T		S-55 conversion by Aviation Specialties Inc. with 840 shp Garrett-AiResearch TSE331-3U-303N turboshaft. Deluxe 'Elite' version by Vertical Aviation Technologies. 50 conversions.
S-56	H-37A HR2S-1 Mojave	Large military transport/assault helicopter with 36-troop capacity, retractable tailwheel u/c and two 2100 shp P&W R-2800 piston engines on stub wings driving single main rotor. Prot. XHR2S-1 Bu.133732 FF 18 Dec. 1953.
S-57		Jet powered VTOL convertiplane project. Not built.
S-58	HSS-1 Seabat	All-metal 2 crew/16 pax military utility helicopter for U.S. Navy with simplified S-55 dynamic components, fixed tailwheel u/c and one 1525 shp Wright R-1820-84 piston engine. Prot. XHSS-1 Bu.134668 FF 8 Mar. 1954. 49 built under licence in France by Sud Est. Westland production as Wessex with turbine power.
S-58	HSS-1N	All-weather/ night capable version of HSS-1 with revised u/c legs, automatic stabilisation and improved avionics. Also built by Mitsubishi from Sikorsky kits.

Sikorsky S-56 H-37A, 50617

Type No.	Designation	Notes
S-58	HSS-1F	HSS-1 fitted with two GE YT-58 turboshafts in nose. Prot. FF 30 Jan. 1957. Later SH-34H.
S-58	HUS-1 UH-34D	U.S. Marines 12-troop version of HSS-1. HUS-1A fitted with amphibious floats. HUS-1G for U.S. Coast Guard SAR duties, HUS-1L for Antarctic support ops. HUS-1Z fitted with VIP interior for Presidential transport.
S-58	H-34A H-34B H-34C	U.S. Army version of HSS-1 with 18-troop capacity. Some converted to VH-34A with VIP interior and emergency flotation bags. HH-34D and UH-34D are ex HSS-1 aircraft transferred to USAF. 136 built by Sud Est.
S-58	H-34G.III	18 HSS-1N for West German Navy and 52 for the Army with Wright R-989-C9HE engine.
S-58	UH-34G UH-34J	HSS-1 with ASW equipment removed and reconfigured for transport and utility use. 14 converted to HH-34J SAR aircraft.
S-58B		Civil version of H-34 for passenger or cargo transport with Wright R-989-C9HE-2 engine.12700 lb TOGW. 18 built.
S-58C		Civil passenger-carrying model with two starboard side entrance doors and six cabin windows each side. 12700 lb TOGW. 17 built.
S-58D		Development of civil S-58A with increased 13000 lb TOGW.
S-58E		S-58 with 13000 lb TOGW.
S-58F		S-58B with 12500 lb TOGW.
S-58G		S-58C with 12500 lb TOGW.
S-58H		S-58D with 12500 lb TOGW.
S-58J		S-58E with 12500 lb TOGW.
S-58T		S-58 fitted with P&WC PT6T-3 twinpack turboshaft. Prot FF 26 Aug. 1970. Kits built by Sikorsky but 160 conversions carried out by California Helicopter International.

S-58T, N870 *(Sikorsky)*

Type No.	Designation	Notes
S-58BT		S-58B fitted with S-58T kit. 13000 lb TOGW.
S-58DT		S-58D fitted with S-58T kit . 13000 lb TOGW.
S-58ET		S-58E fitted with S-58T kit. 13000 lb TOGW.
S-58FT		S-58F fitted with S-58T kit. 12500 lb TOGW.
S-58-HT		S-58H fitted with S-58T kit. 12500 lb TOGW.
S-58JT		S-58J fitted with S-58T kit. 12500 lb TOGW.
S-59	H-39	S-52 converted to XH-59 with installation of one 400 shp Continental XT-51-T3 (licence-built Artouste) turboshaft. First of two Prots s/n 49-2890. FF 1 June 1954.
S-60	Skycrane	Flying crane helicopter with S-56 rotor head, blades and other components. Two 2100 h.p. Pratt & Whitney R-2800 piston engines mounted on stub wings. Fixed tailwheel u/c configuration. Prot. N807 (c/n 60.001). FF 25 Mar. 1959.
S-61	HR3S-1 H-3	Amphibious anti-submarine helicopter with outrigger floats powered by two 1175 shp GE T58-GE-6 turboshafts. Prot YSH-3A Bu.147137 (c/n 61.001). FF 11 Mar. 1959.
S-61A	CH-3A CH-3B	Standard transport version of S-61 for military applications.
S-61A	CH-124	41 for Canadian Navy. 37 assembled in Canada by UACL.
S-61	SH-3A	Japanese production by Mitsubishi.
AS-61A	ASH-3D	Italian production by Agusta.
S-61A-1		8 for Danish Air Force.
S-61A-4		40 for Malaysian AF as the 'Nuri'.
S-61A-5		One modified aircraft for Danish Air Force.

Sikorsky S-61N, G-LINK

Type No.	Designation	Notes
S-61B	SH-3A HSS-2 Sea King	USN version of SH-3A for sonar and anti-submarine missions with two 1250 shp T58-GE-8 engines, increased fuel and improved sonar system.
S-61B	SH-3D Sea King	SH-3A fitted with 1400 shp T58-GE-10 engines, increased fuel and improved sonar system.
S-61B	VH-3D	11 USMC models for Presidential transport.
S-61B	HH-3A	Armed rescue variant of SH-3A with long-range tanks, minigun installation and armour plating.
S-61B	RH-3A	Nine SH-3A converted for mine countermeasures with towed AMCM raft capability.
S-61B	SH-3A	Japanese production by Mitsubishi.
S-61D		Proposed S-61 for USMC with deep square-section fuselage with rear loading doors and high-set tailboom. Not built.
S-61D-2	Sea King	Westland built version of SH-3D. Four pattern a/c supplied by Sikorsky.
S-61D-3	SH-3D	Six for Brazil.
S-61D-4	SH-3D	Seven for Argentina.
S-61E	RH-3E	CH-3C with 1500 shp T58-GE-5 engines fitted with mine countermeasures equipment.
S-61F	NH-3A	One SH-3A for high speed research with modified lower fuselage, enlarged fin and tailplane, retractable u/c, no sponsons, six-blade rotor and two J60-P booster engines mounted on stub wings. FF 21 May 1965.
S-61L		28-pax civil version based on S-61A but with stretched non-water sealed fuselage, no floats, fixed u/c and baggage compartments in lower fuselage. FF 6 Dec. 1960. 11 built.
S-61N		S-61L with amphibious hull and external floats, enlarged vertical tail, retractable main gear and two 1250 shp CT-58-110-1 turboshafts. 126 built.

Sikorsky S-62, PH-NZB *(via MJH)*

Type No.	Designation	Notes
S-61NM		One S-61L with S-61N tail fin, stabiliser and undercarriage.
AS-61N-1	Silver	Agusta model with short fuselage.
S-61R	CH-3C	USAF long-range version with fuselage-mounted sponsons, tail loading ramp, retractable tricycle u/c, gun fittings and two 1300 shp T58-GE-1 engines FF 17 Jun. 1963.
S-61R	CH-3E	CH-3C with 1500 shp T58-GE-5 engines. Some CH-3Cs upgraded.
S-61R	HH-3E HH-3F Jolly Green Giant	Combat-SAR version of CH-3E with refuelling probe, armour plating and overload fuel tanks on external stub wings. Some converted from CH-3E. HH-3F for USCG.
AS-61R	HH-3F Pelican	Italian production by Agusta for Italian Air Force
S-61V	VH-3A	Nine VIP versions of SH-3A for Presidential use by Executive Flight Detachment.
S-62		8/12 pax amphibious helicopter using S-55 blades, rotor head, gearboxes etc. with boat hull and outrigger floats containing retractable main u/c. Powered by one 1050 shp GE T58-GE-6 turboshaft. Prot. N880 FF 14 May 1958.
S-62A	HH-52A HU2S-1G	Production S-62 for civil customers and USCG as 'Seaguard'.
S-62B		S-62A with S-58 dynamic components and 1250 shp GE T58-GE-8 turboshaft.
S-63		Proposed version of S-62 with S-58 dynamic components and 1250 shp GE T58-GE-8 turboshaft. Became S-62B.
S-64A	CH-54A Tarhe Skycrane	Developed S-60 with two P&W 4500 shp T73-P-1 turboshaft engines, tricycle u/c, enlarged cockpit pod and increased lifting capacity. Provision for removable universal military pod. Improved CH-54B with higher gross weight. Prot. N625Y FF 9 May 1962.

Sikorsky S-65C-2 *(Sikorsky)*

Type No.	Designation	Notes
S-64A	CH-54B Tarhe	CH-54A with two 4800 shp T73-P-700 engines, higher gross weight, twin main wheels and new rotor blades.
S-64E		Commercial version of CH-54A. 9 built.
S-64F		CH-54B remanufactured for civil use by Erickson Air Crane Co.
S-65A	CH-53A Sea Stallion	Heavy single-rotor assault helicopter for USMC with 38-troop capacity, S-64 dynamic components, rear loading ramp, retractable tricycle u/c and two 2850 shp GE T64-GE-6 turboshafts mounted in external fuselage pods. Prot. YCH-53A s/n Bu151613 FF 14 Oct. 1964.
S-65A	RH-53A Sea Stallion	15 CH-53A fitted with two 3925 shp T64-GE-413 turboshafts, refuelling probe and machine gun positions for mine countermeasures patrol.
S-65A	HH-53B Super Jolly	Eight CH-53A for USAF fitted with two 3080 shp T64-GE-3 turboshafts, refuelling probe, armour plating, pilot ejection seats, three 7.62-mm miniguns, external hoist and extra tanks etc. for long range search-and-rescue. FF 16 Mar. 1967.
S-65A	HH-53C CH-53C Super Jolly	HH-53B for USAF with 3925 shp T64-GE-7 engines for SAR duties. CH-53C is transport version.
S-65A	CH-53D VH-53D Sea Stallion	CH-53A for USMC with enlarged 55-troop capacity cabin, fitted with two 4380 shp T64-GE-415, gun positions and refuelling boom. VH-53D is staff transport VIP version.
S-65A	RH-53D Sea Stallion	CH-53D for US Navy fitted similarly to RH-53A for mine countermeasures.
S-65A	CH-53G	German Army version with two T64-GE-7 engines, built by VFW-Fokker.
S-65A	HH-53H MH-53H MH-53J	41 HH-53C converted for Special Operations Forces with night rescue infra-red systems and terrain following radar and T64-GE-415 engines.
S-65C		44-pax commercial transport version of CH-53 with airstair doors, passenger windows, lengthened nose and increased fuel. One CH-53 converted but not developed to production.
S-65C		Designation used for export military CH-53.
S-65C-2		Two Austrian AF CH-53. Also designated S-65Oe.
S-65C-3		Israeli Air Force version of CH-53D. 28 delivered.
S-66		Proposed advanced aerial fire support system helicopter for US Army AAFSS competition. Not built.
S-67	Black Hawk	Two-seat high speed attack helicopter with small detachable wings, fin and tailplane, S-65 dynamic components, 5-blade rotor and two 1500 shp GE T58-GE-5 turboshafts. Retractable tailwheel u/c. Prot. N671SA FF 27 Aug. 1970.
S-68		No details known.

Type No.	Designation	Notes
S-69	XH-59A YH-59A	Advancing-blade concept aircraft with two counter-rotating rotor blades, fixed twin-fin tail unit powered by one P&W PT6T-3 turboshaft. Prot. 71-1472 FF 29 Jul. 1973. Three built.
S-70A	UH-60A Black Hawk	Military tactical utility transport helicopter for US Army, National Guard, US Customs etc. to meet UTTAS specification, with 3 crew plus 11-troop capacity, fixed tailwheel u/c, conventional fuselage with fin and full span controllable tailplane. Powered by two 1560 shp General Electric T700-GE-700 turboshafts mounted on cabin roof driving four-blade main rotor. Prot. YUH-60A s/n 73-21650 (c/n 70.001) FF 17 Oct. 1974. Also JUH-60A trials aircraft and GUH-60A ground instructional airframes.
S-70A	EH-60A EH-60C Black Hawk	66 UH-60A converted with Quickfix IIB electronic battlefield communications jammer system, large external dipole DF antennae, whip aerial and large IR suppression exhaust shrouds.
S-70A	MH-60A MH-60L Black Hawk	30 UH-60A modified for special operations with FLIR, door-mounted minigun, auxiliary fuel tanks etc.
S-70A	YEH-60B SOTAS	Eight UH-60A for US Army Standoff target acquisition system development with belly-mounted rotating radar antenna, long-stroke u/c and ground data link. Prot. s/n 23714 FF 6 Feb. 1981.
S-70A	VH-60A VH-60N Black Hawk	Nine VIP version of SH-60B for USMC Executive Flight Detachment with weather radar, special comms equipment and executive interior.
S-70A	HH-60D Night Hawk	Prototype combat rescue S-70 for USAF. s/n 23718.

Sikorsky S-70C, N3124B

185

Type No.	Designation	Notes
S-70A	MH-60G HH-60G Pave Hawk	106 UH-60A converted for USAF as long-range deep penetration rescue or special missions helicopters with refuelling probe, additional fuel and high-spec avionics and flight control systems.
S-70A	MH-60K	Special operations variant for US Army similar to MH-60G but with higher gross weight, external Stinger missile points, chin-mounted FLIR, external tanks on shoulder-mounted pylons, twin 23-mm door-mounted guns and 1875 shp T-700-GE-701C engines. Prot s/n 26134 FF 26 Feb. 1992.
S-70A	UH-60L Black Hawk	UH-60A with 1857 shp T700-GE-701C engines and uprated transmission and infra-red suppression shrouds.
S-70A	UH-60Q Black Hawk	UH-60L modified for high-density medevac missions with 9 litters and updated avionics. One prot. and 3 pre-prod. built to date.
S-70A-1L	Desert Hawk	Eight UH-60L for Saudi Arabia medevac with air conditioning, six-litter provision, improved avionics, rescue hoist etc.
S-70A-2		Designation allocated to possible German order.
S-70A-3		Designation allocated to possible Spanish order.
S-70A-4	Black Hawk	Designation allocated to possible Swiss order.
S-70A-5	Black Hawk	24 S-70C delivered to China and Philippines.
S-70A-6	Black Hawk	Proposed UH-60A troop transport for Thai Air Force.
S-70A-7		Designation allocated to possible Peru order.
S-70A-8		Designation allocated to possible Brazilian order.
S-70A-9	Black Hawk	39 UH-60A for RAAF (later Australian Army). All assembled by Hawker de Havilland.
S-70A-10		Designation allocated to possible Israeli order.

Sikorsky S-76

Type No.	Designation	Notes
S-70A-11		Three UH-60A for Royal Jordanian AF.
S-70A-12	UH-60J	S-70 built by Mitsubishi for JASDF and JMSDF.
S-70A-14		Two VIP versions for Brunei Government.
S-70A-15		Designation allocated to possible Swedish order.
S-70A-16		WS-70L as developed by Westland.
S-70A-17		12 UH-60A for Turkish police inc. two VIP versions .
S-70A-18	UH-60P	Eight UH-60L for South Korea. Some assembled by Korean Air.
S-70A-19		Proposed Westland version of S-70.
S-70A-20		VIP model for Thai Government.
S-70A-21		Two VIP models for Egyptian Government.
S-70A-22		Three VIP models for Korea.
S-70A-23		Designation allocated to possible Algerian order.
S-70A-24		10 UH-60L for Mexican AF.
S-70A-25		Two for Moroccan Gendarmerie.
S-70A-27		Two for Hong Kong Aux.AF.
S-70A-28		95 for Turkish Armed Forces. 50 aircraft assembled by TUSAS Havacilik ve Uzay Sanayi A.S. in Turkey.
S-70B	SH-60B Sea Hawk	Naval version of UH-60 with IBM-fitted integrated ASW and anti-shipping electronics to LAMPS-III specification. Fitted with two 1690 shp T700-GE-401 (later 1900 shp T700-GE-401C) turboshafts, rotor brake, automatic rotor folding, folding tail, dual tailwheel, extra port cabin door, single main cabin windows, external Mk.46 torpedo hardpoints, increased fuel and flotation equipment. 13768 lb TOGW. Prot YSH-60B Bu.161169 FF 12 Dec. 1979.
S-70B	SH-60F Ocean Hawk CV-Helo	Short-range version of SH-60B with search radar, MAD and sonobuoy dispenser and Bendix dipping sonar.
S-70B	HH-60H Sea Hawk	SH-60F with threat detection and countermeasures equipment, cabin-mounted machine guns and Hellfire missile pylons for special warfare support and combat rescue equipment.
S-70B	HH-60J JayHawk	US Coast Guard medium range SAR helicopter based on SH-60B with provision for external fuel tanks, nose mounted search radar and rescue hoists.
S-70B	SH-60R	Upgrade programme for SH-60 to SH-60F standard.
S-70	CH-60	Combat support version of S-70 for US Navy with UH-60 fuselage and SH-60 transmission etc.
S-70B-1	Sea Hawk	Six SH-60B for Spanish Navy with Bendix AN/AQS-13F dunking sonar.
S-70B-2		Eight SH-60B with modified avionics and radar for Royal Australian Navy.
S-70B-3		Seven SH-60B for Japan JMSDF as pattern aircraft for SH-60J and UH-60J.

Type No.	Designation	Notes
S-70B-6		Five armed naval ASW versions for Greece.
S-70B-7		Six SH-60B for Royal Thai Navy carrier-based SAR and maritime patrol.
S-70C		Commercial version of S-70A for civil or military customers with two GE CT7-2C turboshafts, revised window layout etc. Prot. N7601C.
S-70C	Firehawk	One S-70 equipped for fire-fighting with underslung bucket dispenser.
S-70C-1		14 for Taiwan for SAR duties.
S-70C-2		24 S-70C for China based on SH-60B.
S-70CM-1	Thunderhawk	Ten SH-60B frigate-based ASW model for Taiwan Navy.
S-71		No details known.
S-72	RSRA	Three-seat research helicopter for NASA testing of rotor systems. Based on S70 fuselage with tailwheel u/c, small wings and fin/rudder assembly. Powered by two 9275 shp GE T58-GE-5 turboshafts driving a single 5-blade rotor. Prot NASA545. FF 12 Oct. 1976. Two built.
S-72X1		S-72 modified to X-wing rotor system research vehicle powered by two 1500 shp GE T58-GE-10 and two 9275 shp GE TF-34-GE-400A turboshafts. Prot NASA741.
S-73		No details known.
S-74		No details known.
S-75	ACAP	Research helicopter with composite airframe and powerplant and rotor system of S-76. 8470 lb TOGW.
S-76	Spirit	12-passenger high performance executive helicopter with integral fuselage/boom, fin and tailplane, retractable tricycle u/c and 10000 lb TOGW. Powered by two 650 shp Allison 250-C30 turboshafts driving four-blade main rotor. Prot. N762SA (c/n 72002) FF 13 Mar. 1977.
S-76	Mark II	S-76 with improved ventilation, Allison 250-C30S turboshafts, improved dynamic system, additional maintenance access etc.
S-76A+		S-76 conversion with two 700 shp Turboméca Arriel 1S turboshafts. 17 converted to date.
S-76A	Mark II	S-76 with 10500 lb TOGW and improved transmission.
S-76B		S-76A MkII with two 980 shp P&W PT6B-36B turboshafts and 11400 lb TOGW.
S-76B	Shadow	S-76B fitted with nose mounted crew pod for research into systems for LHX light helicopter programme. Prot. N765SA (c/n 76.005).
S-76C		S-76B with two Turboméca Arriel 1S1 turboshafts, increased fuel tankage/range and higher (11700 lb) gross weight.
S-76C+		S-76C fitted with two 855 shp Arriel 2S1 engines and FADEC system. Prot. F-WJDI.

Type No.	Designation	Notes
H-76	Eagle	Multi-mission military helicopter based on S-76A Mk.II with Fantail anti-torque tail rotor, external armament stub wing, modified fuel tanks etc. Prot. N3124G (c/n 760303) FF Feb. 1985. Later titled AUH-76. Also flown with anti-torque fan in shrouded tail installation.
S-77		No details known.
S-78		Civil version of S-70 with enlarged cabin and retractable u/c.Originally Model S-70C-20. S-78-29 had enlarged fuselage for 29 pax. Project abandoned.
S-79		No details known.
S-80	CH-53E Super Stallion	H-53 for USN and USMC with larger diameter 7-blade main rotor and three 4380 shp GE T64-GE-416 turboshafts. Large braced articulated tailplane, tail pylon angled to port and foldable tail section. Prot. YCH-53E Bu.159121 FF 1 Mar. 1974.
S-80M	MH-53E Sea Dragon	CH-53E for mine countermeasures with AMCM equipment, new station-keeping nav systems and enlarged sponsons for additional fuel.
S-80M-1	Sea Dragon	MH-53E for JMSDF without refuelling probe and with Fujitsu PNS nav system.
S-92C	Helibus	Proposed 19/22 passenger civil transport helicopter with external sponsons for fuel and u/c retraction, S-70 rotor head and other dynamic components and two 1750 shp GE CT-7-6X turboshafts. First of five prototypes to fly in 1998.
S-92IU		S-92 in utility configuration for international customers.
	RAH-66 Comanche	Light attack and reconnaissance helicopter developed by Boeing and Sikorsky with tandem two-seat stepped cockpit, retractable tailwheel u/c, chin-mounted 20-mm Gatling gun, shrouded 8-blade tail fan and two LHTEC T800 turboshafts driving an advanced five-blade bearingless composite main rotor. Prot. FF 4 Jan. 1996.

Left: Sikorsky S-92 mockup

Right: Sikorsky XHJS-1 Bu.30368 *(via EM)*

Military Designations

The U.S. Military designations given to the various Sikorsky helicopter models were as follows:

Model	Name	USAF	US Army	US Navy	Marine Corps	USCG	Total Delivered
S-51	Dragonfly	H-5 R-5		HO2S HO3S			232
S-52		H-18		HO5S			91
S-55B	Chickasaw	H-19A, SH-19A HH-19A	H-19C UH-19C	HO4S-1	HRS-1 HRS-2		288
S-55D	Chickasaw	H-19B UH-19B SH-19B	H-19D	HO4S-3 UH-19F	HRS-3 CH-19E	HO4S-3G HH-19G	789
S-56	Mojave		H-37A/B		HR2S-1		156
S-58	Choctaw Seabat Seahorse	H-34A	H-34A CH-34A VH-34A	HSS-1 HUS-1L LH-34D SH-34G UH-34D	HUS-1 HUS-1A UH-34E	HUS-1G HH-34F	827
S-58	Choctaw	SH-34J	H-34B H-34C LH-34D	HSS-1N	HUS-1L HUS-1Z VH-34D		385
S-61	Sea King	CH-3A CH-3B CH-3C CH-3E HH-3E		SH-3A HH-3A RH-3A SH-3D SH-3G SH-3H SH-3J	VH-3A VH-3D	HH-3F	520
S-62						HH-52A	99
S-64	Tarhe SkyCrane		CH-54A				97
S-65	Sea Stallion Super Jolly	HH-53B HH-53C CH-53C HH-53H		RH-53A RH-53D VH-53D	CH-53A CH-53D VH-53F		375
S-70	Black Hawk Sea Hawk Night Hawk Rescue Hawk Ocean Hawk Jay Hawk	HH-60A HH-60D HH-60A MH-60G HH-60G	UH-60A UH-60L EH-60A EH-60C MH-60K MH-60L	SH-60B SH-60F HH-60H	VH-60A VH-60N	HH-60J	1388
S-80	Super Stallion Sea Dragon			MH-53E	CH-53E		248

WESTLAND

UNITED KINGDOM

In common with many other military equipment manufacturers, Westland Aircraft Ltd viewed the end of World War II as a somewhat mixed blessing. 1945 was a moment for the company to take major decisions on the products they should build for peacetime markets. There were potential military contracts for the aircraft that Westland had traditionally built and one of these materialised as the Wyvern which had been initiated in early 1944. However, the strategic review settled on helicopters as being the leading new technology with potential – even though existing designs suffered from poor stability and vibration and were relatively limited in lift capacity.

The direction was a wise one, because it positioned Westland as the leading helicopter producer in the United Kingdom and this was reinforced by the decision to start off with licence production of an existing design rather than following the time-consuming trail of development of an original model. On 10 January 1947, Westland management signed a licence agreement for the company to build the Sikorsky S-51 helicopter, including the right to modify the design and to market it outside the United States. The S-51 was a successor to the Sikorsky R-5 and was one of the first truly practical rotary wing machines. Six pattern aircraft were delivered from Sikorsky's Bridgeport, Connecticut plant, but the Westland WS-51 Dragonfly had many differences and was extensively re-engineered and fitted with an Alvis Leonides engine of higher power than the Sikorsky's Wasp Junior.

The first Dragonfly (G-AKTW) was flown in October 1948, and in the following year a contract was awarded for 13 aircraft for the Royal Navy. The initial roles of these aircraft were for carrier-borne rescue duties and they were fitted with folding rotor blades to facilitate hangar storage. The RAF also received three HC.2s which were sent immediately to assist in the Malayan jungle for casualty evacuation with external stretcher panniers. Ultimately, 98 Dragonflys were delivered to the British forces with a number of different versions of the Leonides powerplant. The civil version, the WS-51, was acquired by a variety of customers who had watched experiments by British European Airways with three of the Sikorsky machines. One WS-51 was fitted with spray bars by Pest Control Ltd and another was bought by Silver City Airways. A further 24 WS-51s were exported to military users including Japan, Iraq, France, Yugoslavia and Ceylon. The last Dragonfly was finally retired in 1969.

Westland also developed the Widgeon, which was a much improved Dragonfly with a 520 h.p. Leonides engine. The Widgeon had a new forward fuselage with a wider and longer cabin so that a passenger could sit beside the pilot with three further passengers on the rear bench seat. There was a port-side nose hatch which would allow direct loading of stretchers. It also used the Sikorsky S-55 gearbox, rotor shaft, rotor head and blades.

HELICOPTERS AND ROTORCRAFT

Three WS-51s were converted to Widgeons and a further 12 new production aircraft were built. Two of these were sold to the Hong Kong Defence Force.

Having established both their credentials as a helicopter manufacturer and a good relationship with Sikorsky, Westland went on to take up licence rights to the Sikorsky S-55, which offered a substantial improvement in load capacity over the S-51. The S-55 had a large square passenger cabin with wide loading doors for bulky cargo, and one pattern aircraft (G-AMHK c/n 55016) was imported to get production underway. The WS-55 Whirlwind was not re-engineered as extensivley as the S-51 had been, but Westland did make changes to the main gearbox. Again, the main customers for the Whirlwind were the British forces which had already had some experience of the S-55 through operation of a batch of 25 Sikorsky-built ex U.S. Navy machines delivered under MDAP.

The Whirlwind Series 1 was fitted with the 600 h.p. Pratt & Whitney R-1340, and 92 military aircraft were delivered as the HAR.Mk.1, Mk.2, Mk.3 and Mk.4 together with 44 civil Srs.1s. The Series 2 which followed was powered by the Alvis Leonides, and 134 military and 19 civil examples were built. Finally, the Series 3, with an upgrade to the Bristol Siddeley (later Rolls-Royce) Gnome turbine based on the General Electric T58, was delivered as the military Mk.9 to Mk.12 (70 units) and the civil Series 3 (5 units). Early Pratt & Whitney-powered Whirlwinds had the original straight tailboom of the Sikorsky S-55, but with the introduction of the Leonides engine the distinctive 'broken back' boom was introduced to improve main rotor blade clearance.

The first HAR.Mk.1 was delivered in July 1954 to the Royal Navy. Whirlwinds served with all the British services for search and rescue, anti-submarine warfare, assault transport and medical evacuation. Two were delivered for use by the Queen's Flight with upgraded 740 h.p. Leonides engines, and export deliveries were made to 16 customers including the French Navy and to the Yugoslav Air Force and Navy. Several of the latter are believed to have been built under licence in Yugoslavia. Of the 68 production civil Whirlwinds, 25 were sold to Bristow Helicopters which used them for operations in Nigeria and to support the early North Sea oil platforms.

In 1956, Royal Navy requirements for a new anti-submarine helicopter with capacity to carry a dipping sonar and a full load of sonobuoys and light torpedoes prompted Westland to approach Sikorsky once again, for a licence to build the S-58 Seabat. With experience of reworking the Whirlwind airframe to take the Gnome turboshaft engine, Westland proposed to fit the S-58 airframe with an 1100 shp. Napier NG.11 Gazelle turbine. The prototype was a Sikorsky-built machine which was converted and given the military serial XL722, and first flew with the new engine in May 1957. This was followed by a pre-production batch of eleven development aircraft which tried a variety of nose

Westland Lynx, XX153 *(Westland)*

shapes and detail engine installation features. The new helicopter, which was named Wessex, went into production initially for issue to the Navy's 700(H) intensive trials unit. The early Wessex variants were tasked as anti-submarine helicopters, but the Royal Marine Commandos and the RAF soon started to receive transport variants and the Queen's Flight re-equipped with all-red HCC.4s with VIP interiors and upgraded avionics.

Some 320 British military Wessexes were delivered, and 42 export deliveries were made to Ghana, Iraq, Brunei and the Australian Navy. Westland also converted 45 Wessex HAS.1s to HAS.3 standard. The first Wessex model for the RAF was the HC.2, which was fitted with twin Gnome engines, and this led to the Navy's HU.5 which was used for tropical operations. A special civil model, the Wessex 60, was certificated, and almost all of the 20 built flew with Bristow Helicopters on North Sea oil support. These operations finally ceased in 1981 following three accidents to the Wessex 60 fleet.

The 1957 Defence Review and subsequent aircraft industry overhaul resulted in all the smaller helicopter companies – Bristol, Fairey and Saunders Roe – being absorbed by Westland. These acquisitions brought existing models with them, but in practice it was only the Saunders Roe P.531 which survived to become a production model. The British Army had operated the Saunders Roe Skeeter as a battlefield observation and liaison helicopter with some success, and the P.531 was designed as a turbine-powered replacement with increased accommodation. The early prototypes were shown to be underpowered and unable to meet the Army specification, but the subsequent P.531-2, developed under Westland's management, was found to be effective and was ordered as the Westland Scout AH.1. Built at the former Fairey factory at Hayes, the Scout entered service in March 1963. A total of 149 Scouts was built for the British Army, which used them in several policing and war situations including the crises in Malaya, Brunei and Aden and also in Northern Ireland. External pylons were fitted to many Scouts to carry Nord SS.11 wire-guided missiles and other external weapons. Westland also sold a small number of Scouts to overseas air arms including those of Jordan and Uganda.

The Westland Wasp was a naval derivative of the P.531-2, the development of which paralleled that of the Scout. However, the Wasp differed from the Scout in many detailed respects. The main fuselage pod was longer and the undercarriage was a swivelling four-wheel arrangement rather than the skids of the Scout. This was to facilitate landing on the helicopter decks of Royal Navy frigates. The Wasp's vertical fin was narrower and a small single tailplane replaced the large underslung unit of the other machine. Provision was made for a pair of Mk.44 torpedoes to be carried under the belly. Ninety-eight Wasps were eventually completed with a handful being delivered to Indonesia, the Netherlands,

Westland Lynx HMA.8

193

Malaysia and South Africa. New Zealand also received eight Wasps, of which two were former Royal Navy aircraft, and seven refurbished R.N. Wasps were delivered to Brazil in 1977.

Inevitably, the demand grew for larger and more powerful helicopters for the British forces. In 1951, Westland had attempted to produce a heavy passenger machine based on the Sikorsky S-56. Two examples of the Westminster were flown but neither the military nor commercial markets were ready for such a helicopter and the project was dropped. Eight years later Westland returned to Sikorsky to take out a licence for production of the S-61/SH-3A Sea King. In 1966, in view of a heightened Soviet threat which required long-range ASW capability, it was decided to replace the Wessex with the Westland-built version of the Sea King. The initial orders for Westland Sea Kings came from the Royal Navy, and four pattern examples (c/n 61-393 to 61-396) were acquired from Sikorsky to speed up the production process. The British Sea King was fitted with a pair of Rolls-Royce Gnome H.1400 turboshafts and with a Louis Newmark Mk.31 automatic flight control system.

Initial Sea King procurement was for 56 HAS.1 variants, and the first was delivered to 700(S) Squadron for service development in August 1969. This version was later developed into the HAS.2 with increased power, and the HAS.5 with a longer interior cabin to accommodate the Sea Searcher radar. Shortly after, the West German Navy ordered 22 Air-Sea Rescue variants as the Mk.41, and this prompted orders from the RAF for a similar SAR version designated HAR.Mk.3. The Sea King was then developed for the Egyptian Air Force as a 21-seat general utility transport, without the external floats and under the name 'Commando'. Subsequently, this model was ordered for use by the Royal Marines as the HC.4 and was used extensively in the Falklands War. The Sea King was such a flexible aircraft that it was equipped with increasingly sophisticated equipment for a wide range of roles. Perhaps one of the most unusual installations was the Thorn-EMI Searchwater radar, which used an inflatable radome which could be extended on an arm from the starboard cabin door. Westland exported Sea Kings to India, Norway, Belgium, Pakistan, Australia and Qatar.

It would be fair to say that, until the early 1960s, Westland had had limited experience of original helicopter design – although they were expert in modification and production of the existing Sikorsky designs. At this time, a number of original design studies were produced and the WG.3 emerged as a new Army tactical helicopter. Westland also entered into talks with Aérospatiale in France because of common requirements in the British and

Westland Scout, XP897

French forces for a modern range of helicopters. An inter-governmental Memorandum of Understanding was signed on 17 May 1965, providing for cooperation in development of these new machines. On the French side, the SA.330 Puma and SA.341 Gazelle were already in development by Aérospatiale. Westland's WG.13 was a neat solution to the gap in capacity between these two machines.

As far as the Puma was concerned, Westland was responsible for assembly of 48 aircraft ordered by the RAF, and approximately 30% of the original fabrication of these machines was done at Yeovil, with the remainder coming from Toulouse. Larger numbers of Gazelles were required by the British forces and parallel production lines were established in France and England, with Westland completing 262 examples.

Design and marketing leadership of the medium-capacity helicopter rested firmly with Westland. Dating back to the WG.3 design of 1963, the WG.13 was originally intended to use rotor blades from the Bristol 192 and the gearbox of the Whirlwind driven by a pair of Pratt & Whitney PT6A turboshafts. The design evolved over the next seven years with an increase in power, and the user definition changing many times. The first of 13 planned development Lynx helicopters flew at Yeovil on 21 March 1971, laying the ground for a British Army utility model, an RAF trainer, an ASW aircraft for the Royal Navy and a French Navy ASW and liaison version. The Lynx embodied many innovative engineering features, including a French-designed semi-rigid four-bladed rotor.

The initial batch of 100 Lynxes were destined for the British Army (AH Mk.1), Royal Navy (HAS. Mk.1) and the French Aéronavale (Lynx Mk. 2). The naval variants had a wheeled undercarriage rather than the skids of the AH Mk.1, and the French naval version had a hatch in the main cabin floor for operation of the Alcatel dipping sonar which had been specified. The naval variants were also fitted with the deck-landing harpoon system to facilitate operations from frigate helidecks fitted with the necessary grille surface. Westland also proposed the Model 606 civil variant of the Lynx, but the substantial costs of certification of a civil variant were not seen to be justified by the market studies and the '606 was eventually abandoned.

There did appear to be a market for a larger version of the Lynx, which led Westland to develop the WG.30. This combined the Gem 41 engines and dynamic components of the Lynx with a new larger-capacity fuselage. In its initial configuration the Westland 30 (as it became known) was seen as a primarily civil helicopter with accommodation for 19 passengers. Its design followed conventional lines with the engines placed above the box-section cabin compartment, a deep well-glazed cockpit in front and a high-set tailboom

Westland Sea King AEW.2A, XV650 *(Westland)*

with tailplane, twin fins and a tail rotor behind. The Westland 30 went into production on a private venture basis with the prospect of orders from British Airways Helicopters, Airspur of Los Angeles and Omniflight who operated Pan Am shuttle services between the downtown New York heliports and JFK Airport.

Unfortunately, the Gem engines caused continual problems and the Westland 30s in the United States were progressively withdrawn. Westland subsequently introduced further variants with General Electric CT7 engines, but the largest order – for 24 aircraft for Pawan Hans in India – was for the Gem-powered Series 100-60. These were delivered to India for use on oil and gas support work, but a series of three accidents in an 18-month period led to the Westland 30s being grounded and the whole production programme was wound up in early 1988 after 41 examples had been built. Westland had also attempted to develop the Westland 30 for military use, but the Puma was so well established that there was little interest in a new medium-weight aircraft.

In the mid-1970s the Royal Navy formulated a requirement for a successor to the anti-submarine Sea King, which resulted in Westland's WG.34 project. Due to a similar requirement from the Italian Navy, the British and Italian Governments came to an agreement for joint development of a new helicopter and this led to the establishment of European Helicopter Industries. The EH.101 is separately described and, with the Super Lynx, forms the major production effort in hand at Westland's Yeovil factory. Westland became part of the GKN Group in April 1994, following a progressive acquisition of its shares from United Technologies and others. The current major programme is the EH.101, although the company has been involved in development of a variant of the Sikorsky S.70 with RTM.322 engines, and application of the S.70 to the Saudi 'Al Yamamah II' programme. Westland has also responded to the British Army's requirement for a new gunship helicopter with a variant of the AH-64 Apache.

Production Details

Westland construction numbers were somewhat complex with four main batches of numbers (prefixed WA) for those models initiated by Westland, together with separate batches based on the Fairey and Aérospatiale serial systems for the later models. Some missing numbers were allocated to cancelled military batches and some serial numbers were reallocated on upgrade to a later model or on reallocation to a different military order. The first and second batches covered Dragonflys and Whirlwinds starting at WA/H/1 and WA.1 respectively. The third batch, commencing WA.1, started with the Wessex but later included Westland Bell 47s, all the Sea Kings and the final few production Whirlwinds. The Lynx has a new batch, omitting the familiar WA prefix and commencing at c/n 1. All new aircraft built by GKN-Westland are now in this form. The

Westland Wasp HAS.1, XT431

Wasp and Scout were built by the former Fairey factory and continued the Fairey system commencing at c/n F.9541. The Gazelle and Puma used serial numbers within the respective Aérospatiale batches, commencing at c/n 1001 in each case. Westland have also allocated separate build numbers to many models, consisting of a three-letter prefix (the last letter of which denotes the year of manufacture) and a number – and these are sometimes quoted to add to a very confusing system.

Production Details

Serial batches and production numbers are as follows:

Model	Serial Batch	Number Built	Notes
S-51 Dragonfly	c/n WA/H/1 to WA/H/149.	149	
WS-51 Widgeon	c/n WA/H/140 to WA/H/152.	12	
S-55 Whirlwind	c/n WA/A/1, WA2 to WA419, Plus c/n WA490 to WA496, WA612/613 and WA692/693 in main Wessex batch.	364	Some c/ns not used for complete aircraft. WA/A/1 was initially WA/H/55001.
S-58 Wessex	c/n WA.1 to WA309; WA460 to WA504; WA528 to WA563; WA614 to WA628; WA686 to 699; WA732; WA739 to WA743.	382	Some c/ns not used for complete aircraft.
WS-59 Westminster	c/n WA.1 & WA.2.	2	
Bell 47G Sioux	c/n WA310 to WA459; WA505 to WA527; WA564 to WA611; WA700 to WA731.	253	
Sea King	c/n WA630 to WA685; WA744 to WA869; WA874 to WA1007 up.	337+	
Wasp	c/n F.9541 to F9544; F.9550 to F9616; F9657 to F.9692; F9717 to F.9734.	125	Former Fairey system. Integrated with Scout.
Gazelle	Within Aérospatiale c/n 1002 to 2106 up	262	Integrated with Aérospatiale prod'n.
Scout	c/n S2/8437,38,40,41,43,46,47 F9472 to F.9511; F.9517 to F.9540, F.9617 to F.9655, F.9693 to F9716, F.9735 to F.99744, F.9758 to F.9762.	149	Integrated series with Wasp. Former Fairey and Saro c/n system.
Lynx	c/n 1 up.	406	
Puma	Scattered in batch c/n 1039 to 1220 and c/n 1622 to 1659. Early a/c also allocated Fairey c/ns F.9745 to F.9752.	48	Integrated with Aérospatiale prod'n. Some a/c also given Westland (Fairey) c/ns as shown.
Westland 30	c/n WA.001, 002 to 040, 901	41	

HELICOPTERS AND ROTORCRAFT

Model Information

Details of all Westland helicopters which reached flight status are as follows:

Type/Name	Notes
WS-51 Dragonfly	Sikorsky S-51 re-engineered to U.K. standards. Four-seat helicopter with single wood/metal 3-blade rotor, fixed tricycle u/c, all-metal mixed construction fuselage and powered by one 500 h.p. Alvis Leonides 521/1 piston engine. Prot. G-AKTW (c/n WA/H/1) FF 5 Oct. 1948.
WS-51 Mk.1A	Civil Dragonfly with deluxe interior.
WS-51 Mk.1B	Mk.1A with 450 h.p. Pratt & Whitney R-985-B4 engine.
Dragonfly HR.1	Royal Navy version of Mk.1A with air rescue winch and utility spec.
Dragonfly HC.2	RAF version with 540 h.p. Leonides 524/1 engine and external panniers for medevac.
Dragonfly HR.3	R.N. version with metal rotor blades for carrier guard duties.
Dragonfly HC.4	HC.2 with metal rotor blades and new servo control system.
Dragonfly HR.5	25 HR.1 and HR.3 upgraded with 540 h.p. Leonides 523/1 engine.
Widgeon	Civil WS-51 with 10-inch forward fuselage extension and reprofiled nose. Five seats. Powered by one 520 h.p. Alvis Leonides 521/2 engine with S-55 rotor head.
WS-55 Srs.1 Whirlwind	Sikorsky S-55 for civil customers modified to U.K. standards. Single rotor helicopter with two-seat crew compartment in nose above engine bay and lower main cabin for 8 pax. Fitted with 3-blade metal main rotor, 4-wheel u/c, inverted -V tailplanes and one 600 h.p. Pratt & Whitney R-1340-40 piston engine. Prot. G-AMJT (c/n WA/H/1) FF 12 Nov. 1952. Some fitted with amphibious floats.
Whirlwind HAR.1	Search & Rescue and general transport version for Royal Navy.
Whirlwind HAR.2	RAF variant of HAR.1 with interior equipment variations. French Navy version named 'Elephant Joyeux'.
Whirlwind HAR.3	Developed HAR.1 for R.N. with 700 h.p. Wright 12-1300-3 engine. Some aircraft with 'broken back' tailboom.
Whirlwind HAR.4	HAR.2 with upgraded R-1340-57 engine.
WS-55 Srs.2	Srs.1 with 'broken back' tailboom, horizontal tailplane, broader tailfin and 750 h.p. Alvis Leonides 755 engine.
Whirlwind HAR.5	3 Srs.2 conversions of HAR.3 airframes for R.N.
Whirlwind HAS.7	Anti-submarine version of Srs.2 with belly torpedo bay.
Whirlwind HCC.8	VIP model for Queen's Flight with deluxe 4-seat interior, extra cabin windows and 750 h.p. Leonides 160 engines. 2 built.
WS-55 Srs.3	5 Srs.2 fitted with 1050 Rolls-Royce Gnome H.1000 turboshaft.
Whirlwind HAR.9	16 HAS.7 aircraft upgraded to Srs.3 standard with Gnome engine.
Whirlwind HC.10	RAF tactical transport version of Srs.3.
Whirlwind HCC.12	2 VIP version of Srs.3 for Queen's Flight with 4-seat deluxe cabin.

Type/Name	Notes
WS-59 Westminster	Large transport helicopter for up to 40 passengers with single main 5-blade rotor and gearbox from Sikorsky S-56, tailwheel u/c, tubular frame fuselage structure with metal cladding for passenger role or open frame for utility/crane role. Powered by two 2920 shp Napier Eland E220 turboshafts. Two built. Prot. G-APLE (c/n WA.1) FF 15 June 1958.
Wessex	Sikorsky S-58 re-engined with 1100 shp Napier Gazelle NG.11 turboshaft. Prot XL722 (ex Bu.141602) FF 17 May 1957.
Wessex HAS.1	Wessex with 1450 shp Gazelle 161 turboshaft for R.N. anti-submarine warfare role. Also commando assault variant.
Wessex HC.2	RAF transport model for 16 troops with twin 1350 shp Bristol-Siddeley Gnome H.1200-110 turboshafts, redesigned gearbox and strengthened airframe. Also HAR.2 for rescue duties.
Wessex HAS.3	43 HAS.1 converted with 1600 shp Gazelle 18/165 turboshaft, new auto flight control system, improved search radar, collar round rear gearbox housing and radome on rear fuselage.
Wessex HCC.4	2 HC.2 for Queen's Flight with 4-seat deluxe passenger cabin.
Wessex HU.5	HC.2 for commando operations with twin 1350 shp Bristol-Siddeley Gnome 110 turboshafts.
Wessex HAS.31	27 Export HAS.1 with 1575 shp Gazelle 13/2-162 for Royal Australian Navy. Later upgraded to HAS.31B with 1600 shp Gazelle 22/165.
Wessex 52	12 HC.2 for Iraqi Air Force.
Wessex 53	2 HC.2 for Ghanaian Air Force.
Wessex 54	One HC.2 for Sultanate of Brunei.
Wessex 60 Srs.1	20 Civil Wessex with twin 1350 shp Gnome 110 turboshafts and fitted with 16 passenger seats and civil-spec nav/com package.
P.531	Saro-designed 5-seat light military helicopter with single 4-blade main rotor and fixed 4-leg u/c. Powered by one 400 shp Blackburn-Turboméca Turmo 603 turboshaft positioned aft of cabin. Prot. G-APNU (c/n S2.5267) FF 20 Jul. 1958. 2 built.
P.531 Mk.0	P.531 with 960 h.p. Blackburn Nimbus A.129 engine.

Westland Wessex HC.2, XR502

HELICOPTERS AND ROTORCRAFT

Type/Name	Notes
P.531 Mk.2	Developed P.531 with skid u/c, broader tailfin and small tailplane, increased gross weight and 635 shp Blackburn Nimbus A.129 engine. Prot. G-APVL (c/n S2.5311) FF 9 Aug. 1959. Second prot. G-APVM fitted with 1050 shp De Havilland Gnome turboshaft.
Scout AH.1	Production P.531 for British Army powered by 1050 shp Rolls-Royce Nimbus 101 turboshaft.
Wasp HAS.1	Developed Scout for anti-submarine use on Royal Navy frigates with fully-castoring four-leg u/c, narrower fin and single tailplane and 1050 shp Nimbus 103 turboshaft engine. Prot. XS463 FF 28 Oct. 1962.
Sioux AH.1	Westland-built Agusta-Bell 47G-3B-1 for Army Air Corps with 270 h.p. supercharged Lycoming TVO-435-B1A engine. Some produced as dual control Sioux HT.2.
Bell 47G-4A	Trainer version of Bell 47 with unsupercharged 305 h.p. engine. 16 built for Bristow Helicopters.
Sea King	Sikorsky S-61D (SH-3D) built by Westland with two 1400 shp Bristol-Siddeley Gnome turboshafts driving five-blade main rotor and five-blade tail rotor, plus new electronic power control system. Four Sikorsky SH-3D aircraft used as prototypes – XV370 to XV373.
Sea King HAS.1	Naval anti-submarine Sea King with Ekco AW391 search radar in dorsal radome aft of gearbox 'hump', and capacity for 4 Mk.44 homing torpedoes. First aircraft XV642 (WA630) FF 7 May 1969.
Sea King HAS.2	HAS.1 with two 1535 shp Gnome H.1400-1 turboshafts, new gearboxes and new six-blade tail rotor. First aircraft XZ570 (WA838) FF 18 June 1976.
Sea King AEW.2A	HAS.1 converted to carry retractable Thorn-EMI Searchwater AEW radar extended on boom from starboard main door. 9 conversions.
Sea King HAR.3	RAF version of HAS.2 equipped for search and rescue with advanced Decca navigation, increased fuel and modified winch system. First aircraft XZ585 (WA851) FF 6 Sept. 1977.

Westland Whirlwind HAR.10, XJ723

Type/Name	Notes
Sea King HC.4 Commando	Transport version of HAS.2 for Royal Marine Commandos without search radar etc., fixed u/c without flotation sponsons. Mk.4X had additional u/c structure, extra windows and dorsal 'dustbin' radome.
Commando Mk.1	5 Commando version of Sea King HAS 1 with fixed u/c without flotation sponsons and sand filters, delivered to Egypt as Mk.70.
Commando Mk.2	Export version of Commando HC.4 for Egypt and Qatar. Mk.2B with VIP interior. Mk.2E with ECM equipment and two additional side radomes. 27 built.
Sea King HAS.5	HAS.2 with longer interior cabin to accommodate advanced MEL Sea Searcher radar, larger dorsal radome and new dunking sonar. Most HAS.2s converted to HAS.5 standard. First aircraft XZ916 FF 1 Aug. 1980.
Sea King 41	23 HAS.1 for German Navy with increased fuel and no sonar system.
Sea King 42	HAS.1 for Indian Navy. Mk.42A to HAS.2 standard. Mk.42B with H.1400-IT engines for high temperature/altitude operations. Mk.42C built as transport model with nose radome.
Sea King 43	11 HAS.1 as SAR aircraft for Royal Norwegian Air Force.
Sea King 45	6 HAS.1 for Pakistan Navy.
Sea King 47	6 HAS.2 for Egyptian Navy.
Sea King 48	5 HAS.3 for Belgian Air Force air sea rescue duties.
Sea King Mk.50	12 HAS.2 for Royal Australian Navy with ship-to-air refuelling system.
Commando 70	Commando Mk.1 and Commando Mk.2 for Egypt.
Puma HC.1	SA.330E Puma built jointly by Westland and Aérospatiale for RAF with two 1320 shp R-R-Turboméca Turmo III.C4 turboshafts. First aircraft XW241.
WG.13 Lynx	Military tactical medium helicopter with single four-blade main rotor and four-blade tail rotor mounted on conventional fin/boom. Twin skid u/c. Accom for two crew and max 10 troops. Powered by two 900 shp. Rolls-Royce RS.360 Gem turboshafts mounted above cabin. Prot G-BEAD/XW385 (c/n WA.001) FF 21 Mar. 1971.
Lynx AH.1	Army and Royal Marines spec. Lynx for transport and anti-tank use with Hughes TOW missiles. First a/c XZ170 FF 11 Feb. 1977.
Lynx HAS.2 Navy Lynx	Naval ASW model with fixed tricycle u/c for shipboard operation, folding tail and harpoon deck landing system. Longer nose radome housing Sea Spray search radr. First a/c XZ227 FF 10 Feb. 1976.
Lynx HAS.3	HAS.2 with two 1120 shp Gem 41-1 turboshafts and increased gross weight. Some a/c with modified nose radar array.
Lynx Mk.2	Version of HAS.2 for French Navy with modified tactical control system.
Lynx Mk.3	Army anti-tank/transport version with WG.30 tail, lengthened forward fuselage, deeper rear fuselage and 1260 shp Gem 60-3 engines. Prot. ZE477 FF 14 June 1984.

Type/Name	Notes
Lynx Mk. 4	Lynx Mk.2 for French Navy with Gem 41-1 engines, modified transmission and increased gross weight.
Lynx AH.5	AH.1 with 1120 shp Gem 41-1 engines.
Lynx AH.7	AH.5 with increased gross weight, improved cockpit layout, redesigned composite tail rotor. Some conversions from AH.1.
Super Lynx	Developed Navy Lynx with 1120 shp Gem 42 turboshafts, composite BERP rotor blades incorporating 'spade' tips, extended range and payload, advanced dipping sonar and 360-degree radar.
Lynx HAS.8	HAS.3 with BERP rotor blades, increased weights, 1120 shp Gem 42-1 engines and new tactical management system. 3 a/c converted from HAS.2/HAS.3.
Lynx AH.9	HAS.8 with fixed tricycle u/c, additional external armament mountings and jet exhaust diffusers. Also named 'Battlefield Lynx'.
Lynx Mk.21	9 HAS.2 for Brazilian Navy with modified nav equipment.
Lynx Mk.25	6 General duties HAS.2 for Royal Netherlands Navy as UH-14A.
Lynx Mk.27	10 ASW version of R.Neth.Navy Mk.25. designated SH.14B.
Lynx Mk.28	Tropical version of AH.1 for Qatar Police. 3 built.
Lynx Mk.80	Danish Navy version of HAS.3 without foldable tail. 8 built.
Lynx Mk.81	8 HAS.3 ASW aircraft for R.Neth. Navy designated SH.14C.
Lynx Mk. 86	Similar model to Mk.80 for Royal Norwegian AF. 6 built.
Lynx Mk.88	19 HAS.3 with Gem 41-2 engines and non-foldable tail for German Navy.
Lynx Mk.89	3 HAS.3 for Nigerian Navy.
Lynx Mk.90	3 Mk.80 for Denmark with improved avionics.
Lynx Mk.95	5 HAS.3 for Portuguese Navy with Racal tactical data system.

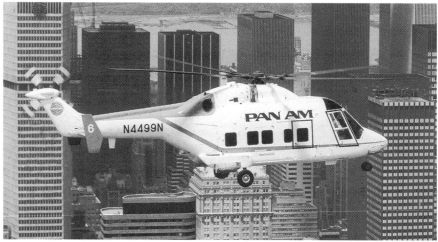

Westland 30, N4499N *(Westland)*

Type/Name	Notes
Lynx Mk.99	Super Lynx for Korean Navy.
Super Lynx 100	Export version of naval Lynx HMA.8.
Super Lynx 200	Super Lynx powered by LHTEC CTS800-4N engines.
Super Lynx 300	Super Lynx 100 with glass cockpit and new navigation system and integrated weapons suite.
Westland 606	Proposed 14-seat civil development of Lynx with alternative P&W PT6-34 turboshafts.
WG.30	Development of Lynx with new enlarged box-section fuselage, modified tail section with full tailplane incorporating end-plate fins, fixed tricycle u/c and two 1135 shp Gem 41-1 turboshafts. First of two Prots. G-BGHF (c/n WA.001/P) FF 10 Apl. 1979.
Westland 30 Srs.100	Production WG.30 for civil customers.
Westland 30 100-60	Srs.100 with 1260 shp Gem 66-3 engines.
Westland 30 Srs.200	Military version of WG.30 with two 1712 shp General Electric CT7-2B turboshafts. Prot. G-ELEC (c/n 007). FF 3 Sept. 1983.
Westland 30 Srs.300	Srs.200 with five-blade main BERP rotor, strengthened rear fuselage, modified u/c and improved gearbox. Prot. G-HAUL (c/n 020) FF 5 Feb. 1986.
P.277	Anti-tank helicopter jointly developed with VFW-Fokker with tandem cockpit, fixed tailwheel u/c and twin turbine engines. Not built.
WG.34 EH.101	See European Helicopter Industries chapter.
Gazelle	See Aérospatiale.

Westland Widgeon, H-4001 *(Westland)*

OTHER MANUFACTURERS

Many other manufacturers have built helicopters and other rotary wing craft in small production numbers and as prototypes. There are also a great number of manufacturers of kit helicopters who produce safe and effective machines for construction by amateurs. The following selected profiles of the more interesting and unusual rotorcraft companies illustrates the great diversity and originality of helicopter and autogyro development since World War II.

ADAMS-WILSON   USA

This company was the manufacturer of the Adams-Wilson XH-1 – a single-seat helicopter with an open-frame fuselage and 34 h.p. Triumph motorcycle engine, designed by T.G. Adams and P. Wilson of Lakewood, California. The prototype, N23P first flew in November 1958, and the type was sold as a kit to amateurs as the Model 101 Hobbycopter. The subsequent Model 102 had a strengthened structure, 50 h.p. Triumph engine and fibreglass cockpit shell.

AERO   CZECHOSLOVAKIA

The CZAL (Aero) factory at Karlin, led by Jaroslav Slechta, developed the XE-1 two-seat helicopter project in 1947, fitted with twin inter-meshing rotors and a 100 h.p. Praga M-197 engine. This led to the XE-II (OK-FYA) which flew on 14 December 1949. It was an open single-seater with a single three-blade main rotor and 75 h.p. Praga D engine. The fuselage of the XE-II was subsequently fully enclosed. It was developed into the proto-type HC-2 Heli-Baby two-seater which had an all-metal fuselage/boom, fixed tricycle undercarriage and 80 h.p. Praga DH engine driving a three-blade rotor. This prototype flew on 3 March 1954, and an order for 200 was announced. It is not clear how many examples were finally delivered, but the HC-2 served with the Czech Air Force for some years.

The HC-2 was followed by the HC-3, which was an enlarged four-seater based on the HC-2 but with a four-leg undercarriage, englarged cabin section and an M-108H engine

Aero HC-2 Heli Baby *(via MJH)*

mounted above and behind the cabin. Three prototypes were tested (OK-15 to OK-17) but the type did not reach production.

AEROCENTRE   FRANCE

The Helicopter Division of SNCAC was established by Réné Dorand and designed and built three prototypes of the NC.2001 Abeille helicopter, the second of which was flown on 28 June 1949, following ground destruction of the first machine. It had twin intermeshing two-blade rotors, an all-metal fuselage with an extensively glazed nose and accommodation for five people. The undercarriage was a fixed tricycle type and it had a tailplane with twin fins. The NC.2001 was powered by a 450 h.p. Renault 12S00 piston engine. The project was discontinued on the dissolution of SNCAC in 1949 with only one flight having been made.

AIR & SPACE   USA

The U-17 gyrocopter was the brainchild of Raymond E. Umbaugh, an agricultural fertilisers manufacturer and enthusiast for the unique properties of autogyros. His U-17 design was a tandem two-seat machine with a slim low-set tailboom and a single fin and tiny T-tailplane. The prototype, N43U (c/n 1), was built for Umbaugh by the Fairchild Engine & Airplane Corporation at Hagerstown, Maryland. It made its first flight in mid-1959 and was powered by a 260 h.p. Lycoming engine.

The second prototype, designated U-18, was redesigned to eliminate the fairly unsatisfactory stability problems of the first prototype. This aircraft (N102U c/n 1F) was fitted with a 180 h.p. Lycoming O-360 and, initially, with a V-tail. The stability problems were still not resolved, however, and a new triple tail with a central rudder was installed. This improved the Umbaugh to the point where it was awarded its Type Certificate (1H 17) on 12 September 1961. Ray Umbaugh embarked on an ambitious plan to market the U-18,

Air & Space 18A, N6155S

placing an order for 10,000 units with Fairchild ! A large network of dealers and distributors was set up in the United States but Umbaugh started to run into trouble because the manufacturing output of the U-18 was too slow to meet the demands of dealers for demonstration aircraft.

The dealers, who had paid large franchise fees took over Umbaugh, the agreement with Fairchild was terminated and manufacturing moved to Florida. The company finally collapsed with just four aircraft completed and flown. The design was then acquired by Air & Space Manufacturing of Muncie, Indiana which made some modifications to the tail unit and commenced manufacture of the Air & Space 18A. Again, Air & Space was faced with dealer pressure for aircraft and set out to raise capital for expansion. This funds-raising exercise resulted in accusations from the Securities & Exchange Commission of irregularities in the commercial claims made to new investors and, though the company's management was eventually cleared of wrongdoing, the costs and delay resulted in the company's collapse. A total of 99 production aircraft had been registered (c/n 2F to 100) though only 67 of these appear to have been actually completed.

The assets of Air & Space then went into storage but were eventually reinstated by one of the dealers, Don Farrington of Paducah, Kentucky. Lacking the rights to the type certificate, Farrington Aircraft set up a programme to remanufacture existing aircraft with a modified collective pitch system, fibreglass engine cowlings and new composite blades. Farrington has also developed an amateur-built kit gyrocopter with some features of the U-18 known as the Farrington Twinstar. This has an open fibreglass cockpit shell, a large twin-fin tail unit and a main rotor mounted on a tubular steel pylon. It is powered by a 150 h.p. Lycoming O-320 and the first prototype, N72DE, first flew in 1993.

AIRMASTER   UNITED KINGDOM

Airmaster Helicopters of Camberley, Surrey designed and built the prototype of a low-cost two seat helicopter designated Airmaster H2-B1. The prototype, G-AYNS, first flew in February, 1972 powered by a 100 h.p. RR-Continental O-200-A engine. It had an enclosed cabin, skid undercarriage, open tubular boom structure with a conventional tail rotor and a two-blade main rotor. Development was later abandoned and the prototype withdrawn from use in 1973.

AISA   SPAIN

In pre-war years Aeronautica Industrial SA (AISA) was involved in work on certain early Cierva-type autogyros. In 1953, AISA produced designs for the experimental IH-51 ultra-light helicopter with tip-mounted pulse jet propulsion, and the H-52 which was of conventional layout but featured a single-blade main rotor. Neither design was built, but, in 1974, the company started construction of the prototype AISA-GN, which was an all-metal four-seat autogyro with a small stub wing, three-blade main rotor, twin booms and a fixed tricycle undercarriage. After prolonged development, the prototype was flown on 20 July 1982, powered by a 300 h.p. Lycoming IO-540-K1A5 engine. The prototype was damaged in September 1982, and the project was then abandoned.

AISA GN *(via MS)*

AMERICAN AIRCRAFT   USA

American Aircraft International of San Diego, California has developed the Penetrator two-seat gunship helicopter. This is based on an extensively modified Bell UH-1B Iroquois with a tandem two-seat cockpit, new fuselage shell incorporating flat armoured panels and a passenger cabin with two bulged observation windows. The Penetrator is fitted with stub wings, a skid undercarriage (or optional retractable tricycle gear), a lower fuselage rear-facing gun turret and two forward-firing cannon. The prototype (N3080W ex U.S. Army 63-8508) is powered by a 1300 shp. Avco Lycoming T52-L-13 turboshaft.

AMERICAN HELICOPTER   USA

The American Helicopter Company was first formed in 1947 and later acquired by the Fairchild Engine and Airplane Corporation in 1954. The first project of the company was the two-seat open-cockpit XA-5 'Top Sergeant', which was based on the lower fuselage and undercarriage of a Sikorsky R-6 with an open rear boom and small rudder. It was driven by two tip-mounted 95 lb. AJ 8.75 pulse-jet engines driven by a fuselage-mounted compressor, and made its first flight in January 1949. This was followed by the single-seat XA-6 'Buck Private' with the same pulse-jet propulsion and a simple open frame structure. American Helicopter then constructed the XA-8 single-seat collapsible helicopter under a U.S. Army contract, flying the first aircraft in June 1952. This had an enclosed cabin with a small tubular boom and V-tail and, once again, rotor-tip mounted AJ 8.5 (XPJ49-AH-3) pulse jets. A series of five XH-26 'Jet Jeeps' were built and evaluated by the U.S. Army and USAF.

AMERICAN SPORTSCOPTER   USA/TAIWAN

Ultrasport 496 N496SC

American Sportscopter (ASI) was formed in 1990 to produce an ultralight helicopter to FAR Part 103, which was designated Ultrasport 254. This kit-built machine first flew in July 1993. It is a single-seater with a semi-enclosed composite fuselage structure, skid undercarriage and a tubular tailboom with tailplane and twin fins and a tail rotor enclosed in a large circular shroud. It is powered by a 55 h.p. Hirth 2703 engine mounted behind the cockpit rear bulkhead. The Ultrasport 331 is a larger version of the 254 falling within the American 'Experimental' category (FAR Part 21.191g), with increased range and higher gross weight. This first flew in December 1993. It was followed by the Ultrasport 496 two-seater which commenced flight testing in July 1995. It has a wider cabin than the '331 and uses a 95 h.p. Hirth F.30 engine. The Ultrasport helicopter kits are manufactured in Taiwan.

AVIAN   CANADA

Avian Industries was established by a group of ex-Avro engineers in Toronto in 1959 to develop a two-seat autogyro known as the Avian 2-180 Gyroplane. This small aircraft had an all-metal egg-shaped fuselage with a tandem two-seat cockpit in the front enclosed by a large bubble canopy, and a 180 h.p. Lycoming O-360-A engine in the rear driving a pusher propeller inside a circular duct. The Gyroplane was fitted with a fixed tricycle undercarriage and had a three-blade rotor fitted with compressed air tip nozzles to assist 'jump starting'. The

Avian Gyroplane C-MTV-X *(via MS)*

prototype (CF-LKF-X) first flew in early 1960 but was subsequently damaged beyond repair, and it was followed by a second similar aircraft (CF-MTV-X) on 16 February, 1961. Avian then built the first of three pre-production prototypes (CF-NWS-X) with a larger annular duct, no tail fins and a more extensively framed cockpit canopy. These were followed by a 'certification prototype' (CF-JTO-X) which had further canopy modifications, spring steel undercarriage legs and a 200 h.p. Lycoming IO-360 engine. The Avian 2/180 was certificated in 1968, but it seems that the company went out of business shortly thereafter without starting production.

BANNICK   USA

Lester J. Bannick developed the Bannick Model T Copter (N9989Z) in 1964. This was a simple open-frame gyrocopter, similar to the Bensen Gyrocopter with a wooden rotor and a pusher 65 h.p. Lycoming engine. It was marketed in the form of plans for home construction. Bannick then completed the prototype of the Bannick Model C Copter which flew in 1967. It used the rotor system of the Model T with a streamlined glass-fibre fuselage incorporating a large tail fin and a 135 h.p. Lycoming engine. No further details of development are known and it is believed that the Model C was eventually abandoned.

BAUMGARTL   BRAZIL

Paul Baumgartl was an Austrian who had worked on three helicopter designs during the war years before emigrating to Brazil. He experimented with a number of light helicopters in the 1950s and 1960s including the single-seat PB-60 unpowered ground-towed rotor kite, and the PB-64 which was an ultra-light single-seater with a minimal tubular fuselage structure. The PB-64 had an unusual pulse-jet propulsion arrangement with the two 30 lb.s.t. ITA jets fitted to a transverse stabilising beam set at right angles to the rotor. The aircraft had no tail rotor but was fitted with a small rudder. Baumgartl subsequently built his PB-63 under Brazilian Air Ministry funding. This was a conventional helicopter with a single seat and semi-enclosed cabin, powered by an 85 h.p. Continental C.85 engine. No production of any of these designs was undertaken.

BENDIX   USA

In 1944, Vincent Bendix (of washing machine fame) established Bendix Helicopters (later renamed Helicopters Inc.). The Bendix designer, Martin Jensen, devised the Bendix Model J single-seater which used a system of coaxial rotors and was driven by a 450 h.p. Pratt & Whitney R-985 piston engine. This was followed by the Model K with an enclosed tube and fabric fuselage but with a much smaller 100 h.p. Continental C-100 engine. The Model K (NX41817) made its maiden flight in June 1945, but Bendix eventually ceased operations in 1949 without achieving certification.

BENSEN   USA

Arguably the most popular amateur-built rotorcraft is the Bensen B-8 Gyrocopter. Igor Bensen experimented with a number of gyroglider designs in the 1950s and sold plans for the B-5 and then the improved B-6, B-7 and B-8. These machines were based on a central girder with a pilot's seat mounted in the nose, a tricycle undercarriage beneath and a vertical mast carrying the free-spinning rotor. Eventually, Bensen created the B-7M and B-8M Gyrocopters which had a McCulloch engine mounted behind the pilot. The first B-7M was flown on 6 December 1955. The later B-8M had a larger rectangular vertical tail and the B-11 was fitted with a teetering rotor hub and a larger rotor. Bensen also built the B-9 Little Zipster with coaxial rotor blades, and the B-13 which flew in March 1963, and was a true light helicopter. These were followed by the B-12 Skymat flying platform machine and the B-10 Prop-Copter (N56U) which flew in August 1958, and had twin vertical lift propeller/rotors. Many thousands of Bensen B-7M and B-8M plans and kits have been sold.

BORGWARD   GERMANY

The German car manufacturer, Borgward set up a helicopter division in 1956 under the leadership of Prof. Heinrich Focke. A light three-seat helicopter, the Kolibri I, was designed and the prototype was flown at Bremen on 8 July 1958. This prototype had an unclad tubular fuselage with a forward cockpit enclosed with bubble canopy, the 260 h.p. Lycoming VO-435-A1B engine in the centre section and a conventional tail boom. The Kolibri was fitted with a V-tail carrying two tail rotors at the tips. The main rotor was a three-blade steel unit with a fully articulated hub and adjustable friction dampers. Only one prototype Kolibri was built and development was abandoned with the liquidation of Borgward.

Borgward Kolibri *(via MS)*

BREGUET   FRANCE

Constructed on behalf of the Société Francaise du Gyroplane by Breguet, the G.IIE first flew on 21 May 1949, at Villacoublay-Velizy to the south of Paris. This prototype had an all-metal fuselage with a tall fin and small T-tailplane. It used the coaxial rotor approach to torque-neutralisation and had a cabin for five people and a fixed tricycle undercarriage. The 240 h.p. Potez 9E engine was buried in the fuselage behind the cabin, and three-bladed all-metal rotors were used. The G.IIE was found to be underpowered and it was re-engined with a 450 h.p. Pratt & Whitney Wasp Junior – in which form it became the G.III. Following testing in 1951 development was discontinued and F-WFKC was donated to the Musée de l'Air.

CHU   TAIWAN

The Humming Bird light helicopter was designed by Major-General C.J. Chu in China during 1945. His Model A Humming Bird was a tiny coaxial helicopter with an enclosed fuselage pod and a 125 h.p. Kinner engine, which was destroyed in ground testing. The subsequent Humming Bird B was similar, but it is not clear whether either helicopter flew – and the Humming Bird B was abandoned in China when Chu fled to Formosa. In 1952, he produced a small tandem-rotor helicopter known as the CJC-3 which was a side-by-side two-seater with a centrally-mounted 190 h.p. Lycoming engine and fixed four-leg undercarriage. No further information is available.

Chu CJC-3 *(via MS)*

CICARE   ARGENTINA

The Cicare 1 and Cicare 2 were lightweight helicopters designed and built by Cicare Aeronautica which was established in 1972 by Augusto Cicare in Buenos Aires. The Cicare 1 single-seater was an open-frame machine with a small windshield to protect the pilot, and a coaxial rotor system. The larger Cicare 2 had two seats and was a conventional design with a three-bladed main rotor driven by a 180 h.p. Lycoming O-360 piston engine, and with a two-blade tail rotor mounted at the end of an open tubular boom structure. The prototype made it first flight on 18 May 1965. The prospective production version was the Cicare III Colibri – later renamed the C.K.1 – three-seater. This differed from the Cicare 2 in having a tapered tube tailboom, four-blade rotor and a 200 h.p. Cicare 4C-27 engine in an open centre-section mounting. The first Cicare C.K.1 (LV-X-62) flew in September 1976, but subsequent development is believed to have been terminated.

Cicare embarked on a new helicopter development in 1986 under contract from the Argentine Government which had a requirement for a light trainer and agricultural helicopter. The CH-5 single-seater was built as a test vehicle for the dynamic systems of the new machine, and this had an open frame fuselage with a tubular tailboom, and a 64 h.p. Rotax engine mounted behind the pilot and driving a two-blade composite main rotor. It flew on 8 July 1987. This was followed by the definitive CH-6-AG prototype which made its maiden flight on 22 April 1988, but funding was withdrawn in 1988 and development abandoned. It is believed that the CH-6 has been reintroduced recently as the Helifly ground trainer.

CIERVA/ROTORCRAFT   UNITED KINGDOM

Rotorcraft Ltd was established with backing from Mitchell Engineering in the early 1960s to produce a new two-seat design by J.S. Shapiro. The Grasshopper in its definitive form had a fuselage somewhat similar to an enclosed sports car with a small v-tail and a skid undercarriage. It was powered by a pair of 65 h.p. Walter Mikron piston engines mounted in the nose. These drove a pair of two-blade coaxial rotors mounted on a pylon which emerged just ahead of the cockpit windshield. G-ARVN, the prototype, flew in March 1962, but was withdrawn from use the following spring when funding was withdrawn following the death of the owner of Mitchell Engineering, and the project was abandoned.

Rotorcraft was then reconstituted as the Cierva Rotorcraft Ltd, subsidiary of The Cierva Autogyro Co., and work commenced on the new Grasshopper Mk.III which was based on the dynamic systems of the earlier aircraft, but with a new four-seat fuselage incorporating a slim tailboom with a fin and rudder and powered by two 135 h.p. Rolls-Royce Continental O-300 piston engines. This was designated CR.LTH-1 (otherwise known as the CR-Twin) and the first aircraft, G-AWRP (c/n GB-1) first flew in 1969 followed by G-AXFM (GB-2) later that year, and a third pre-production machine, G-AZAU (GB-3) in mid-1971. This latter aircraft was fitted with 210 h.p. Continental IO-360-D engines, and the production variants were to be the CR.420 with 210 h.p. Continental TSIO-360-A engines and the CR.640 with 320 h.p. Continental Tiara T6-320 engines. Development was eventually abandoned in 1975 due to lack of further financial backing.

Cierva CR.LTH-1 Grasshopper 3, G-AXFM *(via MS)*

Rotorcraft Grasshopper, G-ARVN *(via MS)*

CITROEN MARCHETTI   FRANCE

In the mid-1970s the Citroen car company set up a design team under Charles Marchetti to produce a light two-seat helicopter. The Citroen-Marchetti RE.2 was a streamlined machine with a skid undercarriage and clear glazed nose cockpit, and it was powered by a 180 h.p. Comotor 624 Wankel rotary engine. The sole prototype, F-WZAB made its maiden flight on 24 December 1975, and underwent development testing until mid-1977, when it was discontinued due to continuing problems with the transmission system.

CSIR   SOUTH AFRICA

The Council for Scientific and Industrial Research (CSIR) designed an experimental auto-gyro in 1965 as a lead-in to a possible production machine to be manufactured by South African industry. The prototype (ZS-UGL) had an egg-shaped fuselage with a full plexi-glass nose bubble enclosing the two-seat cabin, and a twin fin tail unit mounted on external tubular struts. The SARA-II had a fixed tricycle landing gear and a simple rotor pylon with a two-blade main rotor. The machine was driven by a pusher propeller at the rear, powered by a 180 h.p. Lycoming O-360-A piston engine. This aircraft made its first free flight at Swartkop Air Base near Pretoria on 30th November 1972. The lessons learned with the SARA-II were applied to a new design – the SARA-3 – which also had a fuse-lage pod with a two-seat cabin and rear mounted O-360 engine, but used a new twin-boom tail unit with large rectangular tail surfaces. It also embodied a novel fully-automatic vari-able geometry rotor head which assisted rapid takeoffs by automatically moving the rotor blades from zero pitch to takeoff pitch as the rotor disc was tilted. The prototype, ZS-UIT, made its initial flight on 1 August 1977, and was subsequently used for experimental research.

CTA   BRAZIL

The BF-1 Beija Flor was designed in 1956 by Professor Focke at the Centro Tecnico de Aeronautica at the military research and overhaul centre at São José dos Campos. A

CTA Beija Flor *(via MS)*

two-seater, the Beija Flor had its 225 h.p. Continental E225 engine fitted in the nose, with a short coupling to the rotor pylon which was mounted centrally in front of the crew. An open structure tubular steel tail boom carried a pair of tail surfaces and a small tail rotor. The prototype flew on 1 January 1959, and went through extended flight testing until it was damaged in an accident. It is thought that further work on the Beija Flor was then abandoned.

CURTISS WRIGHT   USA

The VZ-7AP Flying Jeep was a research vehicle aimed at creating a battlefield utility helicopter for the U.S. Army. It consisted of a central beam structure with the pilot's station at the front and four outrigger rotor mountings behind. The rotors were driven by a 425 shp Turboméca Artouste IIB turbine fitted in the centre section. Two examples were delivered to the Army for testing in 1959. Curtiss Wright also built an experimental tilt-rotor research aircraft, the X-100, which had a fairly conventional aircraft fuselage and vertical tail, with a single seat in the nose. It was fitted with a stub wing with swiveling wingtip rotor pods. An 825 shp Lycoming YT53-L-1 turbine was fitted in the rear fuselage, and the jet exhaust was emitted from a tail nozzle to give directional stability. The X-100 first flew in March 1960. This aircraft was followed by a larger tilt-rotor machine, the Model 200. This had a fuselage with capacity for six people, and two stub wings mounting four tilt rotors. It was commissioned under a USAF contract, and two prototypes of the X-19A were built and flown in 1963 powered by two 2200 shp Lycoming T55-L-5 turboshafts.

DE LACKNER   USA

Donald de Lackner's Cloudster, built in 1946, had a tube and fabric fuselage with a four-leg undercarriage. There was a small enclosed two-seat cockpit in the nose and two three-blade rotor pylons – one at each end of the fuselage. The 135 h.p. Lycoming engine was housed at the back of the machine and drove the forward rotor via a long transmission shaft. Only one Cloudster was built. De Lackner then moved on with his designer, L.C. McCarthy, to design a flying platform helicopter, and a new subsidiary company, Helivector Corporation, was formed to develop this machine. This DH-4 featured an unusual arrangement of a pair of coaxial rotors mounted beneath the platform on which the pilot stood, and the company built 13 examples for evaluation (c/n 1 to 13) including the prototype, N64N. These were powered by a 55 h.p. Kiekhafer Mercury engine. The company subsequently built the DH-5 (N852 c/n 14) which followed a similar layout, but used a 40 h.p. engine and a tailboom carrying a horizontal control surface. None of the de Lackner helicopters reached full scale production.

DEL MAR   USA

Del Mar Engineering Laboratories of Los Angeles built a series of single-seat personal helicopters for possible use by the U.S. military forces. These all consisted of a simple open frame supporting a pilot's seat in front of an engine with rotor mast and a tubular tail boom with tail rotor. The DH-1A Whirlymite Scout (N3349G) flew on 15 June 1960, and used an 80 h.p. Kiekhafer Mercury piston engine. Several other versions were announced, but it is not clear how many were actually flown. The DH-1B was identical to the DH-1A except for using a Titan turbine engine. The DH-1C Whirlymite was an unmanned target drone version and the DH-1E Spotter was fitted with TV and infrared sensors. The DH-1D Whirlymite Packer, which was intended for troop supply tasks and the DH-1F Whirlymite Spotter were both fitted with the Titan engine. Del Mar also built several ground-based training versions including the DH-1G, DHT-1 and DHT-2. They also produced an advanced machine, the DHT-2A Whirlymite Scout with an 85 shp AiResearch GTP30-91 turboshaft which flew in May 1963.

DOAK   USA

In 1957, Doak Aircraft Company of Torrance, California, built a prototype of the Doak Model 16 VTOL test aircraft. This had an open frame fuselage with short wings, a conventional fin/rudder and tailplane and an 840 h.p. Lycoming T53 turbine engine fitted in the fuselage centre section, with its exhaust system ducted to form a controllable nozzle in the tail. Two ducted fans were fitted at the wingtips and these could be rotated through 90-degrees to provide vertical or forward flight. The prototype (U.S. Army 56-9642) was built under a military contract as the VZ-8 and rights were subsequently sold to Douglas.

DORNIER   GERMANY

During the period 1968 to 1971, Dornier AG constructed 348 Bell UH-1D Iroquois for the West German Luftwaffe, HEER and Police. This followed a period of experimentation into rotorcraft by the company, which had commenced with a small open single-seat battlefield helicopter designated Do.32. This had a triangulated tube structure supporting the pilot's position, and a box-section rear beam to which a vertical tail and the 100 shp BMW 6012 turbine were fitted. The Do.32 could be folded up for ground transport. The prototype (D-HOPF c/n 320001) first flew on 29 June 1962, and Dornier built two further examples. They also built a developed Do.132 five-seater (D-HEIS) with a fully enclosed fuselage, but it is not known if this was flown. The company also built three examples of the Do.31E experimental VTOL transport, which featured a circular section fuselage and stub wing with wingtip vertical lift units containing eight Rolls-Royce RB-162-4D lift jets, and two Bristol Pegasus turbofans in underslung wing pods. The first Do.31E (D-9530 c/n E-1) was flown on 10 February 1967, but the design progressed no further after testing was completed.

Dornier Do.132, D-HEIS   Dornier Do.32

DRAGON FLY   ITALY

Dragon Fly Srl. was formed by the Angelo and Alfredo Castiglioni brothers at Cucciago in northern Italy to build a small side-by side two-seater which was, initially, designed for their own personal use as an easily transportable machine for use in archaeological exploration. Two prototypes of a single-seat model were built and flown in 1989 as a precursor to the two-seat production model. The Dragon Fly 333 is technically an ultralight, but is built to JAR Part 27 standard and was approved in 1996 under the Italian VLR (Very

Light Rotorcraft) standard. Dragon Fly production was set initially at three per month, and the first production machine was delivered in late 1993. Production totalled 51 (up to c/n 51-97) by mid-1997. The all-metal Dragon Fly has an enclosed pod fuselage with fixed skid and a tubular tailboom carrying a T-tail with a two-blade tail rotor. The main two-blade rotor is mounted above and behind the cabin and is driven by a 105 h.p. Dragon Fly/Hirth F30.A2 two-stroke engine. The Dragon Fly can also be delivered as a drone for military use.

Dragon Fly

ELISPORT   ITALY

The CH-7 Angel has been designed by Elisport of Turin and is sold as a kit to amateur builders. It is a single-seat machine with a fully enclosed cabin in a tiny streamlined pod, with a Rotax 582 engine mounted in the centre section, and a strut-braced tubular tailboom carrying a small fin and two-bladed tail rotor. The Angel has a two-bladed semi-rigid composite main rotor.

Elisport CH-7 Angel, N8AB

FIAT   ITALY

In 1959, the Societa per Azioni Fiat was awarded an Italian Defence Ministry contract to design and build a medium capacity helicopter for use by the Italian Air Force. Fiat's Model 7002 had an unusual flat-sided semi-round fuselage section with a small girder tailboom on which was mounted a shrouded tail rotor. The rear quarter of the main fuselage housed a Fiat 4700 turbine which drove a compressor feeding cold tip nozzles on the two-blade rotor. The Model 7002 could carry two crew and up to five passengers. The sole prototype flew on 26 January 1961, but development was discontinued in 1963. Fiat then designed a new high-speed three-seat helicopter, designated Fiat 7005, which had a pusher propeller mounted immediately behind the rotor pylon. This was not built and Fiat discontinued helicopter development in 1967.

Fiat 7002 *(via MS)*

FILPER   USA

Under the direction of William Orr, Filper Research designed a novel helicopter using the 'Gyroflex Rotor', which employed special balance weights fitted to the roots of the rotor blades instead of conventional flapping or lead-lag hinges, or other hub stability devices. This concept was tested on the Filper Helicopter (N9712C) which had fore and aft rotor pylons and the pilot sitting astride a central beam which also carried the engine. The commercial development, however, was the Filper Beta 100A. This was a tandem rotor machine with a two-seat cabin and pylon at the rear, and the engine with the forward pylon in front. This curious arranagment resulted in the pilot being unusually far from the front of the helicopter. The Beta 200 prototype (N5000F c/n CA-0001) was first flown on 26 May 1966. Filper planned several versions of the Beta with either two seats (Model 200A and 300) or four seats (Model 400A and 600A). The four-seat models had a fuselage which was stretched by 36-inches and the first Beta 400A (N5003F c/n A-0003) was flown on 13 July 1967. The Beta models had various powerplants – namely the 210 h.p. Continental IO-360-E (Model 200A), Allison 250-C18 turbine (Model 300) and 250 h.p. Continental IO-520 (400A). Details of the Model 600A are unknown. Registration records show that 32 Betas were completed, comprising two Model 100As,

29 Model 400As and one Model 600A (c/n CA-0001 to CC-0032), but there is some doubt as to whether all of these were completed. It is believed the company ceased operations in 1969.

Filper Beta 400A, N5005F

FIRESTONE   USA

The Firestone Aircraft Company of Akron, Ohio was a subsidiary of the Firestone Tyre and Rubber Company which took over rights to a number of the Pitcairn Autogyro Company designs via an acquisition of G&A Aircraft of Chicago in 1944. G&A Aircraft had previously built six examples of the XO-61 two-seat gyroplane for the U.S. Army. This experience was applied to the design of a new helicopter for the U.S. Army, designated Model 45. The Model 45 was a conventional pod and boom helicopter with tandem seating, a fixed tricycle undercarriage and a three-blade main rotor. The original Model 45B design used a 126 h.p. XO-290-5 engine and the Model 45C (military XR-9A) was a development with a two-blade rotor. However, neither of these was actually built and the prototype (which carried the identity 6001) was designated XR-9B and was fitted with a 135 h.p. Lycoming O-290-5 engine. Firestone also built a civil version, the Model 45D (NX58457), with side-by-side seating but development of helicopters was abandoned by Firestone in 1947.

Firestone XR-9B, 6001 *(HGM Collection)*

GLATFELTER   USA

Edward W. Glatfelter was a former design engineer with Boeing-Vertol. In the mid-1950s he experimented with new control systems for helicopters and designed a rigid rotor system. This was tested on his XRG-65 single-seat design, which had a steel tube structure and incorporated parts of other helicopters including a Bell 47 tail rotor, Piasecki HUP main rotor blades and various Sikorsky components. The single example (N6576D) flew in June 1959.

GLUHAREFF   USA

Eugene Gluhareff established a development company in 1952 to carry out research into pressure-jet powered light helicopters. He built the MEG-1X personal strap-on helicopter rig which used a single-blade rotor with a tip-mounted G8-2 engine and followed this with the MEG-2X which had a two-blade rotor. His final design was the MEG-3X which was based on a dish-shaped platform on which the pilot would stand and a two-blade rotor revolving underneath the platform. No commercial development was undertaken.

GLENVIEW   USA

The two-seat 'Humming Bird' was originally designed by William E. Hunt. It was developed in 1947 by Frontline Helicopter Corp. as the 'Flyride' and the prototype (N544A) made its first flight in January 1948. It was a streamlined all-metal monocoque helicopter with an automobile-style forward fuselage and forward-swept rotor pylon. Power was provided by a 125 h.p. Lycoming engine. The Flyride had a single control stick to operate all functions and a system of linkage of blade pitch to the engine speed. Frontline Helicopter was acquired by Glenview Metal Products and the machine became the GMP-1 Flyride. It was upgraded with a 135 h.p. Lycoming in 1953 and was advertised to the public as the ideal personal helicopter – but it was short lived and lapsed into obscurity.

GOODYEAR   USA

Well known for its airships, the Goodyear Aircraft Corporation developed a small open-frame single seat helicopter which made its first flight on 9 May 1954. This prototype (N62N c/n 1) was designated GA-400R Gizmo and followed classic lines with the pilot seat on the forward frame, a narrow tailboom with a tail rotor and the 32 h.p. Mercury 55 engine mounted amidships and driving a two-blade main rotor. It was followed by the GA-400R-2 and GA-400R-3 (N69N c/n 2J and N 53A c/n 2M) which were powered by a 38 h.p. Johnson two-stroke engine. Like many contemporary ultra-light helicopters the GA-400R did not progress beyond prototype stage.

GUIMBAL   FRANCE

The two-seat Cabri G2 light helicopter was designed by Bruno Guimbal, a Eurocopter engineer, and the prototype (F-PILA c/n 01) made its first flight at Marseille-Marignane in April 1992. Powered by a 150 h.p. Lycoming, it has a fenestron-type tail rotor and three-blade main rotor. The Cabri is built largely of composite materials and development has continued at Aix-en-Provence with restricted DGAC certification being issued on 18 April 1994.

Guimbal Cabri, F-PILA

GYRODYNE   USA

The Gyrodyne Company of America was established by Peter J. Papadakos in 1946. Gyrodyne acquired rights to the five-seat Helicopters Inc. (Bendix) Model J and developed this as the Gyrodyne GCA-2 (N74101). The GCA-2, an all-metal helicopter, had a coaxial twin rotor layout, with a five-seat cabin and a rounded fuselage with twin fins. It was subsequently modified to become the GCA-2A Helidyne, with twin 100 h.p.

Gyrodyne GCA-2, N74101 *(HGM Collection)*

Continental auxiliary engines mounted externally on strutted outriggers to give additional forward speed. It flew in this form on 30 November 1949. A further GCA-2C (N6594K c/n 1002) was built but later abandoned. In 1956, Gyrodyne entered the competition to produce a single seat 'personal' helicopter for operation off destroyer heli-decks for fleet observation, and for battlefield support, and built ten examples of the XRON-1 for the U.S. Navy. These also had a coaxial rotor layout and a 40 h.p. Nelson H.59 engine – later replaced by a 60 h.p. Porsche. This experiment led to development of the QH-50 unmanned drone versions of the XRON-1 and Gyrodyne delivered over 60 production QH-50Cs for operation from Naval frigates.

HELICOM   USA

In the mid-1960s, Helicom Inc. of Palm Springs, California, produced a small single-seat kit-built helicopter named the Commuter Junior. This was an open-frame machine with a 90 h.p. Continental C90-12F engine mounted amidships and driving a two-bladed main rotor. In its prototype form it had a fixed tricycle undercarriage but this was changed to a skid undercarriage on the definitive version, and the pilot seat was provided with a flat-sided cockpit enclosure and perspex windshield.

HELICOP-AIR   FRANCE

The Helicop-Air L.50 Girhel was a side-by-side two-seat gyrocopter built in 1959. It had a substantial wing and three-fin tail unit. The cabin was enclosed by a fully transparent canopy, with the rotor pylon mounted centrally, and the Girhel was powered by a 90 h.p. Continental C.90 engine mounted in the nose. It is not clear whether the prototype (F-WJCO) actually flew.

Helicop-Air Girhel, F-WJCO *(Via MS)*

HILLMAN   USA

Douglas Hillman was an enthusiastic amateur builder who carried out several helicopter experiments in the 1970s and built the Hillman Wankel-B, and then the two-seat Hillman Green Hornet and Turbo Hornet IIA. In 1979, Hillman joined Rudolph Enstrom to develop the Hillman 360. This streamlined three-seat light helicopter bore some resemblance to Enstrom's earlier designs with a fully enclosed fibreglass and metal fuselage,

Hillman 360 *(via MS)*

tricycle undercarriage and a Lycoming HIO-360-C1A piston engine driving a two-blade rotor. The prototype was built at Stellar Air Park near Phoenix, Arizona, and flew on 15 October 1981. Unfortunately, Douglas Hillman died during the period of testing of the Model 360 and the design was abandoned.

HINDUSTAN   INDIA

Hindustan Aircraft, as India's national aviation industry organisation, has manufactured a large range of indigenous and licensed designs over the years. Its Bangalore factory took out a licence with Aérospatiale to manufacture the SA-315 Lama five-seat helicopter, which was named Cheetah in Indian service. The first aircraft flew in October 1972, and approximately 190 examples have been built to date (including 17 from Aérospatiale components) – practically all of which have been delivered to the Indian Army. HAL then took a further licence to manufacture the SE.3160/SA.319B Alouette III, which is known as the Chetak, and was already in service with the Indian Air Force. Again, the majority of the 280-odd aircraft which have been built have gone for military use but approximately 20 are in Indian commercial service. Scant information is available on serial numbers but it is believed that Cheetahs are in the range c/n CH-001 to CH-190, and Chetaks are c/n AH-001 to approximately AH-281.

In July 1984, HAL started development of a new 12-seat helicopter known as the ALH (Advanced Light Helicopter) which was designed with assistance from MBB in Germany. It followed a similar layout to that of the BK-117 although it is a larger aircraft. The twin 1000 shp Turboméca TM333-2B turboshafts are mounted above the cabin and drive a four-blade composite main rotor. The ALH makes use of an advanced integrated dynamic system which combines several rotor control features into an integrated module. The civil prototype ALH (Z-3182) first flew on 23 August 1992, at Bangalore, followed by a second civil aircraft (Z-3183), an Army version (Z-3268) and a navalised prototype (N.901) with Allied Signal CTS800 engines and a retractable tricycle undercarriage. Development is continuing with the prospect of Indian Government orders for up to 200 examples.

Hindustan ALH, Z.3182 *(Hindustan)*

HUNTING PERCIVAL UNITED KINGDOM

In 1951, a Helicopter Division was formed by Hunting Percival and design work commenced on a medium-sized helicopter designated P-74. This machine had a teardrop-shaped fuselage with the two-seat cockpit in the nose and a large cabin running the full length of the fuselage. Beneath the cabin floor was a Napier Oryx gas generator which fed compressed air to the tips of the three rotor blades. The prototype was completed in the spring of 1956, carrying the military serial number XK889. Ground testing commenced but the Oryx engine was insufficiently powerful and the P.74 failed to fly. It was planned to fit a more powerful Rolls-Royce RB.108 turbine, but the rationalisation of the helicopter industry later that year resulted in the P.74 project being cancelled.

Hunting P.74, XK889 *(via MS)*

JOVAIR – McCULLOCH USA

The Helicopter Engineering Research Corporation was established by D. K. Jovanovich in Philadelphia immediately after the war. His initial design concept was for a coaxial rotor helicopter which had a large three-blade primary rotor and a secondary two-blade unit – but also had a small tail rotor. This design did not get further than the drawing board, but Jovanovich was influenced by his design team, who had largely come from Piasecki, to create the JOV-3 tandem rotor machine powered by a 100 h.p. Franklin engine. It had a neat fuselage of steel tube covered with aluminium and fabric, with a tricycle undercarriage and a forward cockpit for two occupants seated in tandem. The rear pylon allowed the rear rotor to turn on a higher plane than the forward rotor so that the arcs could overlap safely.

The JOV-3 prototype (N9000H c/n 1) was built and flown in 1948. It was subsequently fitted with a 125 h.p. Lycoming O-290. Jovanovich transferred the design to the McCulloch Motors Corporation and a new prototype, the McCulloch MC-4 (N4070K c/n 101) was constructed – this time with a 165 h.p. Franklin 6V4-165-B32 powerplant.

McCulloch gained the interest of the U.S. Army and built three examples of the MC-4C, which were designated XH-30 (serials 52-5837 to 52-5839 c/n 001 to 003). These were substantially similar to the earlier variants, but had a further power increase to a 200 h.p. Franklin 6A4-200-C6 engine. The U.S. Navy also received two similar XHUM-1s (Bu. 133817 and 133818 c/n 1001 and 1002). Unfortunately, neither the Army nor the Navy could find a role for the MC-4 and McCulloch subsequently lost interest, with three of the five evaluation aircraft being returned to Jovanovich. One example of the HUM-1 exists at the Pima County Museum in Arizona, and an XH-30 is held at the Fort Rucker U.S. Army Museum.

Jovanovich formed Jovair Corporation and modified the first production MC-4C (N4071K c/n 1000) into the four-seat Jovair Sedan 4E. Another engine upgrade took place with fitment of the Franklin 6A-350, and the Sedan was given a type certificate in 1962. One further Sedan 4E was built (N6570C c/n 101). Jovair also built one example of the Jovair 4A (N4091K), which was a stripped-down open-frame version of the Sedan for training and general utility tasks. They intended to produce the Model 4ES with a super-charged 225 h.p. Franklin 6AS-335, and a Model 4U crop spraying variant, but plans for these were eventually abandoned.

Jovair lost heart over the Sedan and the design rights were sold to Hughes, but they designed a small two-seat autogyro, the J-2, which was flown in June 1962. This prototype (N4068K c/n 1) was an all-metal machine with side-by-side seating, tricycle undercarriage and a stub wing mounting twin booms with a conventional tailplane and tailfins. The autogyro rotor was mounted above the cabin and the J-2 was powered by a180 h.p. Lycoming O-360 engine which drove a propeller mounted behind the cabin.

At this stage, McCulloch returned to take charge of the Jovanovich helicopters and went on to certificate the J-2 in May, 1970. The J-2 then went into production with the first delivery to Colley Equipment in April 1971. The production target was an output of two aircraft per day but just 96 examples (c/n 001 to 096) had been completed when produc-tion ceased. The design was then taken over by Aero Resources of Gardena, California, (believed to be a reconstitution of McCulloch) but it appears that they produced no further examples of the J-2.

Jovair JOV-3, N9000H *(HGM Collection)*   McCulloch J-2, VH-MGP

KAYABA   JAPAN

During the war, Shiro Kayaba, head of the K.K. Kayaba Seisakusho, experimented with a Kellett KD-1A autogyro and built a virtually identical aircraft for Japanese Army tests. After the war, in 1952, Kayaba returned to rotary wing experimentation with the Heliplane. This was a compound helicopter fabricated from the fuselage and Continental E-180 engine of a Cessna 170 light aircraft, with a rotor mounted above the cabin roof and low-set stub wings to which the undercarriage was attached. The three-blade rotor was fitted with small ramjets which were used for takeoff and landing and the rotor would rotate freely in horizontal flight when the Heliplane was being driven by the normal propeller. It first flew in 1954.

KELLETT   USA

Kellett was a famous prewar name in the design and production of autogyros, culminating in the wartime delivery of a batch of YO-60s to the USAAF. In 1943 the company changed to helicopter development with a two-seat military machine – the XR-8 – which had twin side-by-side 'Synchropter' intermeshing rotors, and a tubby tube and fabric fuselage with a fixed tricycle undercarriage. Powered by a 245 h.p. Franklin engine the XR-8 (s/n 43-44716) first flew on 7 August 1944. It was followed by a second prototype, the XR-8A (s/n 44-21908) with two-bladed rotors. The company then moved on to an all-metal machine, the XR-10 (later XH-10), which was a scaled up all-metal version with capacity for 10 passengers or six stretcher patients. This had a similar rotor system and was powered by two 525 h.p. Continental R-975 engines positioned in nacelles on the fuselage sides. Again, two prototypes were flown (s/n 45-22793 and 22795) the first taking to the air on on 24 April 1947, but this crashed in October 1949, and the project was abandoned. A proposed KH-2A 16-seat civil helicopter remained unbuilt.

Kellet KH-15 *(via MS)*

Kellet XR-8, 43-44714 *(HGM Collection)*

Kellet XH-10, 522793 *(via MS)*

Kellett also designed the large flying crane XR-17, which was taken over by Hughes and built as the XH-17, and the KH-15 Stable Mable single-seat personal helicopter. The open frame KH-15 used a pair of Reaction Motors rocket engines fitted at the rotor tips, and first flew under sponsorship from the Office of Naval Research on 13 May 1954. It was fitted with a patented gyro stabilisation system but, despite showing remarkable flight characteristics, it progressed no further.

KHARKOV   SOVIET UNION

The KhAI-24 autogyro was built by the Kharkov Aviation Institute in the mid-1960s. Its fuselage resembled that of a conventional light aircraft with a tandem two-seat cabin, twin tail fins and an M-332 engine in the nose. It was fitted with a fixed tricycle undercarriage and a three-blade main rotor. There is no indication that more than the single prototype was ever built.

LANDGRAF   USA

Fred Landgraf established the Landgraf Helicopter Corporation in the early years of the War, and flew a prototype of his single seat Landgraf H-2 as a development machine for a series of three-seat (H-3) and 5/8 passenger helicopters (H-4). The Landgraf concept involved twin outrigged rotor pylons carrying three-bladed wooden rotors, which were fitted with ailerons to allow the direction of travel of the machine to be changed. The all-wood H-2 first flew on 2 November 1944, powered by an 85 h.p. Pobjoy R engine. Testing of the H-2 continued until 1949 but withdrawal of military funds resulted in the demise of the Landgraf company. They did, however, grant rights to Firth Helicopters Ltd in England and they built the prototype 'Firth Helicopter' using the fuselage of the Planet Satellite light aircraft. This machine (G-ALXP) was built in 1954 but never flew.

LOCKHEED   UNITED STATES

Lockheed started a programme of helicopter research in the mid-1950s. The CL-475 (N6940C) was a two-seat machine with a slab-sided tube and fabric fuselage, and fixed tricycle undercarriage equipped with a 140 h.p. Lycoming VO-360-A1A piston engine mounted above and behind the cockpit. It flew on 2 November 1959 and was used to develop a successful rigid rotor concept. It was followed by the Model 186 which was subject of a U.S. Navy research award.

Two examples of the Model 186 were built (Bu. 151262 and 151263) initially as the XH-51A, followed later by a single XH-51N. The first of these flew on 2 November 1962. The XH-51A was a streamlined two-seat machine which was able to test the high-speed characteristics of the rigid rotor system as a result of the installation of a 550 shp Pratt & Whitney PT6B-9 turboshaft engine. Lockheed subsequently fitted the second aircraft with a stub wing and an externally mounted Pratt & Whitney J60-P2 turbojet on the port side of the fuselage. In this form it achieved a maximum speed of over 300 mph. Lockheed also built two examples of a commercial version, the Model 286, which was intended as a civil helicopter for the business aviation market. The prototype (N286L) flew on 30 June 1965, but despite extensive marketing little interest was created and Lockheed abandoned the concept.

Lockheed's final foray into the helicopter field came in 1964 when it responded to the U.S. Army's AAFSS request for a battlefield gunship helicopter. Lockheed designed the AH-56A Cheyenne which was a large machine with two seats, a stub wing and retractable tailwheel undercarriage. The Cheyenne was fitted with a 3925 shp General Electric T64 turboshaft engine and could carry a large array of Hughes TOW anti-tank missiles, 7.62-mm minigun, XM140 cannon and other armament. Ten Cheyennes were built (s/n 66-8826 to 66-8835 c/n 186-1001 to 1010) the first of which flew on 21 September, 1967. Unfortunately, stability problems and the loss of one of the prototypes led to the cancellation of the programme in 1972. The U.S. Army had already adopted an 'interim' solution with the Bell HueyCobra and it became clear that this was a more cost-effective solution than the highly complex Cheyenne.

LUALDI   ITALY

The Air Lualdi & C. SpA was formed by Carlo Lualdi in 1953 and became established as the Italian agent for Hiller Helicopters. They designed their own light helicopter, the two-seat ES.53, which flew at Campoformido in September 1953, and used a Hiller-type rotor design with a controllable transverse secondary rotor. This was followed by the L-55, which was an all-metal machine with a skid undercarriage and a fully enclosed cabin, with the 180 h.p. Lycoming O-360 engine mounted in the nose and driving a rotor pylon which was carried in a housing in the centre of the cabin. This prototype was followed by an improved L-57, with a larger-diameter main rotor and a modified flight control system. In turn, this led to the definitive four-seat L-59, which had more extensive cockpit transparencies and a 260 h.p. Continental IO-470-D engine. One prototype was built for Lualdi by Aermacchi (I-GOGO – later MM576) for civil and military testing, and the commercial type certificate was issued in August 1961. Lualdi is believed to have closed down in 1963 without putting the L-59 into production.

Lualdi L-59

MANZOLINI   ITALY

The Libellula was the brainchild of Count Ettore Manzolini. It was very similar to the Sud Djinn in external appearance with an open framework fuselage and fixed skid undercarriage. Manzolini devised a coaxial rotor system for the Libellula and flew his prototype

on 7 January 1952. This was followed by the Libellula II which used a higher powered 105 h.p. Walter Minor 4-III engine and had an enclosed cockpit. This aircraft, I-MANZ, gained an RAI type certificate in 1962, but no manufacture was undertaken.

Manzolini Libellula III I-MANZ *(via MS)*

MASCHELIN   BELGIUM

The M.58 Masquito has been designed by Paul and Stefaan Maschelin of Kortrijk and was under testing for JAR certification in mid-1997. The Masquito is a side-by-side ultra light two-seater of all-composite construction with a pod and boom fuselage, skid under-carriage and a 65 h.p. Rotax 582 engine.

MONTE-COPTER   USA

Monte-Copter Inc. was established in 1953 in Seattle to design and build light helicopters. The first design was the Model 10, which was a two-seat machine with a large bubble canopy and a tailboom mounting a tailplane with large twin rudders. The two-blade rotor had control paddles similar to the Hiller system. It was driven by a 135 h.p. Lycoming O-290 engine which generated cold airflow to the rotor tips. This piston engine was then replaced by two externally-mounted Turboméca Palouste turbojets. The prototype, N68P, flew in 1955 and was later modified to become the Model 12, with a single tail fin. Monte-Copter then built the three-seat Model 15 Triphibian (N69P) which flew in 1960. This was a very streamlined machine with a boat-shaped fibreglass fuselage, forward-sliding canopy, small stub wings with sponsons to house the main wheels and a small full depth rudder. It was powered by a 200 h.p.Continental gas generator housed in the rear fuselage feeding compressed air to the rotor tip nozzles.

NHI   NETHERLANDS

The SOBEH Foundation (Stichting voor de Ontwikkeling en Bouw van een Experimenteel Hefschroefvliegtig) was established in the early 1950s to research and build small ramjet-powered helicopters designed by J. Meyer Drees. The SOBEH-1 helicopter, which flew in 1954, was an open-frame single-seat machine with a skid undercarriage. Two small ramjets were fitted at the tips of the two-blade rotor, which embodied an automatic pitch adjustment system, and the pilot controlled the machine through a suspended overhead stick The SOBEH-1 was written off through ground reso-nance, but was succeeded by the SOBEH H-2 (PH-NFT) which was flown in May 1955. The H-2, was an improved version with a large windshield and a tiny strutted tail unit with a small anti-torque propeller. It was taken over by Nederlandse Helicopter Industrie N.V. which was formed by Aviolanda and Kromhout and based at Rotterdam, and they refined the design into the two-seat NHI-3 Kolibri.

The first NHI-3 (PH-NHI) flew in May 1956, and featured a more substantial cabin enclosure and a stronger tail unit. The power units were two 55 h.p. NHI TJ-5 ramjets but these were upgraded to the more powerful 100 h.p. TJ-5A in production aircraft. The main role for the Kolibri was in crop spraying, for which role it had spray tanks mounted beneath the fuselage floorpan with standard spraybars. An initial production batch of ten aircraft (c/n 3002 to 3011) was initiated in 1958 for customers in Dutch New Guinea, the United Kingdom, Germany and Israel. Further development of the Kolibri ceased after the company was acquired by Aviolanda in May 1959.

NHI H-3 Kolibri, PH-NHI *(via MJH)*

OMEGA   USA

Bernard W. Sznycer, a former engineer with Pitcairn, developed the three-seat SG-VI-D helicopter in Canada in the mid-1940s. He was assisted by Selma Gottlieb and supported by Engineering Products of Canada Ltd (CanAmerican). The sole prototype, CF-FGG-X, flew on 9th July 1947, and gained its Canadian type certificate in February 1951. It had an enclosed cabin and open tubular tailboom and was powered by a 178 h.p. Franklin GA-4-165-BGF engine positioned horizontally above the tailboom. This drove a four-blade main rotor with a complex control system. It was subsequently upgraded to become the SG-VI-E with a 200 h.p. Franklin 6A4-200-C6 engine.

The SG-VI-D did not go into production and Sznycer started a new company, Allied Aero Industries, in the USA to develop and build the Omega SB-12 utilty helicopter. This had a flying crane layout, with a forward four-seat crew pod and an open tubular rear fuselage and fixed tricycle undercarriage. A metal cargo box could be suspended beneath the fuselage mid-section. The BS-12 (N267B c/n 156) used two 210 h.p. Franklin engines positioned end-to-end above the rear fuselage. The prototype flew on 29 October 1956, and was followed by a revised version – the BS-12B (N290B c/n 1001). The Omega design was progressively upgraded with detail design changes, notably to the cabin pod and to the engines. The BS-12D-1 (N285B c/n 1002) had two 260 h.p. Lycoming O-540 engines and a five-seat cabin. The second BS-12D-1 (N286B c/n 1003) was fitted with supercharged Franklin 6AS-335 engines and redesignated BS-12D-3. In 1960, the investors backing the Omega designs withdrew support and further development was terminated.

Omega BS-12D-1, N285B *(via MS)*

PIASECKI   USA

Having left the Piasecki Helicopter Corporation, Frank Piasecki set up Piasecki Aircraft Corporation and became involved in the Agusta 101G large transport helicopter and also embarked on research under government contracts into compound helicopters. The company built a prototype of the Pathfinder 16H-1 (N616H) which first flew on 21 February 1962. This machine had an all-metal monocoque fuselage with a small low wing, a forward-swept pylon mounting a three-bladed rotor and an annular tail duct with a pusher propeller and directional vanes. It was subsequently modified with a stretched fuselage and a 1250 shp General Electric T58 turboshaft engine to become the Model 16H-1A and then to Model 16H-1C Pathfinder III configuration with a 1500 shp T58-GE-5. A nine-seat development, the Model 16H-3J was not proceeded with.

REVOLUTION   USA

In 1994 Revolution Helicopters of Excelsior Springs, Missouri announced their kit-built Mini-500. This single-seater could easily be mistaken for a scaled-down Hughes 500D with its egg-shaped fuselage pod, slim tailboom and T-tail. The Mini-500 is powered by a 67 h.p. Rotax 582 engine and over 350 kits have been sold, with examples flying in Holland, South Africa and Brazil as well as substantial numbers in the United States.

Revolution Mini-500 PH-RHC

ROTORCRAFT   USA

The 1950s saw a rash of 'personal military helicopter' designs which were seen as giving mobility to the soldier in the field. Several companies were given development contracts by the U.S. Army, including the Rotor-Craft Corporation. Rotorcraft had acquired rights to the rigid rotor designs of the Landgraf Helicopter Company and built an experimental machine known as the XH-II Dragonfly which used the Landgraf rotor system mounted in tandem – but so closely positioned that they overlapped. This was eventually abandoned and Rotorcraft produced the RH-1 Pinwheel single-seat helicopter to meet the U.S. Army specification. The Pinwheel had a 'quadripod' frame layout, with the pilot sitting in the centre of the structure with a pair of liquid nitrogen tanks positioned behind him to feed Reaction Motors XLR-32RM rocket motors mounted at the rotor tips. The Pinwheel, which flew in 1954, was eventually abandoned as being too complex for Army operations.

ROTORWAY   USA

In 1958, B.J. Schramm set up a company to market a single-seat amateur-built helicopter known as the Schramm Javelin. This machine had a tubular steel structure with a formed aluminium body shell and was powered by a 100 h.p. Mercury powerboat engine. It first flew in August 1965. Schramm subsequently redesigned the Javelin as the Scorpion, and he formed Rotorway Aircraft Inc. to market kits for this revised version, and claimed that 250 were flying by 1970. The Scorpion Too followed, and this had an expanded fuselage structure with a two-seat fibreglass cabin enclosure and a 140 h.p. Evinrude marine engine.

Rotorway Exec 162F, N14897

With Scorpion Too kits being successfully marketed, Rotorway moved on, in 1980, to a much more sophisticated two-seater – the Exec. This was a streamlined machine based on the Scorpion Too with an all-metal monocoque and glassfibre fuselage shell and a 152 h.p. Rotorway RW-152 water-cooled piston engine. It was subsequently upgraded to Exec 90 standard with a large number of detailed alterations. The design was further changed in 1995 to become the Exec 162F with a FADEC electronic control system. Over 200 Execs are flying.

Rotorway Scorpion Too, ZS-UIW

RYAN USA

In 1956, The Ryan Aeronautical Company was awarded a contract by the U.S. Army to develop an ultra short takeoff aircraft. This single-seat VZ-3 Vertiplane was not a helicopter, but more a deflected thrust aircraft. It had a conventional fixed wing aircraft layout with a T-tail, tricycle undercarriage and short span wings with drooped tips which mounted a pair of large propellers driven by a Lycoming T53 turbine buried in the fuselage. The key to the near-vertical takeoff ability of the VZ-3 was the huge flaps which extended to an almost vertical position and provided airflow deflection to give vertical lift. The VZ-3 prototype (56-6941/NASA235) made its maiden flight on 21 January 1959, and was eventually retired in 1963 after testing at NASA-Ames.

SCHEUTZOW USA

Webb Scheutzow designed a small two-seat helicopter with a patented low-cost 'Flexihub' rotor head which relied on rubber mountings for the two main rotor blades and required no lubrication. The Scheutzow B was a side-by-side two seat helicopter with the classic layout of an enclosed fibreglass cabin, an engine in the centre section, tubular open frame rear boom and a fixed skid undercarriage. The prototype, N564A (c/n 101), flew on 26 January 1967, followed by three further examples (c/n 102 to 104), but the type failed to gain a Type Certificate and development was abandoned in the early 1970s.

Scheutzow B, N592A *(via MS)*

SILVERCRAFT   ITALY

Silvercraft Italiana and SIAI-Marchetti jointly designed an all-metal three-seat helicopter, the SH-4, the prototype of which (I-SILX) made its first flight in March 1965. It was a robust little machine with a skid undercarriage and a high-set tubular corrugated tailboom with a small fin and tailplane and a two-blade tail rotor. The SH-4 was powered by a 235 h.p. Franklin 6A-350-D piston engine and the main rotor had two blades and a transverse mass-balanced stabiliser bar similar to that on a Bell 47. Certification was achieved in September 1968, and the SH-4 went into production at Silvercraft's works at Sesto Calende in basic form, and as the SH-4/A for agricultural use and as the SH-4/C with a supercharged Franklin 6AS-350-D1 engine. A total of 21 SH-4s were completed (c/n 01 to 021) with individual examples being exported to Brazil, South Africa, France and Holland. One aircraft was delivered to the Italian Air Force.

Silvercraft then designed and built the SH-200 which was a more streamlined two-seater with a low-set boom, large bubble windshield, T-tail and a 205 h.p. Lycoming LHIO-360-C1A engine. This helicopter (I-SILD) made its first flight on 12 April 1977, but Silvercraft abandoned this development and ceased helicopter activities in 1979.

Silvercraft SH-4, ZS-HDR

SIEMETSKI   GERMANY

The single-seat ASRO 3-T was built by Alfons Siemetzki and made its first flight on 29 December 1961. This experimental helicopter was an open-frame machine of conventional layout, with a rudimentary windshield to protect the pilot, a skid undercarriage and a BMW 6002 turboshaft engine mounted amidships. The ASRO-3 was used to develop the ASRO-4 which had a fully enclosed fuselage pod and tapered tubular tailboom, and was fitted with a 130 shp MAN-Turbo 6012 turbine driving a three-blade rotor. This machine flew in May 1964, and was tested for some while before being abandoned without achieving certification.

SPITFIRE   USA

Spitfire Helicopters of Media, Pennsylvania was founded by John J. Fetsko and developed a three-seat helicopter based on the Enstrom F-28A powered by a 420 shp Allison 250-C20B turboshaft engine. The first prototype (N4890 c/n 042) was converted from an existing F-28A airframe, and a second machine designated Spitfire Mark II had a stretched cabin section and upgraded engine. It was intended to build the Spitfire Mark II and the further develped Mark III and Mark IV in a new facility in Malaga, Spain, but this proposal was not pursued.

VFW   GERMANY

In the late-1960s, VFW (Vereingte Flugtechnische Werke) built an experimental open gyrocopter modelled on the Bensen B.8M. This VFW-H2 was unusual in having ducted rotor blade tip jets supplied from the 72 h.p. McCulloch engine. The engine itself was mounted behind the pilot and drove a two-blade pusher propeller. The H2 (D-HIBY) was followed by a more sophisticated machine – the H3 Sprinter which had a completely enclosed fuselage structure with a three-seat cabin, slim low-set tailboom with a V-tail, and a tricycle undercarriage. The powerplant was an Allison 250 turboshaft which, again, provided compressed air to the tips of the three rotor blades for vertical takeoff and also drove two large multi-blade ducted fan propellers mounted on the fuselage sides which provided forward power. The H3 was further developed into the H5 which was similar in layout but had a larger cabin with five seats. The first of two prototype H3s (H3-E1, D-9543) flew in early 1970 without the external fan propulsion units. It was intended that the H5, would be followed by the H7 7/8 seater (construction of which was apparently started but not completed) and the much larger H9. As it turned out, however, further development was abandoned in 1972 following the merger of VFW and Fokker.

VICTA   AUSTRALIA

Well known for its two-seat Victa Air Tourer fixed-wing trainer, Victa's aviation division designed a small two-seat gyroplane, the Model 67. The prototype, which was designed by John Blackler, was registered VH-MVB and flew in May 1962. It was a neat machine with a tricycle undercarriage, twin-fin tail unit and a two-blade main rotor with a pusher propeller driven by a 180 h.p. Lycoming engine. The prototype logged 150 flights and 20 hours of test flying time, but was abandoned due to financial constraints.

WAGNER-HTM   GERMANY

The Helikopter Technik Wagner, formed by Josef Wagner, designed a series of helicopters with coaxial rotors during the 1960s. The earliest test models were fairly rudimentary machines built to test the concept, and one design was a roadable machine titled the Rotocar III. The first production-standard prototype to fly in July 1965 was the Wagner Sky-Trac 1 (D-HAJE), which still had a frame structure but was fitted with a 260 h.p. Franklin 6AS-335-B engine, and had a sliding canopy forming an enclosed cabin for the single pilot. A second machine was built (D-HARB) which was fitted with a pontoon landing gear and a longer boom with a V-tail. The subsequent three-seat Sky-Trac 3 (D-HAJI) had a more complete cabin structure and was fitted with spray bars and underslung tanks for agricultural chemicals. Wagner also built a prototype (D-HAGU) of the Aerocar roadable helicopter, powered by a 260 h.p. Franklin 6AS-335-B engine, which had a complete body shell with twin fins and four wheels linked to an automobile drive system for its ground transport role. It was first flown in 1965. It was subsequently rebuilt with a Turboméca Oredon turbine engine.

After extensive development work had been carried out, the Wagner designs were passed to a new company, Helikopter Technik Munchen (HTM) in 1971. HTM abandoned the Aerocar, but built a new prototype of the FJ-Sky-Trac (D-HHTM) in tandem two-seat configuration, as a utility helicopter with a 260 h.p. Lycoming IO-540 engine. This still had the coaxial rotor system but was extensively redesigned to accommodate the new engine and cockpit layout. HTM then went on to build two examples of the HTM Skyrider (D-HTMS and D-HHTF) which reverted to the configuration of the Sky-Trac with a four-seat cabin and a fully enclosed streamlined structure. The Skyrider was an attractive machine with a skid undercarriage and V-tail, which commenced flight testing on 21 February 1974. Unfortunately, HTM was forced to abandon further development in 1975 through lack of further funding.

HTM Skyrider, D-HHTF *(via MS)*

Wagner Sky-Trac 3 D-HAJI *(via MS)*

YAKOVLEV   SOVIET UNION

The Yakovlev OKB started development of helicopters after the war and designed an experimental machine, the Yak-EG with a coaxial rotor system. A prototype of this helicopter was tested in 1947/48 following which it was decided that the coaxial rotor layout should be developed by the Kamov bureau, and Yakovlev moved on to other helicopter configurations. They produced a design designated Yak-100 which was externally similar to the Sikorsky S-51. The first of two prototypes of this helicopter flew in 1948, but the Mi-1 was adopted as the standard light helicopter for the Soviet forces and the Yakovlev design was dropped.

In 1951, Yakovlev was directed to design a large 40-troop military transport helicopter. The result was the Yak-24, which was a tandem rotor helicopter with dual fixed undercarriage units at front and rear, a V-tail and four-blade rotors driven by 1430 h.p. ASh-82V engines. The Yak-24 had a large glazed nose section containing the cockpit and a rectangular-section cabin in the centre section. The four prototype examples of the Yak-24 were fabric-covered and suffered many ground and in-flight resonance problems, and they did not achieve the design load specification. Ultimately, modifications were made to the rotor blades which resolved the vibration difficulties. The Yak-24U was flown and this went into production for the Soviet army. It had an all-metal fuselage and numerous design improvements including twin fins. Several civil variants were built, including the Yak-24K VIP model which had a shorter fuselage and airstair door, and the Yak-24A airline version with larger cabin windows. It is thought that only a few of these versions were actually produced and the main production variant was the military version of which many hundreds were completed.

Yakovlev Yak-24

INDEX